Talk to Me:

What educators (and others) can learn about de-escalation from hostage negotiators

Emma Van Der Klift

Talk to Me:
Copyright © 2019 by Emma Van Der Klift
All rights reserved. No part of this publication may be reproduced, distributed, or transmitted in any form or by any means, including photocopying, recording, or other electronic or mechanical methods, without the prior written permission of the author, except in the case of brief quotations embodied in critical reviews and certain other non-commercial uses permitted by copyright law.

tellwell

Tellwell Talent
www.tellwell.ca
ISBN
978-0-2288-1569-3 (Paperback)

Table of Contents

ACKNOWLEDGEMENTS ix
FOREWORD xi
INTRODUCTION: CALL OFF THE SWAT TEAM AND BRING IN THE NEGOTIATORS xv

My Journey xviii
Educators: Unprepared and Shocked xix
Student Voices xx
I Don't Have Time, and You Don't Know the Kids I Work With! xxi
When You're Stuck…Bring in More People xxii
It's Not Another Model xxiii
But Wouldn't Life Be So Much Easier If There Was a Recipe We Could Follow? xxv
Are There Specific Skills We Can Learn? xxvi
How the Book Is Organized xxvi
A Few Words on Language xxviii
In Conclusion: A Confession or Two xxix

CHAPTER ONE: DEFINING THE PROBLEM (OR I DID MY HOMEWORK) 1

Reframing Behaviour as Conflict 1
Classroom Management 3
Educators Caught in an Ideological Cross Fire 3
Behaviourism in the Classroom 4
Positive Behavioural Intervention and Support 5
Student Perceptions 13
Lack of Training 15
Structural Issues 18
Systemic Issues: Zero Tolerance 18
The Unfortunate Catch 22 20
Teacher Beliefs 21

CHAPTER TWO: HOSTAGE NEGOTIATION (IT'S NOT THE SWAT TEAM) 25

A Brief History of Hostage Negotiation 26
What Exactly Do Negotiators Do? 27
Talking to Negotiators 28

CHAPTER THREE: RELOCATING THE PROBLEM 30

Choosing a Constructive Narrative 30
Shifting the Narrative 34
Just a Person in a Bad Place 36
Narratives at School 39
Taking an Anti-pathology Stance 44
Max 45
Smarten Up versus What's Up 47
An Example 49
In Summary 51

CHAPTER 4: RELATIONSHIP 52

Federal Agents Say the Darnedest Things 52
The Problem with Pop Behaviourism 56
The Three Rs 59
But Doesn't Relationship Building Take a Long Time? 63
The Two by Ten Study 64
Because He's Nice 66
Support and Expectations 69
An Example: "Fill the Bucket" 70
In Summary 74

CHAPTER FIVE: EMPATHY 75

What Is Empathy? 76
How exactly is empathy created, and is it really possible to be empathetic to people you don't approve of? 77
Empathy Isn't Always Involuntary: It's a Decision and a Discipline 78

An Example 79
We Have the Best Professional Development Sitting
Right Here in our Classrooms! 84
The Limits of the Golden Rule: A Caveat 85
In Summary 85

CHAPTER SIX: CURIOSITY 87

The Importance of Silence 89
"Is There Anything Else?" 90
Hold onto Your Dreams! 91
It's a Process 93
Skating on the Surface 93
What Would You Say If You Did Know? 94
Specificity 95
What Part of "No" Don't You Understand? 96
My Favourite Role Model 99
"Mom, What's a Spaz?" 101
Now, Class, Say 'Em 102
The Million-Word Essay 103
In Summary 104

CHAPTER SEVEN: LISTENING 105

The Physiology of Listening 107
Active Listening 108
A Cautionary Note 110
A Few Stories 113
Hearing Aids and Flying Fathers 121
Listening at School and at Home 123
In Summary 124

CHAPTER EIGHT: SELF-MANAGEMENT 125

Be Prepared 127
Lessons from Labour Negotiations 129
People Will Try to Make You Feel the Way They Feel 132
A Story 132

Motor Mimicry and Emotional Contagion 134
You Can't Take It Personally! Or "I Just Love It When a
Kid Tells Me to F$%# Off!" 137
A Cautionary Tale 137
In Summary 138

CHAPTER NINE: DYNAMIC INACTIVITY 139

Don't Just Do Something, Stand There! 139
Spilling Wind 140
Breathing Lessons 144
Make the Room Bigger 145
I Don't Have Time for Dynamic Inactivity! 149
In Summary 152

CHAPTER TEN: FACE SAVING 153

What Exactly Is "Face"? 153
Isn't Face Saving Just Placation? 154
Losing Face 155
We Don't Lose Face When We're Alone 155
"PE Doesn't Stand for Physical Education. It Stands for
Public Embarrassment." 156
"She's a Sweet Lady, But It's Not Professional What
She Does" 157
"If You Go in Blazing Guns with Kids, They Just Don't
Buy It" 159
Personal Face Is Always a Fighting Issue 159
"I Have Never Seen a Hostage Situation or Any Act of
Violence that Was Not Preceded by Some Loss" 161
"He Had to Get Out with Dignity" 162
Saving Face: An Active Process 163
In Summary: What Can You Do to Help? 166

CHAPTER ELEVEN: THOUGHT INTERRUPTION 170

I'll Have Your Wallet 174
In Summary 175

CHAPTER TWELVE: PROBLEM SOLVING 178

Go Slow to Go Fast 178
Sit In the Snowbank 179
Lessons from Waco: A Cautionary Tale 180
Daniel 187
Page believes that a disruptive person is metaphorically drowning: 189
This Is Your Brain on Stress Hormones 189
A Personal Story 190
What Should We Do When We're the Ones Drowning? 192
Ask the Experts 194
"I Didn't Just Come for the Juice and Cookies, You Know!". 195
Three Important Components of Problem Solving:
Preparation, Practice, and Training 197
Mediation and Negotiation in the Classroom and Beyond... 198
Solution-Focused Problem Solving 200
Four Helpful Questions 201
One Knot at a Time, or Miss Piggy's ThirdLaw 204
Negotiation Is a Series of Small Agreements 205
Some proactive suggestions about supporting an
inclusive, safe school culture are as follows. 206

CHAPTER THIRTEEN: SOME FINAL THOUGHTS FROM NEGOTIATORS AND EDUCATORS 210

Some Last Words from Educators 212

CHAPTER FOURTEEN: COMPARING PARACHUTISTS TO POTTERS 214

In Summary 217

EPILOGUE: SCHOOL SHOOTINGS 221

The Safe School Initiative 222
Technology Will Never Be a Substitute for Relationship 224

An Example of a Proactive School-Wide Response 226
Changing the Conversation 227
A Graphic Example 228
So What *Should* We Do? 230
Who Can We Call on for Help? 231

REFERENCES 233
APPENDIX A: INTERVIEW WITH RON GARRISON ON RESTRAINT AND SECLUSION 257

ACKNOWLEDGEMENTS

If I repent of anything, it is very likely to be my good behaviour.

—Henry David Thoreau

This is for my family, especially my mother, who taught me to hold the dignity of all living things as inviolable. This is also for the children in my family who are still in school (or will be getting there soon): Mieka, Zophiah, Coral, Emiko, and Julianna. May you always have adults in your lives who listen.

Most of all, this is dedicated Norm, my soul mate and partner in all things. So many more cliffs to jump off together, so many more rabbit holes to go down, so many metaphors to mix, so little time! I don't think there is a word coined that describes the synergy we share. In the early days of our relationship, when we were becoming a family, you told me your philosophy of step parenting was to stand behind me with a hand on my shoulder. You've continued that philosophy in facilitating the birth of this book. Thank you—for everything.

There is no copyright on titles. For this I am grateful, since I stole the title from the New York City Hostage Negotiation Team."Talk to Me" is their motto. I hope they will forgive my flagrant thievery. Imitation, as they say, is the sincerest form of flattery.

It turns out that qualitative research is the perfect medium for someone who loves stories. My thanks to the brilliant, perceptive, and deeply humane negotiators, administrators, educators,and students who shared their amazing stories with me. Thanks especially to Ron

Garrison, who planted the seeds for this inquiry so many years ago. And to the following:

Alfie Kohn. Your work has influenced me profoundly. It was a huge honour to have you as my advisor during the early days of this project but a bigger one to call you friend. Thank you also for your second look at this work more recently.

Rich Villa and Jacque Thousand. In addition to the gift of your friendship—a friendship that has endured almost three decades—your generous support, encouragement, practical suggestions, and feedback are gifts I am very grateful for.

Leah Kelley. For your friendship and encouragement, and not least for the daily dose of writing discipline we have shared for well over a year. If Norm step parented this book, we've joked that you've midwifed it.

Lee Davis Creal and Michael Creal. Your enthusiasm for this project, your careful reading and generous comments buoyed my spirits many times during the inevitable periods of self-doubt.

I hope those not mentioned realize the only reason is lack of space. Thanks to all of you who made this project possible and helped me retain a semblance of common sense in the process.

FOREWORD

Listening, curiosity, and empathy nurture relationships. It sounds simple enough. But can delivering safer schools and communities to our students and teachers actually be that simple? As a court-qualified expert in school safety with over thirty years of public-school teaching, school administration practice, and law enforcement experience, I can certify that, yes, it often can be that simple. In this book, that is what Emma Van Der Klift aims to show us.

During my varied professional career, I taught high school students; was director of student services for a California school district; trained teachers in classroom management, conflict resolution, and violence prevention in thirty-eight states and Canada; worked with the United States Departments of Justice and Education as a national school safety consultant; trained police and school security staff; consulted with prison and jail medical staff in seven states; partnered with Lee Canter on school safety planning; testified in eighty-five school law cases; introduced teachers and school administrators to resilience-based student interventions; and incorporated restorative justice programs into school discipline procedures.

Despite promoting these numerous programs over many years, I found that student and teacher relationships emphasizing positive empathetic communication were the most effective way to foster individual and institutional safety and our best hope for negotiating a safe resolution to school conflict, confrontation, or crisis. Like Emma, I believe that none of the programs and models currently on offer to educators will ever take the place of genuine relationships.

I met Emma Van Der Klift and her partner, Norman Kunc, twenty-five years ago at a conference in Austin, Texas. Apparently, they were somehow impressed that a person like me who trained police to negotiate and communicate effectively and empathetically with serious habitual juvenile offenders and gang members would believe and teach educators about communicative relationships as the central key to school safety. Go figure.

Nevertheless, being internationally respected consultants in their own right, Emma and Norm decided they liked what I had to say and that it might be worth offering me a beer after the conference to unfairly extract information from me. How, they asked, does a "fed" survive scrutiny from his peers while promoting nurturing relationships instead of detentions, suspension, expulsion, and even incarceration? It's a good question. While many in the field of education may remain skeptical that such approaches might be really effective, those of us involved in higher stakes negotiation know better. We have learned from decades of experience in both international and domestic negotiation that hard-line approaches do not deliver on their promises. I told Emma and Norm that what we've learned is that schools are not made safer through making them more like prisons.

After this initial conversation and many subsequent decades of friendship sharing the stage at numerous teacher and administration education conferences, Emma asked me to speak more specifically about my experiences with negotiation during times of school conflict and crisis. One of my primary observations regarding student and teacher conflict in schools was that teachers sometimes confront and challenge students in ways that hostage negotiators would never do. Emma was intrigued by this statement and wanted to know more.

A few years later, apparently based on this conversation, Emma began working on a leading-edge interdisciplinary thesis linking confrontational teacher and student behaviours with the de-escalating practices used by hostage negotiators. In 2010, she completed a major research project at Royal Roads University examining how the diverse perspectives of hostage negotiators, educators, and students could be merged to provide a road map to create better empathetic relationships between students and their teachers. Much of that research is contained within this book.

Along with other experts, I shared with Emma how police hostage negotiators, often trained by the U.S. Federal Bureau of Investigation, use empathetic approaches like open-ended questions, mirroring, and paraphrasing to accomplish their goal of nonviolent resolution during times of conflict, confrontation, and crisis. But most important is the way in which negotiators come to view the people they are negotiating with. Rather than seeing these individuals as disordered or as criminals, negotiators understand that individuals in crisis are simply trying to resolve issues in whatever way they can and work actively to help them extricate themselves from these difficult situations without injury or loss of life.

The foundation of Emma's book *Talk to Me* is rooted in a philosophy of partnership between students and teachers. Unfortunately, one of the consequences of educational modernity, especially in countries like the United States and Canada, is that school boards and law enforcement officials continue to believe that paramilitary tactics like active shooter drills, lockdowns, surveillance, and arming teachers will guarantee safer schools.

There is scant evidence that these schemes are actually effective in preparing students and teachers for dealing well with each other during minor conflicts, never mind during a crisis like a school shooting. What research does substantiate is that some of these reactive preparations can actually be developmentally injurious to children (see Appendix A). Better to invest in positive relationships with our community, parents, and students than in combative correctional tactics designed to increase the stress in children's (and teacher's) lives.

In this book, Emma helps us learn from the collective wisdom of hostage negotiators, educators, students, and parents. When we negotiate our way through difficult interpersonal situations, and are confident in successful outcomes because we practice negotiation every day and embrace a philosophy of partnership, we will not need to lockdown our students' lives with fear.

Emma's book does not present the reader with prescriptive answers to hypothetical questions. Rather, she offers answers designed to stimulate more questions. And through this process of questioning, negotiation emerges as an effective pathway to better and safer relationships with our students.

Ron Garrison, MA, MS
Benicia, California

INTRODUCTION:

CALL OFF THE SWAT TEAM AND BRING IN THE NEGOTIATORS

There's an old joke I have heard is actually a Sufi parable. It goes like this:

> A policeman is walking his evening beat on a dark city street. As he approaches a lone streetlight, he notices a man on his hands and knees apparently searching for something.
>
> "What are you doing?" the policeman asks.
>
> "I'm looking for my keys," the man replies.
>
> "Where did you drop them?" the policeman asks.
>
> "Somewhere over there." The man points across the darkened street.
>
> Puzzled, the policeman asks, "If you lost them over there, why are you looking over here?"
>
> "Because," the man replies, "the light is better over here."

When it comes to thinking about students who are labelled problematic through their behaviour, perhaps this is what we've done in education. We've looked where we believe the light is best, or where we were told we *should* look—to the empirical and supposedly evidence-based material and the plethora of model-based interventions that overflow educational bookshelves and libraries. I am not arguing against those weighty tomes, but I am going to suggest that we may have lost those proverbial keys and that we should pull out our flashlights Nancy Drew–style and go back to where we lost them. Maybe the help we need can come from different quarters. In this book, the people I've enlisted to help us find those keys do indeed come from a different part of the street.

This book is based on work I did in 2010 as I completed a master's program in Conflict Analysis. The idea to meld the world of hostage negotiation with the world of education arose from a comment made by a friend and colleague who had experience with both—as an educator and as a federal agent. In the course of a conversation about classroom management and de-escalation, he told me, "Educators routinely do things to confront kids in ways that hostage negotiators would never do." This counterintuitive statement both mystified and intrigued me. It prompted a year's worth of research into the world of hostage negotiation, domestic and international, and a series of fascinating interviews with women and men from all over North America. What I learned surprised and amazed me, and also profoundly influenced my subsequent thinking about the ethics of engagement when relationships are troubled, situations are escalating, and violence is possible.

Specifically, this is a book about the non-coercive, relational, and communication-based approaches that hostage negotiators use to help distraught, barricaded, sometimes suicidal, or even homicidal individuals to de-escalate. These men and women are successful in resolving more than 90 percent of the issues they are called upon to negotiate without loss of life, injury, or the use of coercion (Kohlreiser, 2006). This is a significant statistic, and the negotiators I spoke with told me they believed that 90 percent was actually a conservative estimate. They placed the number at closer to 95 percent. This book is about how we can help someone to de-escalate when they are in crisis and is also, perhaps most importantly, about how we can learn to effectively de-escalate ourselves. It is meant for teachers and others who interact with students labelled difficult or disruptive and offers some ideas I gleaned through research and conversations with hostage negotiators, educators, students, and parents.

There are three reasons why I chose to look at what the field of hostage negotiation might offer educators who struggle to support these students. First, I am ethically committed to the search for non-coercive ways of working with people who are upset and struggling—even, or perhaps especially, those seen as particularly troublesome and unreachable. Second, I strongly believe in the value of "cross-pollination" between various fields of study. Applying the lenses of one field to the issues faced by another can generate unexpected insights and open new ways to think and act. The third reason is personal and ties directly back to my experience as a student in the public school system.

It is probably an understatement to say I was not a model student. As an undiagnosed autistic kid, my attempts to cope with what I experienced as a hostile classroom environment often led me to either retreat into myself or act out in ways that challenged my teachers. Throughout my rocky career at school my report cards were filled with that familiar litany of teacher frustration: "could do better," "needs to pay attention," and "must try harder." When I quit school at age 15, disillusioned and angry, nobody tried very hard to keep me. Luckily, although I did not like school, I did like learning. So I took Mark Twain's advice and didn't let school interfere with my education. I read voraciously and eventually cobbled together an adequate education. I was one of the lucky ones, but I have carried with me a visceral memory of what it felt like to be labelled one of "those" kids—the so-called losers and dropouts.

We know what the statistics are for students who leave school prematurely. Research makes unequivocal links between dropout rates and unemployment, poverty, and even incarceration (Alliance for Education, 2003). We also know that students with learning difficulties and behavioural issues are the students most likely to drop out of school (Alliance for Education, 2009). However, what is less known is that teachers also drop out of school. Statistics on teacher retention show that approximately one in four teachers quit teaching within the first two years (Greene, 2008), often because they feel inadequately prepared to deal with disruptive student behaviour. There is an ironic circularity to this problem. Both students and teachers feel unable to manage the classroom experience, but it is disruptive *student* behaviour that most often gets blamed for the defection.

For the teachers who stay, disruption at school can take up an enormous amount of time, energy, and even financial resources. Confrontations between students and educators can result not only in personal stress for both but also in conflicts that involve families and even the larger community. For example, school personnel may be held legally responsible when incidents erupt and interventions are questioned. Ron Garrison, an international expert in school safety and an expert witness in more than 85 legal cases involving restraint and seclusion, noted that every year in North America students and teachers are injured and even killed during confrontations (personal communication, June 2010). This is a sobering reality and, in this era of school shootings, is top of mind for many. However, it's not always easy to know what to do or how to respond.

My Journey

Over the period of a year, I read everything I could find about hostage negotiation. I perused FBI training manuals and read countless journal articles and books. But perhaps the most interesting part of the process was when I found and had the privilege of interviewing hostage negotiators from all over North America. Notable among these was Dominick Misino, whom I was fortunate to interview three years before his untimely death in 2013. Misino was the negotiator who resolved the Lufthansa Flight 592 hostage taking in 1993. During his career he successfully negotiated more than 200 incidents without a single loss of life, then went on to become an international trainer. I also spoke with John Tost, the Canadian negotiator who successfully negotiated the Headingly Prison riots in Winnipeg in 1996. Another negotiator I interviewed, Robin Burcell, became a forensic artist and now writes best-selling crime novels! Yet another, Andy DeWeese, retired from law enforcement only to become his county's most successful bylaw enforcement officer. He told me he's never had to file a report or actually enforce anything. He credits his success to what he learned on the job as a police negotiator. He doesn't threaten people; he talks to them. Others are trainers and practitioners from both Canada and the United States.

During many hours of interview and discussion, I heard about how negotiators operate, what considerations are most important, and what kind of training they receive in order to do this difficult and sensitive work. I found a philosophy of engagement that surprised me in its unanimity. I found a group of women and men who are deeply committed to non-coercive de-escalation processes. They proved humane and thoughtful, and what I heard changed my view of what is possible when we learn to engage empathetically with people who are deemed irrational or dangerous.

Educators: Unprepared and Shocked

In the course of writing this book I reached out to educators, university professors, deans working in teacher education programs, and school administrators from all over the world. I asked about pre-service training. Almost unanimously I was told that little time or attention was paid to issues of classroom management (a phrase I confess to deeply disliking) in the pre-service training programs they'd attended. They also noted that little had changed in this regard since their days as university students. I learned that educators were usually left on their own to find, learn, and practise the interpersonal skills that appeared most needed. Some responded by taking personal initiative to seek out ancillary training. Many, however, claimed they had no idea where to look.

Teachers told me how unprepared they felt when issues first arose in the classroom. Most left teacher training with the assumption that they would simply learn what they needed to know on the job or through mentor teachers. However, the mentors and supports weren't always there, and there was little practical advice to be had. Teachers told me that despite their desire to learn new and effective approaches, they often found themselves going back to what they'd experienced in the classroom as students with their own teachers, especially when they were under duress. Many expressed discomfort with this but admitted they often just didn't know what else to do besides reproduce what had been done to them. As one assistant principal I spoke with eloquently put it,

> This profession is unique because everyone entering it is an expert. We've all been in the process from a young age. Essentially, teachers do to the kids what was done unto them. And that perpetuates a lot of behaviours that are rooted more in familiarity than a useful teaching practice.

A troubling theme emerged during these conversations. Educators underscored what I was seeing in my review of extant literature: there is still considerable disagreement within the educational sector about exactly how to respond to student disruption. Many schools support programs based on what are considered pragmatic behaviour management premises favouring the application of rewards and punishment. Although many of these approaches claim to be positive, and proponents insist that whenever possible interventions should be made supportively, most continue to operate from a deficit perspective. The assumption is that it is ultimately the student who must change to fit the school. Still others suggest that antidotes to disruption will not be found within the code of conduct but instead through the creation of more interesting, relevant, and self-directed curricula. In this instance it is the school that must change to fit the student. In the face of these contradictions, one has to wonder how teachers are to make sense of this divide and figure out what to do. Further, most of us recognize that even if there is a commitment to one approach or the other, neither is likely to eliminate disruption entirely, since interactive conflict is unavoidable.

Student Voices

This work would be incomplete without including the voices of students. Unfortunately, students are rarely asked for their input—especially students most directly affected by the behavioural procedures and policies that are applied to them at school. It wasn't easy to find literature that showcases the voices of students, particularly those labelled disruptive, but I did find some. In addition, I spoke with students as part of the initial study and afterward as well. I also bring my own experience to this work and that of many of the people I've met in person and online in discussions about this topic.

I Don't Have Time, and You Don't Know the Kids I Work With!

For many years, my husband and partner, Norman Kunc, and I have offered workshops on relational, communication-based approaches to disruption. Unfortunately, these are sometimes criticized as placation, with the underlying assumption that empathy and accountability cannot coexist. "We can't just let kids get away with bad behaviour" is something we often hear. "There need to be consequences" is another. Even for those who want to try a different approach, the concern is that what we're proposing will be time-consuming and inefficient. I started this project because we were consistently hearing the same two objections when conversations centred on what are sometimes called "soft skills"—relationship building, fostering a sense of belonging, empathy, and deep listening. "We don't have time to build relationships" we were often told. At times our ideas would be dismissed as naive, idealistic, or just plain unrealistic. "You just don't know the kids I work with!"

I'll admit to being frustrated by these responses. I believed they represented an abdication of responsibility. But over time I began to rethink my perception. While it is most certainly true that time is at a premium for educators, and it is equally true that I don't know the particular students teachers work with, it became clear that what was being expressed in those two comments was actually deep frustration: frustration with students labelled disruptive, yes, but also frustration with the system's requirements and the unfulfilled promises of a long line of proposed solutions, many of which continue to mandate conflicting approaches. After all, how do you respond supportively to students in a zero-tolerance environment? For many teachers, already overwhelmed with the day-to-day requirements of the classroom, arbitrary changes in curriculum, a decrease in both funding and support, and the increasing standardization of the educational system, it's been difficult to figure out where to turn for assistance or even find the time to do so.

When You're Stuck…Bring in More People

A common problem exists in education—actually in almost any field. Typically, when we try to solve problems, we only talk to each other. Teachers talk to teachers; psychologists talk to psychologists; engineers talk to engineers. Generally, this makes sense. After all, who understands education better than educators? Especially when we are struggling, we want and need the support of our peers. At best, talking to others who understand our challenges can be a source of support and new ideas. The danger, however, is predictable. When we ask the same questions, we tend to get the same answers. Our understandable frustration at finding ourselves stuck in this loop can lead to another problem. Those conversations, rather than bringing forward alternative ideas, can become a litany of complaints and bitterness and devolve into what my friend and colleague Rich Villa refers to as "problem admiration." The more stuck and frustrated we feel, the more we are inclined to indulge in these counterproductive interactions.

Margaret Wheatley (2002) says, "When you're stuck, bring in more people." Unfortunately, when relationships become difficult, many of us are inclined to do the exact opposite. This is often the time we hunker down and try to wrestle the problem to the ground all by ourselves. Sometimes we take this approach because we worry that our struggles may be seen as evidence of our incompetence, but sometimes it's simply because we're exhausted and out of ideas.

When I heard Margaret Wheatley's comment, I began to wonder if the help teachers need could come from unexpected places. Hyman and Perone (1998) looked at the educational policies and practices most likely to contribute to disruptive student behaviour and warned that a move toward a law-enforcement orientation by schools was a move in the wrong direction. Ironically, it is law enforcement to which I turned for ideas. However, hostage negotiators comprise a segment of law enforcement with a different focus. Instead of applying a series of cascading punitive strategies and relying on ultimatums and authoritarian directives, hostage negotiators rely on listening and support to help de-escalate disruptive individuals. Instead of applying an action imperative, negotiators use dynamic inactivity and respond fluidly to the situation rather than reacting to it. Hostage negotiation approaches are non-coercive and non-avoidant, and they rely on communication and relationship-building to create change. The hallmarks of modern crisis negotiation include active listening, self-management, and the development of authentic rapport and empathy. Negotiators insist that although there are some skills that must be learned and practised, the most important part of the process is not about superimposing theories and strategies on a situation or an individual but has to do with being present and flexible and, most important, changing the way we think about people who are in crisis. They also insist that the process is deceptively simple and that it works.

It's Not Another Model

> "Any tool is a weapon if you hold it right."
>
> —Ani de Franco

I begin with a caveat and a warning. I started learning and practising conflict resolution skills almost 30 years ago, many of which are similar to those used by hostage negotiators. I used these skills and ideas profitably in my workplace position as a labour relations director and also in private mediations over the years. What I'd learned was helpful in many ways. However, I began to become concerned that these skills could also be used disingenuously around the time of Michael Brown's death in Ferguson, Missouri, in 2014. Brown's death at the hands of law enforcement sparked outrage about the continuation of systemic racism and inequity in America and precipitated the birth of the Black Lives Matter movement. During the aftermath of the

Ferguson incident, Missouri politicians exhorted members of the fledgling group to tamp down their anger, or else they could not expect their issues to be heard. This expectation—that a dissenting group will be heard only if they state their issues "nicely"—exposes a serious power differential that effectively silences all protest. In the process, it ensures the survival of a problematic status quo: those in power can dictate how difficult interactions and conversations should take place or if they can take place at all.

Leaders in Missouri used the language of conflict resolution. I found this distressing. Since then, it has been my ongoing concern that the skills I talk about in this book could be used to suppress dissident voices or in service of the status quo. These skills must never devolve into tools of suppression or even oppression.

Students who present as "behaviour problems" are sometimes what my late friend Herb Lovett used to call the "social critics" who tell us what isn't working in our schools. Sometimes the way in which those criticisms are raised is difficult for us to interpret, much less respond to positively. It is my hope that the approaches I bring forward here will be used not to silence those resistant voices but to create viable ways to listen to the subtext of what difficult students are trying to tell us. We must ask ourselves: Is a dissenting person a freedom fighter or a terrorist? Is behaviour always evidence of simple noncompliance, or is it a cry for help or evidence of resistance to a sometimes problematic system?

My second worry is that readers might interpret what I've written as an invitation to use these ideas as a step-by-step model. "Just do these ten things in this order, and you'll be fine." That's actually the opposite of my intent. Instead, I hope these ideas will be used flexibly and situationally. My concern with models is that they tend to crystallize ideas and are not always responsive to the diversity of situations we are confronted with or the people we're interacting with. In a model-based approach, we often have only one option or a limited series of options to choose from. When those options fail or fizzle, we're at a loss. What to do now? In some ways it is like the difference between classical music and jazz. In classical music, although musicians can add feeling and nuance, they are required to follow the score quite rigidly. Many models mandate similar rigidity of response. In jazz, improvisation is what makes the music alive and responsive. The actions of one musician prompt the others to create variations. They must be intensely attuned to one another and follow one another's leads flexibly. This is how I hope these ideas will be used.

But Wouldn't Life Be So Much Easier If There Was a Recipe We Could Follow?

Unfortunately, we all know there isn't a recipe when it comes to human relationships, much as we might wish there were. People and relationships are far too complex to fit neatly into pre-packaged boxes. So what I didn't want was to write yet another book of tactics and strategies, another "ten tips for what to do on Monday," or offer more tricks for that ubiquitous "teacher's toolbox."

However, if you're like the many educators I've talked with over the years, it's likely that your toolbox is already overflowing, and further, many of the strategies you've collected are frustratingly contradictory. We probably all secretly wish for some kind of recipe we could follow that would solve our problems efficiently once and for all. However, if I came to you claiming that I (or even the negotiators I interviewed) had the answer to all the issues you face, you'd likely be skeptical. So you should be. In the time you've been teaching, you've likely seen your share of suggested programs and approaches taken on and discarded with disheartening regularity. This has led many teachers I know to harbour cynicism and mistrust of anything labelled "the new best thing" or "flavour of the month."

In this book I neither pretend expertise nor claim a technology. If anything, I am relying on the credibility I've borrowed from the negotiators, educators, students, and others I spoke with and a set of guiding principles. What I hope to do is to provide a series of stories and concepts that may spark new ideas for you. Rather than techniques, they are more about being present than following a formula. They reflect an overarching philosophy of engagement.

To quote two of the negotiators I interviewed,

> You've got to adjust, depending on what the situation is. You've got to be able to change your methods. And it depends on . . . the people you're dealing with.

> There's no template to what we do . . . we modify . . . adapt.

Are There Specific Skills We Can Learn?

Yes. Might they be useful to you in your classrooms? I believe they could be. But here's that caveat again. Unless these approaches are grounded in a philosophy of respect and partnership, of openness and empathy, they will simply be more stuff to collect for that toolbox. The most important thing I learned from the negotiators was not about specific strategies. It was about a change in perspective, finding other ways of seeing and interpreting people and events. They reminded me that this always involves being reflexive, observant, and quick on your feet. As the great South American educational philosopher and activist Paulo Freire (1970) says, praxis must be much more than simply the practical application of a skill. Rather than a habitual response based on what we've done in the past, or a rote series of discrete steps, it should be a process of reflection followed by action, followed by more reflection. In other words, an organic, fluid, and generative process that flows from an ethical, values-based stance.

In short, this is not a book about how to make someone do what you want them to do without them knowing you're doing it. It is, however, a book that will introduce you to some people and some ideas that may be new. It might help you to see the situations you find yourself in through new eyes.

How the Book Is Organized

This book is a blend of journalistic exploration, story, theory, and discussion, and it includes vignettes from hostage negotiators, educators, students, parents, and others. Some stories and metaphors come from my own experiences and others who have personal experience with school discipline programs.

I begin by offering an outline of the problem faced by educators in contemporary Western education. This chapter is the most academic in the book. If that's not your thing, you may want to skip it. However, its purpose is to create some context for what follows.

Next I introduce you to a brief history of hostage negotiation and the way this branch of law enforcement has changed from an "action imperative" policy of "contain, chemicals, and SWAT" to a communication-based process that has its roots in communication theory and psychotherapy.

The next chapter, titled "Relocating the Problem," will introduce the concept of narratives and explore how the narratives we use to make sense of the world influence our behaviour and responses—and how critical it is to question and sometimes intentionally change those narratives.

The following nine chapters are about specific relational crisis negotiation approaches and reflect a synthesis of the things I learned from negotiators. As mentioned, none of the nine ideas are intended to represent a fixed model. Rather, they are intended as ideas that may be profitable to grapple with and consider. They might best be described as "things to think about". Although I have treated them separately, they are all part of a single approach. It's impossible, for example, to create supportive relationships without empathy and impossible to listen well without curiosity. Of course, self-awareness is always necessary! The approaches are as follows:

- Relationship
- Empathy
- Curiosity
- Listening
- Self-awareness/management
- Dynamic inactivity
- Face saving
- Thought interruption
- Problem solving

In the epilogue I look at the issue of school shooting, a topic that today inevitably arises in the context of any discussion about school discipline and safety. I revisit the recommendations of the Safe School Initiative (2003) and the Bystanders Report (2008).

Finally, I have included the transcript of an interview with Ron Garrison, school safety expert and expert witness in 85 cases involving restraint and seclusion.

A Few Words on Language

I've used the term *hostage negotiation* throughout this book, even though it might more aptly be called crisis negotiation, since many of the situations negotiators face don't necessarily involve hostages. Dominick Misino, former head of the New York City Hostage Negotiation Team, told me that more than 80 percent of the issues they are called to negotiate are incidents involving barricaded or suicidal individuals (personal communication, February 2010). Hammer (2007) also suggested that hostage negotiation is more accurately defined as crisis management. In this context, crisis can be defined as "A personal difficulty that overwhelms, or threatens to overwhelm, a person's resources and coping ability or capacity" (Slatkin, 2006, p. 5). Crisis (or hostage) negotiation is the process whereby an outside intervener attempts to de-escalate or disarm an individual and bring closure to a hostage or barricade event through listening and verbal means.

I have deliberately avoided using the word *behaviour* wherever possible. Over time, this word has changed from a verb to a noun and is often used pejoratively—as in "he's a real behaviour problem." We may assume the word *behaviour* is neutral and merely descriptive, but in fact it is more than that. A student assigned the label of behaviour problem as if that label encompassed an entire identity may have significant difficulty becoming free from the globalized weight of such a pronouncement. In this book I suggest that there is no such thing as a behaviour problem; there is only conflict. Making this shift in the way we see disruption has the potential to open space for different and more effective responses.

Many of the stories in this book are true or only slightly altered. In some cases names have been changed to protect identities, but in most I was privileged to have permission to use names. In a very few cases, stories are hybrids. I thank all the people who kindly allowed me to recount their experiences.

In Conclusion: A Confession or Two

Before we proceed with the interesting stuff—what I learned from hostage negotiators, educators, and students is nothing if not interesting—I have a confession to make.

Although this is a book about education, I am not a teacher. The only experience I have in the classroom is as a student, and as mentioned, I wasn't terribly successful. Despite the fact that I have never taught in the classroom, in a strange twist of fate I have been involved in adult education: providing conference keynotes and workshops, and conducting in-service and training for teachers and human service workers in the areas of inclusive education, disability issues, conflict management, and behavioural support for almost 30 years.

I used to feel apologetic about my lack of direct classroom experience. What right did I have to speak to teachers about what goes on in the classroom? However, I've had to rethink that. Perhaps it is exactly because I come from outside the field of education that what I have to offer might be relevant and helpful. I bring you a different perspective, both through my experience as a mediator and negotiator and through my past experience as a so-called disruptive autistic student. Further, because I have had the privilege of travelling internationally to talk with educators about their work, perhaps I can serve as a conduit, bringing their wisdom to you and vice versa.

It is for this reason that I no longer apologize about sticking my nose into the work teachers do. I know how much I have learned from the many wonderful educators I've met over the years, and I hope I've been able to give back something useful. I have had the privilege of time and resources that have allowed me to delve into alternative fields that interest me and bring them forward for your consideration.

I bring to this work both passion and curiosity: passion in support of outliers and outsiders in our school system who struggled like I did, and curiosity about whether the approaches that helped me learn adaptive skills might help others. It's my hope that what I've written might broker a peace between educators, who try valiantly to understand why these students do what they do and ache to find a way to help them, and students, who likewise try valiantly to cope with difficult situations and to understand what adults want from them.

It is from this vantage that I wrote this book. I hope it proves useful.

CHAPTER ONE

DEFINING THE PROBLEM (OR I DID MY HOMEWORK)

> Individual experiences of failure are most often understood as personal events. Such descriptions leave no place to go. Stepping away from an individualistic perspective makes room for the social construction of a larger perspective, one that reaches beyond the limiting idea of the individual . . . as responsible for institutional and systemic failures.
>
> Vikki Reynolds (2010)

> Research is important, not for what it can measure, but for what it can do.
>
> —Patty Lather (1993)

Reframing Behaviour as Conflict

What if there was no such thing as a "behaviour problem?" What if there was only conflict? What might happen if we entertained the idea that calling a difficult interchange conflict could actually make things easier? After all, we can't negotiate a behaviour problem, but we can negotiate a conflict. How might this change in narrative alter the way we respond when we feel challenged?

Labelling someone a behaviour problem is not only unkind, it also isn't particularly helpful. In fact, doing so might make our work more difficult because the term is vague and non-descriptive. It doesn't tell us why a person is doing what they are doing. Perhaps the very act of reframing student disruption as conflict has the potential to open opportunities to find fruitful and alternative responses to challenging situations.

In this chapter, and in this book as a whole, I attempt to create linkages between conflict theory and educational practice. I synthesize some of the literature I reviewed during the initial study that gave rise to this book, hoping to examine the potential for a change of focus about difficult interactions from a remedial, behaviourist view to one in which student disruption is framed more neutrally.

This reframing may be an important first step in bridging what is sometimes called the "research-to-practice gap" in education (Mayer & Furlong, 2010). It suggests the need for an analysis of the nature of the relationship and interactions between the student, the learning environment, the broader culture, and the teacher. In this view, so-called "challenging behaviour" does not occur in a vacuum, nor does it belong solely to the student; rather, it is a function of the interchange. This suggests that confrontations between teachers and students cannot be effectively resolved by simply invoking the code of conduct or applying a series of rewards and punishments in a top-down authoritarian manner but rather through cooperative and collaborative means.

The idea of utilizing conflict processes in schools is not particularly new. Many educators acknowledge the value of peer-mediation programs designed to teach students communication skills (Cohen, 2005; Johnson & Johnson, 1996, 2006). In fact, many schools have implemented peer mediation and restorative justice programs and experienced considerable success with them. However, what may be new is the idea that mediation and negotiation might also have utility between teachers and students during difficult incidents.

Classroom Management

Although the term *classroom management* is uncomfortably fraught with suggestions of control and enforced compliance, Evertson and Weinstein (2006) chose to define it more neutrally as "the actions teachers take to create an environment that supports and facilitates both academic and social-emotional learning" (p. 4). However, even this definition raises complexity. As Martin (2004) pointed out, "The concept of a 'positive learning environment' is both broad and vague" (p. 1) and is subject to interpretations as varied as the individuals who hold them.

Educators Caught in an Ideological Cross Fire

Many educators and, indeed, the wider public have suggested that getting compliance from students through the application of positive reinforcement coupled with negative or even so-called "logical" consequences is the most effective means of managing disruptive behaviour. Others suggest that educators can circumvent the need for either punishment or reward systems by creating more dynamic learning environments, focusing on relationship development and stressing student involvement in all aspects of education. These distinct ideologies do not coexist peacefully within the educational research and practice.

Educators are caught in the crossfire of this debate. Proponents on both sides have made impassioned arguments that centre the discussion on divergent theories of child development, educational philosophy, and issues of pragmatics and efficacy. Bookstores and libraries are filled with advice for teachers, but until recently there has been comparatively little serious research to help make sense of this debate.

In an effort to bring some coherence to the discussion, Freiberg and Lapointe (2006) set out to identify and evaluate classroom management programs currently available to educators. Out of 800 programs, only a small number could be described as evidence-based. They settled on 40 using the following criteria: only school-based programs serving a population of students aged 3 to 18 and selected by at least 1 of 14 relevant organizations were eligible. All programs needed to demonstrate a focus on prevention and intervention and evidence of support, training, and resources. In addition, management processes must have been integrated in both classroom and school (p. 739).

They identified three major themes: (a) moving beyond discipline, with an emphasis on learning and self-control; (b) school connectedness or the need for involvement of all constituents of the school community; and (c) social and emotional development. Two subthemes also emerged: (a) caring and trust, with a strong focus on relationship, attachment, and trust building; and (b) positive school and classroom climate, stressing the influence of the learning environment on student behaviour.

These authors suggested that previous paradigms, which were largely based on a control and compliance orientation, should be replaced with others based on teacher facilitation and student self-direction. In their view, it makes little sense that "in a technological world that expects flexibility, independence, and self-discipline, many schools of the 21st century continue to follow management paradigms of the 19th and 20th century that valued compliance and obedience over innovation, creativity and self direction" (p. 773); they also stressed the need for the development of "student centered learning environments" (p. 774). Pianta (2006) suggested the need for "a focus on relationships rather than discrete behaviors" (p. 704). Conflict processes work well with what these authors recommended. However, the ongoing popularity of programs based on behaviourist approaches that favour the analysis (and counting) of discrete behaviours and the application of teacher-led interventions indicate that these recommendations have been less realized than proponents of self-directed learning had hoped for.

Behaviourism in the Classroom

Lee Canter's (1988) assertive discipline is an older example of a behaviourist approach to classroom management that was widely used in North American schools for several decades. Canter claimed that teachers could not afford what he believed were long-term strategies based on relationship building and democratic problem solving such as those described by Freiberg and Lapointe (2006) and Pianta (2006). According to Canter, when it comes to discipline matters, teachers "need answers, and they need them now" (p. 73). Canter's suggested remedies were simple and swift—reward compliance and punish infractions. This approach is based on a somewhat Skinnerian behaviourist assumption that human behaviour will change only in order to gain a desirable reward or to avoid an undesirable consequence (Skinner, 1972, 1974, 1983). Practitioners like Canter continue to claim statistical success in suppressing or diminishing difficult behaviours in this way, which gives their programs significant appeal for individuals looking for a fast and scripted answer to the pragmatic problem of "what to do on Monday."

Positive Behavioural Intervention and Support

Many educators are questioning both the efficacy and the ethics of punishment and are in the process of shifting to programs that claim to emphasize the positive. Positive behavioural intervention and support (PBIS) is one such program that has found widespread popularity in recent years. Users of the PBIS program stress strategies like verbal praise, token systems, prizes, activity rewards, and public recognition as ways to increase student involvement and facilitate change in school culture (Newcomer, 2007).

At first glance, PBIS appears to offer a new and promising take on the issue of discipline. But is it actually all that new or different from what has gone before? In this context, it might be important to note that like many of its predecessors, the program is firmly located in a tradition of behaviourism and derives directly from the related field of applied behaviour analysis (Horner &Sugai, 2004; Newcomer, 2007). Although proponents insist the program supports a positive orientation, this claim may be misleading (Chui & Tulley,1997; Mulick& Butter, 2005). Rule infractions are still punished, and the list of interventions remains startlingly similar to other approaches:

planned ignoring, time-outs, and removal of privileges or students, detention, segregation, suspension, and even expulsion (Newcomer, 2007). This argument is often countered with a claim that punishment is typically mild and occurs less frequently (Horner, 2000; Lewis et al., 2006)

Alfie Kohn (2018) is concerned that despite claims that PBIS promotes prosocial aims and favours positive interventions, its goal is "to make students do whatever they're told." He adds, "It's all about compliance and conformity" and dryly suggests that given a wholesale reliance on tokens and praise, the program might better be renamed "TKLP, for "Treating Kids Like Pets" (p. 281).

Is treating kids like pets ethical? This is a question that doesn't get much air time in the discussion. However, as Kohn (1993, 2018) says, the question isn't whether you can get people to do what you want by applying either the stick or carrot (because you can, at least in the short term) but rather whether we *should* do so and whether the ends truly justify the means.

When it comes to behaviour management, the PBIS focus is on eliminating "inappropriate behaviour" (Newcomer, 2007). Of course any discussion of appropriate versus inappropriate (not my favourite words under any circumstance) must raise questions of interpretation. It may be that a teacher—or indeed the entire school—values students who stay in their seats with both feet on the floor, look at the teacher when they are speaking, and do whatever the teacher wants immediately. In these schools, this may be considered the benchmark for appropriate classroom behaviour (Newcomer, 2007).

In such a classroom, what happens to the student who needs activity in order to fully engage with what they are learning? If raising a hand before speaking and staying in your seat is what's considered appropriate (and is enforced), what happens to the student with involuntary speech and movement tics? If appropriate behaviour means taking an active part in group work, what happens to the student who requires more processing time and becomes overwhelmed with the intensity of small group interpersonal dynamics? What happens to the student who struggles with transitions?

Although *appropriate* isn't easy to define, proponents of PBIS claim that providing clear rules and expectations will counter this vagueness. It is recommended that there be no more than three to five rules, and students should be made aware of and periodically reminded of these expectations (Newcomer, 2007). While it is certainly difficult to argue against the need for clarity, we should be concerned with three mitigating issues. First, the adoption of generic school-wide rules may override individual teacher discretion, a complaint I heard from several teachers. As one teacher I met at an educational conference in Chicago told me,

> I've been teaching for 40 years. I'm a good teacher, but now I'm spending all my time doing data collection instead of teaching. And because it's a school-wide initiative, we all have to do the same thing. Not once in 40 years have I ever felt I needed to send a student to the principal's office. Now with PBS, I have to. It's all about data collection.

PBIS is a highly data driven program. Proponents defend this by saying they are trying hard to understand the underlying reasons for difficult behaviour. They are looking for antecedents and patterns. However, the way in which this typically takes place is not through asking students for explanations of their own behaviour. Instead, teachers are expected to implement complicated data systems, tracking how often and how long a behaviour occurs by using clickers, timers, clocks, apps, paper and pencil, tables, graphs, and stopwatches. It is assumed this will provide the needed information to address the situation effectively.

But will it? It's interesting to note that even weather researchers have concluded from their experience over the past 20 years that data collection is not an adequate way to predict weather. There are too many variables to make accurate prediction possible. And this kind of prediction only involves wind and air masses, not the complexity of human behaviour!

A second concern is that the lack of student involvement in the creation of rules becomes a lost opportunity for the development of critical thinking skills. Students who are actively involved in the creation of a democratic classroom and have opportunities to question fairness and utility of the rules applied to them will be far more likely to invest in making the classroom work than they will if rules are simply imposed on them.

The third concern is that the way in which the rules are enforced may undermine the goal of a cooperative classroom environment. In support of clarity, teachers are encouraged to act quickly to stop undesirable behaviour. They are told it is critically important to immediately let the student know what is wrong with what they are doing and how the behaviour doesn't fit with previously discussed classroom/school expectations. Curiosity and listening are noticeably absent in this model. Instead, it's a model based on telling. It would seem that in this model, if any questions are asked, they are not asked of students but answered through detailed data collection, which is then collated and interpreted by the adults in the school.

As you will see later in this book, this is in direct opposition to what hostage negotiators and even brain researchers have learned about the role of curiosity and listening in de-escalation processes. It is also entirely possible that an approach based on telling will miss important information that might surface with a few well-placed questions. Consider the following story.

A friend related an incident that occurred many years ago in a large urban high school in southern Ontario. The school had recently committed to becoming fully inclusive, and one of the first students it welcomed into a ninth grade class had a significant disability. In addition to using a wheelchair, she couldn't speak and at that time did not yet have any other reliable way to communicate.

A few weeks into the school year, the teacher came to see the principal in obvious distress. Although her commitment to inclusive education was strong, she'd been faced with something she had no idea how to address. Apparently the young girl in the wheelchair had suddenly taken to masturbating in class. Needless to say, this was neither the time nor the place for such an activity, so the teacher and the assistant had been trying to stop her. They'd tried talking to the girl about appropriate places and times, and when that didn't seem to have an effect, they admitted they'd become punitive, removing her from the classroom into a time-out area and sometimes speaking harshly.

Later, in the staffroom, the teacher asked her fellow educators to help her think through the situation because if it didn't change, they would have to rethink the placement. The school nurse just happened to be in attendance. "Has anyone checked her out physically?" she innocently asked. Conversation stopped while the teacher considered this possibility.

It turned out that the student had a serious yeast infection that was making her uncomfortable and itchy. It was easily remedied.

Unfortunately, it's easy get so caught up in eradicating an undesirable behaviour that we forget to ask the simplest questions. Were the teachers in this scenario completely obtuse? Of course not. However, what we see often depends on where we're focusing our attention. These teachers were focused on understanding the situation in the context of inappropriate behaviour and therefore missed the fact that it was a medical situation. Ruth Meyers, a psychiatrist and physician who has consulted on incidents termed "disruptive and self- or other injurious behaviour" for more than 30 years, claims that in the 7000 cases she's been involved with, the genesis of the so-called behaviour is more often than not a medical issue that can be resolved (personal communication, 2018). However, in many instances the first response is to place the individual on a behaviour program or remove them from the classroom.

Finally, although PBIS is touted as evidence based and widely considered the gold standard for education, many of the studies cited to support its success have been criticized as self-generated and circular (Chui &Tulley, 1997; Mulick& Butter, 2005) and largely reliant on case studies without control groups (Osher, Bear, Sprague,& Doyle, 2010). Many schools in North America are in the process of adopting

PBIS, but perhaps we should worry that they are travelling down a dubious road that isn't substantially different from what has come before and promises more than it delivers.

Although the program was not identified by name, it was recognizable by the processes and structures described by some of the educators I interviewed. I heard mixed reactions. One participant enthusiastically endorsed the approach, claiming it had given staff much needed inroads to addressing issues and provided a way to develop "a common language that we can [use to] interact with students about appropriate behaviour." In his school, they distributed something they called "power cards." Teachers give out cards for "powerful" behaviour (i.e., what the teacher approves of) and conversely give out different cards (powerless cards?) when a student is acting in ways the teacher disapproves of. I assume the first would be redeemed for prizes or privileges, but it was not clear what happens if a student amasses a collection of negative cards. It would probably lead to the same predictable cascade of punitive responses. As one educator noted,

> This is our number one program goal. Students are rewarded for positive behaviour by receiving cards. Where staff were often hesitant to interact with students about either positive or negative behaviour, now we can just walk up to a person and say, "That was really great what you just did there . . . Good job. Here's a card" or, on the negative side of things, walk up to a student and say, "Hey, the way you just spoke to that kid there wasn't very powerful. What could you have done differently so that that student isn't upset?"
>
> Many of our staff would like to think that eventually the kids will intrinsically do positive things without having to receive an exterior type of reward token to do it. I've got a more balanced approach; research certainly would suggest that if you're getting positive attention and rewarded for doing positive things, then the frequency of those behaviours will tend to increase.

But does the research actually support this? Alfie Kohn (1993, 2018) has spent more than 25 years reviewing precisely this research and disagrees. He found that approaches like PBIS with their token and reward systems actually accomplish the opposite of what they intend. He notes that "evidence suggests that when children are rewarded or praised for acting in a caring or helpful way, they subsequently become *less* caring and helpful (102, 173–74, and 288). It's also important to realize that the *goal* of programs like PBIS isn't to help students become sophisticated decision makers or critical thinkers" (p. 281).

Responses to the adoption of a PBIS approach were not uniformly appreciated among the educators I interviewed. One vice principal I spoke with expressed reservations that echoed Kohn's concerns:

> We're wrestling with the role of positive reinforcement. I don't like that you reward with stuff for what you should be doing anyway. If you are internally motivated to do something anyway, it devalues it to give coupons. It takes the locus of control from an internal one to an external one. And that means if the person doing the reinforcement isn't present you might not do that behaviour—[the student] doesn't necessarily own it. And that disturbs me.

I heard stories about behaviour specialists strategically situated in the back of classrooms observing particular students and taking notes. Their presence did not go unnoticed by either the student under surveillance or the other students. Another described a process whereby students considered "at risk" were shadowed by adults with clipboards during class, in the hallways, and even in the lunchroom. It isn't hard to imagine what the student reaction to this might be, and unless the observer has managed the trick of invisibility, it will likely stigmatize a struggling student even further. What we know from studies on quantum mechanics is that the observer will always impact what is observed.

Some might argue that what I've described in this critique are misinterpretations of PBIS goals and values, and highlight inflexible responses. This may be true, in part at least. And it is certainly not lost on me or other critics that many people's intentions are only the best. However, it is inarguable that data collection, rule enforcement, and the application of complicated reward systems remain the biggest hallmarks of PBIS programs, and in that way it remains similar to other behaviourist approaches. PBIS is based on the notion that all behaviour is functional and is used by the child to gain something he or she wants or to avoid something undesirable, and in this way it echoes a behaviourist belief about what motivates people (Gresham et al., 2004). There is a globalized assumption that students engage in behaviours that work for them and are in some way reinforcing. Ross Greene (2008) worries that such assumptions are simplistic and, further, might "lead many adults to the conclusion that those behaviors are purposeful" (p. 36). Greene suggests that for many disruptive students, the issue is not about the need to manipulate, get attention, or avoid work; instead, many of these students lack the skills necessary to manage classroom dynamics. Instead of applying rewards and consequences in an effort to shape behaviour, Greene recommends asking, "What lagging skills help us understand why the kid is getting, avoiding, and escaping in such a maladaptive fashion?" (p. 36). He noted that behaviourist programs—positive or negative—remain ineffective for some members of the school population, stating, "The school discipline plan *isn't working for the kids who aren't doing well*, and *isn't needed for the kids who are*" (p. 8, italics in the original).

Winslade and Monk (2007) go further, and note that "it is tempting to assume that they [students] are lacking in the necessary knowledge or skill to address the problem. However, another explanation is that young people are not used to experiencing themselves as authorities on themselves" (pg. 36). This suggests a need to interrogate our current practices of talking about students without them and instead work to include their voices in discussions that involve them.

I once raised some of these concerns with a prominent proponent of PBIS at an international educational conference. He protested my criticism with a telling response. "But we just don't know what else to do!" This, I thought, was honest.

Student Perceptions

Little attention has been paid to students' perception regarding the discipline and classroom management structures present in schools. In overlooking student voices and perspectives, we miss opportunities to learn how our actions are being interpreted. Students can provide important insight and input about what works, what doesn't, and why or why not.

The students I interviewed were largely unimpressed by token systems and verbal praise. Although none of them identified their school as a PBIS school, they were familiar with the processes.

> In our French program, you could get stamped on a card, when you are good, but it kind of dies out after a few years. It's kind of like a bribe when you are in Grade 8 and 9.
>
> But I don't know if it works for behaviour. I don't think so.

The students described feeling patronized and manipulated by praise. "Nice hand raising? Seriously?"

> I like the way you worked quietly and stayed in your seat? Sheesh.
>
> Next thing you know it's gonna be 'good pencil sharpening'

The students were clear, however, that acknowledgement is categorically different from praise. Praise, they noted, feels condescending. Acknowledgment is helpful in understanding whether you're on the right track.

Interestingly, they also felt that praise was often used disingenuously by teachers, so that a student receiving praise wasn't really being acknowledged for anything meaningful but instead was being used by the teacher to give a coded message to other students: "be like *this* student." This caused embarrassment and anxiety about being identified by other students as a "brownnoser." The biggest complaint

I heard was feeling singled out. Kids, it is clear, dislike being singled out for good stuff or for bad.

Although detentions were sometimes given in their schools, the students were unanimous: "I don't think they really work."

> You can't force them to come in. What are you going to do?

One student said that attempts to enforce whole-class detentions resulted in a cascading problem of tardiness: "When you have to stay for an extra seven minutes in class, they think they're punishing you in their class, but they're really punishing you in the next class!"

Woolfolk Hoy and Weinstein (2006) asked students to comment on what discipline processes worked or didn't work in their schools. Students identified personal caring, listening, "being there," fairness, humour, and the exercise of authority without resorting to humiliation or punitive means as effective teacher behaviours. Conversely, although the threat of punishment was relatively inconsequential to many, students considered the use of insults, public reprimands, and shaming severe enough to be held on par with expulsion. In addition, students reported that such tactics are often more upsetting to bystanders than those to whom they were directed. The students I spoke with agreed.

When asked similar questions, students interviewed by Cothran et al. (2003) identified teacher consistency, confidence, fun, empathy, self-disclosure, good communication and listening skills, caring relationships, respectful tone and manner (i.e., talking *with* students, not *at* them), role modelling, and firm but not mean standards as essential qualities shared by good teachers. They suggested that respect was lost when teachers resorted to threats or aggression, raised their voices, or lost control. Despite a wide demographic and school context, student responses were strongly consistent. Crowley (1993) found that personal relationships, humour, asking for student opinion, answering questions, and clear expectations (both academic and behavioural) were important to a group of adolescents labelled behaviourally disordered. Conversely, she found that teacher rigidity, overuse of discipline, rule enforcement, negative regard, and use of punishments eroded relationships and resulted in pervasive student anger and acting out. These findings were confirmed by Pomeroy (1999) in a study based on interviews with 33 students who were excluded from school. Crowley concluded,

> Positive attitudes toward teachers may lead to positive attitudes toward the subject matter and toward school in general. These attitudes may lead to a greater probability that a student with a behavioral disorder may graduate from high school and become a productive member of society (p. 147).

Students share common themes with respect to what they believe is effective classroom management. They want engaged, caring teachers who listen and provide clear expectations, and they would like to be included in decision making, asked for their opinions, and, above all, respected. Finally, they want to have fun.

It is interesting to note, and germane to this discussion, that "interpersonal and communication skills described by the students are largely missing components of teacher education programs. Effective communication training might be expanded to include active listening, questioning, enthusiasm, and conflict resolution skills" (Cothran et al., 2003, p. 440).

Lack of Training

Despite the fact that classroom management and issues related to student aggression and disruption rank as some of the most important concerns for teachers, it's surprising how little attention is paid to them in either teacher preparation programs or educational research conferences. Reasons for this are unclear. According to Evertson and Weinstein, this may be in part "because classroom management is neither content knowledge, nor psychological foundations, nor pedagogy, nor pedagogical content knowledge" (p. 4). Therefore, "it seems to slip through the cracks" (p. 4).

In a study of 156 public secondary teachers, Spaulding (2005) found that only 16.5 percent had received pre-service education in crisis management, and only 12 percent felt that what they had received was helpful. Although 72.5 percent of the respondents had received a minimal amount of training in more standard non crisis classroom management strategies, "very few of the respondents reported a positive and worthwhile classroom management course" (p. 7), stating that it bore "absolutely no relationship to real life in the classroom" (p. 7). Spaulding reported that 89 percent of the respondents agreed that pre-service courses should be provided to help teachers learn to work effectively with disruptive and aggressive students. However, there is little agreement regarding what the content of such training should be.

The administrators, teachers, and instructors in teacher education programs I interviewed agreed that pre-service training in classroom management and crisis prevention in Canada and the United States is generally inadequate. "I would say it was minimal. Absolutely minimal. I don't remember a course. There may have been one or two lectures, but it wasn't much at all."

> Often it's not touched on at all, and if it is, it's just one quick course.
>
> I don't honestly think that I had a course. . . . I think it was something that would have been discussed at different points and times.
>
> I think it was part of a survey course, once.

All were unanimous in recommending more comprehensive pre-service and practicum training with specific focus on classroom management. In addition, the value of mentorship programs was emphasized: "I think that schools need to try and create in-school mentoring programs where the new teacher is immediately linked up with a more seasoned campaigner."

> Knowing which support levels to go to if you are having challenges in your classroom. It's not a weakness if you're asking for support.

However, others mitigated this with stories of unhelpful mentoring. "Just because she's been there since God was a baby doesn't mean she has all the answers!"

> I think what would help teachers is insight into what the students are bringing into the classroom. I think teachers, to defend them, are so under the gun—testing, too much stuff to do, so they go boom! Get it all done. I think if we can help them understand special needs, behavioural issues, why kids do what they do . . . teacher education is so heavily focused on curriculum.

Another seasoned educator shared an interesting perspective:

> I think long-term, sustained effort is the solution to the problem. And that's what we don't do in schools. We need to identify a number of topics—of which conflict resolution would be one—we need to focus on. And [we need to] continue a long-term strategic effort in that direction. Because if we don't solve those problems, we're not going to be able to teach kids anything.

Still another agreed and recommended specific in-service around conflict management:

> I think some teachers here have been blessed with not having to deal with a lot of really hard core behavioural issues. So when it comes up, and there's some difficult behaviour, their way of dealing with that is . . . I don't want to say it's not very good, but they haven't thought it through. They get annoyed, and just want to send that problem away. So I think that ongoing in-service . . . how to manage conflict with students, and sometimes a conflict with other staff, too.

Structural Issues

It's not an understatement to say that educators work within a system that is subject to both overt and tacit constraints. These structural and external constraints combine to influence how teachers will respond to difficult students, which approaches will be sanctioned and allowed, and which will be more difficult to implement. In the widest sense, the cultural and political expectations placed on schools not only dictate how education will take place but also define the purpose of education itself. These expectations then translate into the mandates and regulations that schools and individual educators must abide by and include not only student–teacher ratios, what will be taught, and how it will be taught but also what disciplinary practices will be followed. Each of these, combined with considerations of school climate and culture, have important implications for the relationship between teachers and students. Although we can acknowledge that individual teachers have a great deal of influence in how those relationships will be developed and fostered, this discussion wouldn't go far enough without acknowledging the role of the systemic pressures teachers face.

Systemic Issues: Zero Tolerance

Contemporary schools are faced with demands for greater academic and social accountability within a context of fiscal constraint. This inevitably translates into that tired old saw—doing more with less. Many educators believe student disruption seriously hinders their ability to meet these competing demands. In an effort to manage this problem, many schools still rely on a process of triage, where difficult students are sent to detention or time-out, relegated to remedial or segregated programs, suspended, or even expelled. Few people I've talked to see these responses as optimal but instead express a sense of desperation: "We just don't know what else to do!" These approaches seem to promise short-term results, and are alluring in a climate of increasing demands. In addition, the many constituent groups that influence how education takes place—politicians, school districts, parents, and even the general public—often support these approaches and accept them within a wider political context of zero tolerance.

Widespread adoption of zero-tolerance policies, in the United States at least, immediately following the 1999 shootings at Columbine is an example of one such complicating systemic pressure (Skiba & Peterson, 1999). These policies mandate unilateral punitive responses to misbehaviour, regardless of any mitigating circumstance or even the severity of an infraction. Examples of children sent home because they carried plastic butter knives to school in their lunch pails and children expelled for having chains on their Mickey Mouse wallets have shown up in the news, but despite the obvious ridiculousness and overreaction to these so-called infractions, it hasn't been enough to move some schools away from a zero-tolerance stance. Proponents of zero-tolerance policies suggest it will give educators the tools they need to discipline effectively and therefore will result in safer schools (Skiba et al., 2006). Implementation is based on the assumption that punishing or removing difficult students will serve as a deterrent to all students, classroom and school climate will improve accordingly, and academic performance will rise. It is assumed that these policies will definitively address public concerns about what is widely believed to be a dramatic rise in adolescent violence.

However, these assumptions have been challenged and even disproved (Daniel & Bondy, 2008; Day, Golems, MacDougall, & Beals-Gonzales, 1995; Pollack, Modzeleski, & Rooney, 2008). With the exception of school shootings, which are separate issues that require a more complex analysis, the incidence of school violence has remained stable and has even declined in recent decades (Astor, Guerra, & Van Acker, 2010). In fact, it has been argued that the use of harsh punishment and the application of metal detectors, guards, and locked schools have been shown to erode school climate and contribute to more problems (Mayer & Leone, 1999). The promise of improved academic achievement and student behaviour has not been found (Skiba et al., 2006). In addition, families and the general public are increasingly critical of what is seen as arbitrary rule enforcement. Henry Giroux (2009) of McMaster University argued that zero-tolerance policies have created "disciplinary practices that closely resemble the culture of prisons" (p. 2); Giroux is worried that schools have become increasingly "militarized" and has famously described this as the "prison pipeline" (p. 2), referring to the practice of sending violators past the principal's office straight into the juvenile justice system.

Although not every school has an openly acknowledged policy of zero tolerance, particularly in Canada, many still utilize the same approaches under another name. Detention, suspension, and expulsion are the last resort of most educational settings in Western countries. What we know is that when success is based on removing the student from the classroom or even the school, the problem has simply been moved back to the community. Unfortunately, the climate of fear and punishment created in the process may cause an increase in the very behaviours schools are trying to change. If we look at the incidence of school shootings in the United States, despite a paucity of clear antecedents, a history of suspension and expulsion is often something the shooters have in common (personal communication, Garrison, 2018; also see the epilogue in this book for a further examination of the issue of school shootings).

In some jurisdictions, lawmakers have suggested amendments to existing legislation to allow for more in-school discretion and the use of alternatives to suspension and expulsion (Wise, 2009). This does not mean the pendulum has swung toward less punitive approaches. Many educators and members of the public believe the only effective response to misbehaviour is punishment, delivered swiftly and decisively, and that softer responses are tantamount to letting students get away with bad behaviour. Kohn (1996) noted that much of the controversy between so-called soft and hard approaches is based on the idea that punishing or doing nothing are the only available options. "Until this false dichotomy is identified and eradicated, we cannot hope to make any progress in moving beyond punitive tactics" (p. 31).

The Unfortunate Catch 22

Most educators understand the need to create a sense of belonging in the school community. It's hard to argue against the notion that belonging is a necessary prerequisite for the development of self-esteem, pro-social behaviour, and even learning. However, many schools make belonging contingent on good behaviour and achievement. Although achievement is easily quantified, good behaviour isn't always clearly defined, making it difficult for some students to conform. Students who don't meet the standards are routinely removed from their classrooms, sent to segregated settings, put into detention, and refused opportunities for social engagement until they demonstrate that they can master the curriculum and behave according to the school codes of conduct. Removing those students who aren't seen to be measuring up has some unintended consequences: students are required to master certain skills and behave in certain ways before they are allowed to belong, but the isolation and lack of belonging they experience in these segregated settings and through exclusionary practices makes it impossible for them to learn the pro-social and academic skills they need. For some students, this translates into an endless catch-22 situation wherein their lack of learning is then used as further justification for their continued exclusion (Kunc, 1992).

Teacher Beliefs

What teachers believe about the nature of education has a strong influence on what they choose to define as disruptive behaviour and how they decide to respond to it. What teachers believe about children and even human nature is equally, if not more, influential. As Greene (2008) stated, "It's your philosophy of kids that's going to guide your beliefs and your actions in your interactions . . . especially when the going gets tough" (p. 10). If, for example, we believe children are inherently destructive, disrespectful, and troublesome, our responses to their behaviour will be quite different than if we believe children are inherently cooperative, constructive, and kind (Kohn, 1996).

Johnson et al. (1994) conducted a study with a group of South Australian educators to determine how they viewed desired student behaviour, why they thought students should behave that way, what assumptions they held about the innate nature of children, what teacher and parent roles should be, and the location of power. Their findings were synthesized into the following four orientations to school discipline: (a) traditional or "teacher-in-charge [with] a number of clear rules and escalating punishments" (Lewis, 2006, p. 1201); (b) liberal progressive, with an emphasis on "shared responsibility, cooperation, and self-discipline" (p. 1201); (c) socially critical, which posited "student disruption as reasonable resistance to oppression" (pp. 1201–1202); and (d) laissez-faire, "which derived from the free choice movement within schooling" (p. 1202). Most teachers interviewed fell into the categories of traditional or liberal progressive, which Johnson et al. suggested reflects the status quo. Very few fell into the category of laissez-faire, an approach considered by most to be too soft and largely ineffective. What is perhaps most interesting is that virtually no teachers self-identified as socially critical.

Johnson et al. concluded there was greater need for educators to interrogate the assumptions and values inherent in education and to recognize the "ideological and political nature of discipline policies and practices" (p. 274). In addition, these researchers found that teacher beliefs about school discipline went "beyond psychological and even classroom related considerations" (p. 261). Responses were highly value-laden, critical of parenting styles and existing societal mores, and often reflected negative overarching theories of human nature. This suggests that when it comes to discipline, belief systems are even more complex and influenced by previous experience and outside forces than those held about other classroom issues.

Pajares (1992) maintained that beliefs continue to be the strongest predictors of behaviour since they are less dynamic and more rigidly held than more recently acquired academic knowledge. In this context, it is important to note that before educators ever reach pre-service training at university, they have likely spent almost two decades in classrooms as students, watching and learning about the practice of teaching from their teachers. By the time they enter teacher preparation, much of what they have observed has been internalized. Fang (1996) reviewed relevant research and found that despite training that contradicted what they had experienced as students, educators were most inclined to teach the way they were taught. Fang's research suggests that the narratives of education and, more specifically, of expected student behaviour are not easily changed. Reconciling more recent educational developments like cooperative learning and self-directed schools with expectations for quiet and compliant student behaviour is therefore likely to remain a daunting enterprise.

To further exacerbate this problem, Pajares (1992) pointed to a problematic self-sustaining cycle: "beliefs influence perceptions that influence behaviors that are consistent with, and that reinforce the original beliefs" (p. 317). Kennedy (1999) likewise noted a double bind faced by educators: "most teachers necessarily hold multiple and conflicting ideals. All of us do. We want teachers who are strict and do not tolerate inappropriate behavior, yet we also want teachers who are sympathetic and sensitive to students' needs" (p. 70).

Finally, Hyman et al. (2006) reported that one third of teachers in the United States considered bullying a normal childhood experience. Seen together with another study showing that 50–60 percent of students reported being bullied by teachers, a troubling connection between teacher beliefs and teacher actions may be drawn (Hyman et al., 2006). Earlier, Hyman and Perone (1998) worried that "victimization of students by school staff, most often in the name of discipline, is seldom recognized as a problem that may contribute to student alienation and aggression" (p. 7). This implies that without confronting the role of beliefs upon practice, it is unlikely change will take place. If educators believe difficult behaviour is simply the result of students making poor choices or having poor impulse control, or that it arises from a perverse desire to manipulate, garner attention, or resist adult control, there will be little room for responses that go beyond the remedial.

While much has been written regarding the influence of teacher behaviour on student learning, there is significantly less research available that attempts to analyze the influence of specific teacher behaviour on disruptive student behaviour (Evertson & Weinstein, 2006). There is, however, a small but promising body of research that begins to re-conceptualize behaviour as the result of interaction and relationship and, consequently, moves us closer to defining the issue as conflict.

Spaulding (2005) was asked by a group of administrators in Texas to conduct research on specific behaviours employed by teachers that either escalated or de-escalated students' aggressive behaviour. She found that "by far, the most common answer to what teachers do that may increase the chances of a violent situation was backing students into a corner" (p. 10). Those interviewed noted that the need for respect was paramount for both teachers and students, but they observed that although teachers expected and demanded respect from students, this was not always reciprocated.

Spaulding found that helpful teacher behaviours included giving students a voice, being proactive, good self-management, getting to know students and working to build relationships, showing respect, having a positive attitude, and being alert for abnormal student behaviour and body language. Instructional, listening, and conflict-management skills were identified as critical. The need for these skills, with an emphasis on self-management, was confirmed in Martin's (2004) study of three novice teachers.

In contrast, behaviours that were seen as triggers for disruption included over-control; a lack of clarity and consistency; humiliation, confrontation, and disrespect—especially in front of other students; not listening; negative attitudes; lack of rapport; taking things personally; unfairness; and having unreasonable expectations. Interestingly, passivity or being "too nice" and teacher isolation were also seen as contributing factors. A majority of Spaulding's respondents identified three specific teacher behaviours that were known to escalate disruption: "social isolation, derogatory comments, and gossip" (p. 13). Participants recommended "showing respect toward students as a way to de-escalate potential violent behavior" (p. 14) and increasing "teachers' awareness of their own behavior and . . . being willing to admit their mistakes and apologize to students" (p. 14).

So what does all this mean, and what can be done to address it? In the remainder of this book, I will introduce you to the philosophy and practices of hostage negotiators.

CHAPTER TWO

HOSTAGE NEGOTIATION (IT'S NOT THE SWAT TEAM)

> Hostage Negotiation can be summarized in one word—COMMUNICATION.
>
> —McMains & Mullin (2006)

Before I began this project, my view of hostage negotiation was largely influenced by television dramas and sensational news coverage. I envisioned helmets, shields, bulletproof Kevlar vests, smoke bombs, guns, throw-phones, bugs, and a lot of authoritarian commands. I certainly didn't see hostage negotiation as non-coercive. As I delved into the literature and began having conversations with real negotiators, I was catapulted into a parallel universe of negotiation theory and practice that I had no idea existed despite all the years I'd been involved in studying and teaching conflict processes.

The first thing I was surprised to learn was that the interventions I'd seen on TV and in the movies, referred to as Special Weapons and Tactics (SWAT), are used less than 1 percent of the time. Instead, negotiators rely on listening, relationship building, empathy, and open-ended questions, and they are successful in resolving more than 90 percent of the incidents they attend without injury or loss of life. These statistics include both international and domestic incidents. The situations we hear about through the media and watch on mainstream television are usually those that have failed. This leads the general public to believe that negotiation is far less effective than it actually is. These statistics initially impressed and convinced me to see if linkages might be profitably made between what negotiators know and do, and what educators know and do.

A Brief History of Hostage Negotiation

Until 1973, interactions between law enforcement and hostage takers or barricaded individuals were conducted in two ways: with a demand for surrender or a tactical intervention, sometimes known as a contain, chemicals, or SWAT approach (Strentz, 2006). The 1971 hostage taking in Attica prison that resulted in the deaths of thirty-nine people, and the deaths of eleven Israeli hostages and four Arab terrorists that took place in Munich during the 1972 Olympic Games, led to questions regarding the efficacy of those approaches. Law enforcement and government recognized the death tolls as unacceptable and began to look for alternative approaches.

Dr. Harvey Schlossberg, a psychologist and police officer with the New York City Police Department (NYPD) was asked to review both the Munich and Attica tragedies as well as other past incidents and to make recommendations about how law enforcement might change its approach and engage differently with people in crisis in order to minimize the possibility of violence and loss of life. With Frank Bolz, also of the NYPD, Dr. Schlossberg formulated a radical new strategy that would later be called the New York Plan (1974). The suggested model was based on communication theory and psychotherapy. The New York Plan was first implemented in 1973 during a hostage incident in a sporting goods store in New York City. Seven people were taken hostage by three armed men. Recognizing that conventional approaches were dangerous, since throwing a smoke bomb into a hardware store would likely have resulted in an even greater tragedy with the possibility of fire and explosion, they opted to try the New York Plan. Although one police officer lost his life at the beginning of the interaction, the incident was resolved without tactical intervention, and the approach overall was considered successful.

Since that time, countless law enforcement practitioners worldwide have been trained in this form of communication-based negotiation. Although most of the theories, principles, and guidelines currently used by negotiators worldwide were developed by the FBI through its Crisis Negotiation Unit, part of the Critical Incident Response Group in Quantico, Virginia, their origins are credited to Schlossberg and Bolz.

In the next section, I briefly introduce you to some of the definitions, considerations, and skills currently taught internationally.

What Exactly Do Negotiators Do?

As mentioned in the introduction, Hammer (2007) suggested that hostage negotiation is more accurately defined as crisis management. Crisis (or hostage) negotiation is defined as the process whereby an outside intervener attempts to de-escalate or disarm an individual and bring closure to a hostage or barricade event through verbal means (McMains&Lancely, 2003).

The philosophy of crisis negotiation is perhaps best described by Goergen:

(a) self-control: the negotiator must control his or her emotions;
(b) approach: de-escalate to lower tension;
(c) empathy: see through the eyes of the subject;
(d) process: listen;
(e) recognition of basic human needs: i.e., security, recognition, control, dignity, and accomplishment (p. 18)

In addition, he noted that the objectives of negotiation must include attention to the development of a climate conducive to anxiety reduction, good rapport, meaningful dialogue, helpful problem solving, and what he called "verbal containment." Verbal containment, understood in this context, is the attempt to keep the subject engaged to avoid further escalation.

In order to successfully resolve crisis incidents, contemporary hostage negotiators rely on a series of communication-based strategies. The *Hostage Negotiation Study Guide*, compiled by the International Association of Chiefs of Police and the Federal Law Enforcement Training Center (2010), listed the following communication skills as essential for crisis negotiators: active listening, normalizing, using "likability" as influence, mirroring, validation, probing, and finding common ground. Rather than removing options—something commonly done in school discipline programs—the authors asked, "Is this a negotiable incident, or can it be made into it?" (p. 4).

The negotiators I spoke with repeatedly stressed the need to foster hope and build perspective. "Hostage takers or people who barricade themselves, I have discovered, are people that have just run out of hope completely," said one negotiator. Another added,

> There are different reasons why people get negative perspectives on things, and when you try to get to the core of what that is, what you try to do is point them in the direction of something that will give them hope or help. I think hope is the big thing.

Talking to Negotiators

During my interviews with hostage negotiators, what was most surprising was the remarkable consistency of content. With virtually no prompting, their comments fell into a series of coherent repeating themes. Over and over, I heard them stress the need for relationship development, the creation of genuine rapport, and the importance of listening. The participants even agreed about how and when to deviate from the approaches they recommended!

Interview content corresponded in specificity and detail to the literature I looked at. Terminology and even turns of phrase were often an uncanny echo of what I had read previously. This was particularly surprising since the negotiators represented a geographic area spanning two countries and thousands of miles. Clearly, the training they received was consistent and well articulated. As one negotiator pointed out, even though there are periodic changes within the field,

> In the final analysis I can promise you right now, they're going to come back to the same things that I was taught from Schlossberg in '86. And I swear in another 10 years I'll be able to sit down here and another guy will do the same thing and that's because people are people and behaviour is behaviour.

These scholars and practitioners unanimously identified relational attunement (empathy), rapport-building, listening, and attention to face issues as the most crucial and central aspects of successful negotiation. Communication-based strategies, as they are used in hostage negotiation, are based on a larger understanding of the dynamics of both escalation and de-escalation that come from an understanding of brain research and typical human physiological changes that occur during stressful events. These ideas and strategies have their roots in the fields of psychotherapy, communication, and conflict analysis, and will be explored in more depth later in the book.

CHAPTER THREE

RELOCATING THE PROBLEM

> *The person is not the problem, the problem is the problem.*
>
> —Michael White

In this chapter I introduce what I believe is the most profound thing I learned from hostage negotiators. It is the philosophy that informs every aspect of their work, and I believe it is something that might make an educator's job easier.

Choosing a Constructive Narrative

In short, it is this: negotiators consciously choose to adopt constructive narratives about the people they are negotiating with. They continuously release judgment in favour of curiosity and empathy and reject negative interpretations of what the person is doing and why. In order to explain how they accomplish this, and why it is so critically important to their work, I must begin with a description of what is meant by narratives in this context.

When most people hear the word *narrative*, they understand it as another word for a story, whether an oral history, a biography, a novel, a blog, or even a work of nonfiction. Sometimes *narrative* is interpreted as an autobiography or the story of our lives. While these are all good examples of a particular use of the word, in this book I use it differently. The narratives I want to talk about are the pervasive and dominant stories that operate underneath our conscious awareness, influencing our ideas, attitudes, and actions.

Winslade and Monk (2007) define narratives as the complex, socially constructed cultural and personal stories we all use to bring coherence to our lived experience. In other words, they are the stories that help us make sense of our lives and the world around us. These stories do more than describe. They work below the surface as a framework that supports us in actively constructing our perceptions. They are the stories we use to make decisions about what is right and wrong, true or false, real or not; about who we should be, what we should do, and what others should be and do.

These narratives are created relationally. They come from what we have learned and assimilated from our families of origin, through our education, religious communities, and the cultural groups we are part of. They also come down through the ages in the form of allegory, fable, cautionary tales, historical accounts, and even morality plays. We internalize the messages contained in these stories and are guided by them. Within these narratives are a series of unquestioned norms that "shape . . . choices, values, feelings and actions" (p. 30) and, perhaps most important in the context of the discussion that follows, shape "what we expect of ourselves and others around us" (p. 30). Like fish in water, we are so familiar with these stories that we rarely question their origins. We take their veracity for granted, and we come to regard them as simply common sense. But are they?

Although it might seem that these narratives represent obvious truths, in fact they are simply a series of assumptions that differ widely from society to society, community to community, and even family to family and individual to individual. They also change over time. Take, for example, our view of the role of women in Western society. It's been less than a hundred years since women gained the right to vote. Before that, women were seen as unable to make the rational decisions necessary to do so. But today women not only vote but also run for office and are elected. What changed? Did women somehow evolve and develop greater rationality? Of course not. What changed was the *narrative* our society holds about women's capabilities and competence. Understanding the shift in this example allows us to recognize that narratives are far more fluid, changeable, and subject to challenge and contradiction than we might immediately recognize. Consider another example.

We are all familiar with the cartographical map of the world, and it is a common assumption that mapmakers show the world accurately. In all modern maps of the world, north is at the top of the map, and south is at the bottom.

But is this representation accurate, or is it an arbitrary rendition of what the world looks like? In 1979, Australian Stuart McArthur challenged this view and developed what he called the Universal Corrective Map, sometimes known as the "upside down" map. The slogan McArthur attached to the map was "Australia: No Longer Down Under."

Although many believe this map corrects a Eurocentric view of the world and a bias favouring the north, in fact early mapmakers all over the world, including Europeans, drew their maps the way McArthur did. There were many other conceptualizations and representations of the world reflected in the way maps were drawn at different times in history. Some showed east at the top or, even more confusing, all views pointing inward. So which is the right way? Perhaps there isn't one. If we look at the world from outer space, the idea of up, down, north, or south becomes ludicrous. Obviously, there is no "upside down" from that vantage point. However, most of us become disoriented when we see McArthur's map since it contradicts a universally accepted narrative we've uncritically carried since childhood.

It is undeniable that life would be easier if there was only one overarching narrative—or map—of what is real and true that we all agreed upon. It's likely we'd rarely be in conflict with one another. However, the truth is that we live in a world rampant with multiple conflicting narratives. There are no singular stories that describe reality in complete or definitive ways, and for every story, there is at least one other story that contradicts it, if not many. Not only do we hold personal narratives that do not line up with the stories of others, but also each of us are walking repositories of multiple and competing narratives that we try desperately to sort through and reconcile. We may have been raised, for example, to believe that women should stay home and raise their children. We may now also believe that women should be financially contributing members of society. This contradiction of narratives can result in considerable personal stress as we try to align them and live accordingly. Consider the following quote from Alice Morgan (2000), a narrative therapist from Australia.

> Our lives are multistoried. There are many stories occurring at the same time and different stories can be told about the same events. No single story can be free of ambiguity or contradiction and no single story can encapsulate or handle all the contingencies of life (p. 8).

However stressful, complicated, and contradictory they may be, we need narratives. These stories give us the ability to organize and interpret our experiences. Without them, we would be adrift in a sea of incomprehensible and unmanageable incoming data. Narratives help us sort through the chaos and create cognitive order for ourselves. But the narratives we live by can become problematic if we mistake them for unquestioned objective reality. We risk becoming rigid and dogmatic, believing that anyone who disagrees with us must be wrong. Thus, learning to question and even replace unhelpful narratives can allow us to choose those that are most useful and discard those that are not. The more lightly we hold our narratives, and the more we learn to question them, the more opportunities for action and influence become available to us. When we understand that the narratives we hold are arbitrary and can change, we open up space to consider alternatives.

So what does any of this have to do with hostage negotiation and, more importantly, education? In fact, as I came to learn and as you will see, understanding how narratives operate in our lives and how they can be consciously chosen or rejected is the basis of successful de-escalation and hostage negotiation.

Shifting the Narrative

Hostage negotiators are trained to shift negative narratives, judgments, or speculations about the character, intent, or possible pathology of the people they are negotiating with before taking action. In order to be effective, they insist that anyone intervening in a crisis must first intentionally challenge and then replace judgment with empathy, listening, curiosity, and genuine concern. If this crucial first step does not take place, those negative perceptions will be communicated to the other person and invariably result in failed negotiations. "It leaks into the conversation," negotiators I spoke with told me.

> No matter how careful you might be when you're talking to the person, if you're judging them they'll know it. People are really sensitive to that. And once you've broken that trust bond, it's almost impossible to get it back. So we can't be impatient or moralistic or bossy. We have to see people differently.
>
> Be genuine. That's important, or they'll know it when you are negotiating.

You want someone that is sincere, too. You don't want to be talking to someone and thinking, "They're just doing their job and they can't wait to go home."

We can say the words, but I think the words will be very different if we don't have the right tone and intent behind them.

Slatkin (2005), an author, researcher, trainer, and hostage negotiator, stressed the importance of setting aside personal opinions and "seeing the individual for what he/she is, a hapless person with a painful dilemma, who has, however misguidedly, attempted to solve it by creating a public crisis" (p. 56). Schlossberg agreed, and added that "if you accept what he's doing as understandable—crazy [sic] in your terms, but understandable to him—then you can learn with him, because what he is doing is purposeful, understandable and goal directed" (1979, p. 17).

An excellent example of what both Schlossberg and Slatkin say is shown clearly through the magic of Hollywood in the movie *John Q* (2002), where audiences are permitted an inside view of what is going on in the mind of a hostage taker (played by Denzel Washington). We come to see him as a hapless father desperate to secure a transplant he believes his critically ill son has been denied. It is difficult to watch this movie without empathizing with the central character and rooting for him, even though we understand that what he's doing is problematic, illegal, and dangerous. What is most interesting about this film is the way the directors take us into John Q's experience, helping us to suspend judgment and come to see him as a tormented person with a legitimate complaint. The hostage negotiators I spoke with intentionally do what this film led the audience to do—move inside another person's experience and reframe it from their perspective.

Negotiators told me that while it might seem justified to most people to label hostage takers and barricaded individuals as disordered and antisocial, doing so would be ineffective, self-defeating, and dangerous, and cause them to overlook important information. Roger Fisher and Scott Brown (1989), international negotiators with the

Harvard Negotiation Project, remind us that before we can negotiate successfully, we must be *unconditionally constructive* (p. xiv). This means doing what is good for the other person and the relationship, regardless of reciprocation. They urge us to "separate the person from the problem. Deal with both, but do not link them" (pp. xiii, xiv).

Although the educators I interviewed most often resisted the temptation to place blame, they noted that negative attribution was not uncommon among members their profession, especially when frustrated by a difficult student. In particular, educators pointed to specific narratives about student intention as most problematic. Viewing students as manipulative, attention seeking, resistant, or reluctant to work made it more likely that their disruptive behaviours would be taken personally.

Just a Person in a Bad Place

How exactly do negotiators make this shift? How does someone release judgment when they're feeling angry or frustrated? Most of us would find it enormously difficult to adopt a mind-set of empathy and curiosity toward hostage takers in these extreme circumstances and might argue that our judgments about them are legitimate. Further, many would be outraged at the idea that we should be empathetic to someone who is threatening innocent people. It may seem that we are not holding the person accountable for their actions and that we are pandering to them. This is consistent with the popular notion that "we don't negotiate with terrorists."

Negotiators, however, disagree and caution against taking such an approach. They tell us that it is a mistake to conflate empathy with condonation. They further believe—and the statistics of their success support this belief—that more can be safely accomplished through the development of relationships than through hard line approaches. This does not mean there is no accountability, but it is recognized that it is important to separate the de-escalation process from decisions that come after. Negotiators stated,

> You can't create a relationship bond if you are judging someone. It just can't happen.
>
> No matter what, you're worthy of respect. Releasing judgment, that's really important.

This process of reframing, negotiators explained, is actually quite simple. In my interviews, I heard the same pivotal phrase over and over again: you have to recognize that this is just a person in a bad place.

This simple phrase represents the ultimate empathetic reframe. Once negotiators make that shift, they are in an improved position to work constructively to help the person arrive at a better emotional place where problem solving might be possible. The first question a negotiator will ask a hostage taker or barricaded person is "How'd we get here today?" *Today*, as one negotiator told me, is the operative word. Then they listen. At that point they do not offer opinions or suggest options. Dominic Misino, former head of the New York City Hostage Negotiation team, told me the NYPD team motto is "talk to me." "It's with good reason that it isn't 'listen to me!'" he added. "Listening helps us to enter into the experience of the other person. We can't do that if we're judging them."

When I told him what I was writing about, another negotiator commented,

> I suppose that if an educator allows annoyance or judgment to creep in, it won't necessarily be seen as a big deal, and the consequences might not be immediate or dire. However, we don't have that luxury. If we can't make that shift in how we see the person we're negotiating with, people die. People die! The stakes are very high for us. Judgment is not an option. Lives depend on it.

The consequences may not at first appear as immediate or dire for educators, but I'd argue that they are. Students may not physically die when we allow judgment, anger, and irritation to overcome us, but the relationships we have with them most certainly will.

Bernard Gassaway (2007), former principal of a school in a socioeconomically depressed part of Bedford-Stuyvesant in New York City, wrote about something he called "suicide by educator." When I called him up to ask about it, he told me he'd read about and been struck by the phenomenon of "suicide by cop," where a person will do things to provoke a lethal police response. He immediately made the connection to his own work in education and called it "suicide by educator". "Suicide by cop" is outlined in the FBI Training Manual (2003). The indicators are as follows:

- An activity purposefully aimed at creating a confrontation with police
- Provocation to achieve a deadly force response

Gassaway believes the indicators are similar for students:

- An activity purposefully aimed at creating a confrontation with an educator
- Provocation to achieve a deadly force response (detention, time out, suspension, and expulsion)

He stressed the importance of creating a positive relationship with all his students. As a self-confessed former difficult student, like the negotiators, he understood how crucial it is to suspend judgment and replace it with listening and empathy. "It's what I wanted for myself," he told me. He also said:

> Kids who are failing, depressed, and have all but given up on school will often do things to provoke extreme responses in us. They will disrupt classrooms, pick fights, and generally try to antagonize us into a punitive response. It includes everything from detention through to arrest. What we don't see is how difficult these students' lives are

and how much they are struggling. They want us to see that but aren't really surprised when we don't.

Gassaway was adamant that educators must resist the tendency to blame and label students. Instead, he explained that his approach was to become as available to his students as possible, creating relationships with every student and listening to what they had to say. While it might be argued that this would be a daunting task in a school of thousands, Gassaway made a point of finding simple ways to connect. From the first day at his new school, he would stand at the door in the morning and greet every single student who arrived. "I knew I was getting somewhere when I went from a 10 percent chance that the student would respond by saying, 'Good morning' to an 85 percent success rate." In addition, he never scheduled meetings until after three thirty, to ensure that he was available to students and staff the entire school day. He also worked hard to learn every student's name:

> I saw this one student in the hallway during classroom hours. I said, "Don't you have somewhere to be, young lady?" She looked at me with a defiant expression and said, "You don't know me."
>
> I looked back at her, smiled, and said, "Get back to class, Bernadette." She was so surprised! I could hear her as she was walking away, "He know me! He know me!"

Narratives at School

Narratives play a huge role in educational practice. Education is rife with narratives that describe what schools should be, how school discipline programs should operate, the role of teachers, and how students should behave. In addition, and relevant to this discussion, there are many overarching narratives that both describe and define students. One way in which these pervasive narratives show up for students labelled disruptive is through the process of deficit identification. Some of the labels difficult students acquire are the result of formal diagnoses, but unfortunately many are based on nothing more than speculation and armchair psychology.

Over the years, we've all heard students characterized by a series of alliterative and alphabetical labels like these. Students may be described as *avoidant, alienated, aggressive, apathetic, abusive, abnormal*, or *attention seeking*. We conceive of them as *disordered, delinquent*, or *disruptive*. Sometimes we call them *deviant, disrespectful, destructive, disobedient*, or even *downright dysfunctional*. They are *defective, defiant*, or just *generally difficult*. In this way, we name our students *hostile, irresponsible, indifferent, insubordinate, lazy, lacking conscience, manipulative, negative, passive-aggressive, psychopathic, rebellious, relationship resistant, sociopathic, troubled*, and *threatening*. Sometimes we say they are just plain *unmotivated*. We have a further arsenal of acronyms with which to label them.

But what do these words mean, and how useful are they? Do they really describe what the student is doing or why they might be behaving in this way? What might happen if, rather than making pronouncements, we asked ourselves what the student is avoiding and why? What are they resisting or alienated from? Why might they be indifferent and unmotivated? Further, what exactly are they disrupting? The characterizations we use in our attempt to make sense of difficult relationships have one thing in common. They are narratives, and like all narratives, none of them can adequately represent a complete picture. They are simply interpretations based on snapshots.

Physician and psychiatrist Ruth Myers tells a story about a young man with fetal alcohol syndrome (FAS) that shows just how limited those snapshots can be. She begins by describing why some actions that appear to be defiance or laziness can be reframed when we have some useful background information about neurology. In this way, knowing something about how people with FAS learn and develop is not used to further pathologize them but instead to come up with better ways to respond:

> The way the neurology works in a person with a classic form of Fetal Alcohol Syndrome (FAS) is that issuing an

order makes it much harder for the person to do whatever it is you want them to do. However, if you ask that person to help you, they're all in. An example might be, "Well, it's time for you to have a bath now." And that won't typically work. What does work is, "Do you think it's time for your shower now?" or "Can you help me get that set up for you properly?" "What's the right way to do that for you?" And that kind of context will help the person retrieve the information they need because those circuits work. What works are questions rather than demands. And questions that invite collaboration rather than compliance.

The other thing that's a neurological struggle for people with FAS is any kind of multistep task that they have to retrieve just purely by remembering, like keeping appointments. It's just that the [brain] circuitry is not well suited to that. One of the ways that people need support is with gadgetry and reminders—but kindly reminders. "You have an appointment in ten minutes. Would you like to take off now?" Or something to that effect. But it's best to use gadgetry reminders rather than continuing to browbeat the person to try and remember or keep their calendar in their head. It also works much better if the person chooses their own gadgets and their own reminders.

Another thing that tends to work really well is humour (when it's shared humour, not demeaning). Like, "You have to strap on your flying shoes now 'cause it's time to . . ." or, you know, goofy stuff. Like, oh yeah, we're just friends helping each other out here, this isn't just me giving you an order.

What I'm thinking about was a First Nations fellow who really taught me this in just wonderful detail. Sixteen years old and he was referred to me—literally described by his teachers as "this guy's a terrible FAS." I just thought to myself, "Oh boy, what an awful way to describe somebody!"

They told me that when he was in school, he was not successful at anything. "We give him clear instructions, and he just chooses to disobey them!" That's basically the whole way he was described by his teachers. And I asked them, "Well, where does he succeed? What does he love? What's important to him?"

They said, "Is that important? Don't you think that's just reinforcing inappropriate behavior?" I'm like, "Oh boy, here we go again."

So he was not succeeding in school. He was not succeeding in any of his lessons, any of his subjects, missing all of his appointments, never on time, never able to do anything. And so I said, "Well, in that case I gotta come see what's going on in school." And they told me, "Oh no, he's busy with some family activities right now." So I asked them, "Well, what's that?" and they told me, "It's the big pow-wow for his particular nation."

So I go because I want to meet him and here's what I see. First of all, without a word of guidance or instruction, he helps prepare the feast. Without a word. The second thing is that, again, with no instruction whatsoever, he puts on the feathers, the beautiful costume, and completes, with his brothers and his father, these beautiful dances, without... He's flawless. And I say [his name was Jimmy Antelope. That's not exactly his name, but it's kind of like his name, for privacy], "Jimmy, you were amazing!" And he said, "Well this is my family. They need me." (personal communication, 2017).

Unfortunately, the negative interpretations we hold about such students carry a great deal of weight and often go well beyond simple attempts to understand and explain what's going on. These pejorative labels may have significant negative consequences for our students—not just in the immediate situation but for their future. They crystallize and perpetuate a negative view and can implant an identity of deficiency, deviance, and dysfunction that students come to internalize and believe about themselves. As narrative practitioner Sara Cobb (2013) reminds us,

> Stories matter. They have gravitas; they are grave. They have weight. They are concrete. They materialize policies, institutions, relationships, and identities that circulate locally and globally, anywhere and everywhere. (p. 3).

In their important book *Reclaiming Youth at Risk*, authors Brendtro, Brokenleg, and Van Bockern (1998) worry that both the formal and informal labels we attach to disruptive students are more than just unkind; they are hostile and counterproductive:

> Alienated children and youth are assigned a multitude of labels, most of them unfriendly.
>
> Most terms are either overtly hostile or overtly patronizing in the long established tradition of blaming the victim. While professional pejoratives may sound more elegant than labels invoked by the public, both are often equally condescending (p.7).

Winslade and Monk, in their book *Narrative Counseling in Schools: Powerful and Brief* (2007), echo these sentiments:

> Words do have effects and ...how we speak about ourselves and about others does matter. Descriptions...have a life of their own, once they have been uttered, that has little to do with the "truth" of the description in the first place. Because children spend a significant part of their early lives at school...the ways they get described at school are powerfully absorbed into their understandings of themselves and others. They must make sense of their own lives in relation to the way in which they are described by significant others in their school lives. (p. 75)

The informal labels that students acquire at school are often fuelled by frustration. When confronted with difficult behaviour, it is hard for most of us to avoid taking things personally. That's when we are most at risk of resorting to unhelpful labelling. However, what negotiators reminded me was that what we may initially understand as a person's deliberate provocation and disrespect may not be as personally directed as we might believe. It may be a person's desperate attempt to engage with us. As one negotiator said, "As long as they're talking, then there is a glimmer that this is going to work out." Furthermore, students who are characterized as dysfunctional may be struggling to extricate themselves from under the weight of the negative and pathologizing narratives they have been assigned. Their behaviour may represent a rebellion, and rather than deliberate disobedience, it may actually be an act of resistance. Considering this possibility may help us assume a stance of solidarity with the student and refuse to take part in further pathologizing conversations and practices.

Taking an Anti-pathology Stance

I was interested to learn that the field of crisis negotiation has steadily moved away from diagnostic profiling of personality types. Although negotiators used to enlist profilers with a mental health background to assess the communication of crisis subjects and recommend strategies based on those assessments, despite what you may see on popular television dramas like *Criminal Minds*, they seldom do anymore. Authors and trainers like Mitchell Hammer (2005) have suggested that such profiling might not only be ineffective but also dangerously inaccurate since it is often difficult to distinguish between a distraught and a mentally disordered individual. Negotiators might then be led to act on faulty assumptions based on generalizations about the subject's pathology. The emphasis today is on helping negotiators to assess what is occurring in the moment and respond accordingly, and on understanding that being emotionally upset is not the same as being emotionally disordered.

> To over-pathologize the observed behaviour patterns of the subject . . . can result in an inaccurate labelling of a

> hostage taker as 'anti-social' when there is no firm evidence to support such a diagnosis. This occurred, for example, during the Waco siege, reflected by the FBI's unproductive obsession with figuring out a psychological diagnosis at the expense of focusing more attention on understanding the interactional dynamics present in the situation.
>
> Once so categorized, negotiators run the risk of attempting to communicate to the supposed disorder rather than attending and responding to the interactional dynamics that take place between the hostage taker and the police negotiator. (Hammer, 2005, p. 52)

The late Herb Lovett, a friend and colleague, used to talk about students with "severe reputations." Their reputations, he noted, precede them into every educational setting they enter, and with each passing year, this "dossier of dysfunction" grows thicker and thicker. Each subsequent teacher becomes more alarmed at the prospect of teaching the child who comes to school with a file like that. It's difficult to overlook, let alone remain uninfluenced by the negative accounts it contains. For many, the child's bad behaviour becomes a foregone conclusion, and every transgression is further evidence of the veracity of the file. This, of course, becomes the proverbial self-fulfilling prophecy. Consider the following true story as an example.

Max

It was recess, and the schoolyard was a boiling mass of children, running and playing in the unseasonably warm sunshine. It took several teachers to monitor the grounds that day since a recent school renovation project had produced several untidy and dangerous piles of lumber, drywall, and nails.

A teacher spotted a fifth grade boy running toward him with a two-by-four in his hand. Alarmed, he ordered the boy to put the wood down. The boy continued to approach, obviously agitated. He was saying something, but he was talking too fast and was too far away for the teacher to make sense of it. Once again he was told to drop the wood. He didn't seem to hear.

"Max!" the teacher yelled, moving forward and grabbing him forcefully by the arm. "You never listen! Put down the wood! Now! You, young man, need to go to the office immediately!"

Max was still talking, but the teacher, angry and upset, was in no mood to listen. He collared the boy and took him directly to the principal's office. The principal and the teacher quickly decided that Max should receive a suspension. It wasn't the first offense for this student, and they felt they should send a strong message about unacceptable behaviour.

"That was a dangerous thing to do," the principal said. "Someone could have been hurt."

"But I was just trying—"

The principal cut off Max's attempted explanation curtly. "No excuses!" Max's mother was called to pick him up. He cried hot tears of anger and frustration as she led him to the car. As they were leaving, the principal leaned into the vehicle and told Max's mother that the police would be calling to follow up on the incident. "We can't have this kind of behaviour. We're taking a serious and harder line approach to it."

"But, Mom," Max protested as they drove away. "It's just not fair! That piece of wood had two big nails sticking out of it, and it was lying in the middle of the kindergarten play area. I was just bringing it back to the pile! I told him and told him, but that teacher just wouldn't listen to me!"

The narratives circulating around Max were so powerful that the adults in the scenario were completely unable to see him or his actions in any other light. Because he'd been in trouble so often before, everyone assumed that this incident was nothing more than yet another similar episode. In this way, Max's reputation so thoroughly preceded him that it completely obscured him. Consequently, an act of altruism (misguided as it may have been) that came from concern for children smaller than himself was misconstrued and converted into an act of defiance.

Being misunderstood engenders strong feelings. "That's not fair!" we hear kids say. It's one of the biggest complaints kids make about adults. A steady diet of misunderstanding creates a child who doesn't any longer care what adults think. *Besides*, the rationale goes, *they always think I'm misbehaving anyway, so I might as well give them what they expect.*

It's easy for us as readers to see this vignette from a meta vantage point, but in similar circumstances it may be much more difficult to step back and recognize that our shared narratives about Max could be faulty and unjust. Unfortunately, it's possible to create the very pathology we think we're working so hard to eliminate. But what if we take the stance that behaviour, like learning, takes place relationally, and our interpretation of a student's motives is only one of a possible myriad of alternative explanations? How might this change what we do?

Smarten Up versus What's Up

Stuart was a young adolescent we met almost two decades ago. He had spent most of his time at school defined as a behavioural problem. Maybe you've heard other children characterized in the same way he was. Over the years he'd been labelled with many of the usual acronyms. In addition, he'd been called manipulative, controlling, power oriented, resistant, a bully, a blamer, and self-centred. It had been suggested that most of his actions were specifically designed to gain attention. On better days, when teachers were feeling more kindly toward him, he'd been called wounded or damaged. They'd speculate that he lacked self-esteem or even evidenced attachment disorder. All in all, the ways in which Stuart had been described, even the kinder ones, firmly located the problem as a deficit within him. This left little room for alternate interpretations. Stuart carried a great deal of resentment about the way he'd been characterized and treated, and the self-fulfilling prophecy suggested that adult life was going to be difficult for him.

Later in this book, I'll get back to what happened to Stuart. But for now, let's start by contrasting the prevailing view of Stuart held by his teachers and others with what negotiators might say about him. Confronted with Stuart at his most upset, a negotiator's view would likely be strikingly different. They would disregard the negative interpretations and dismiss them as unhelpful, counterproductive, and irrelevant, and would understand Stuart as a person simply trying to solve a problem—again, as "just a person in a bad place." In this view, the problem isn't seen as solely located within Stuart. Instead, it is relationally constituted, a combination or confluence of events that include the environment and the people he's interacting with.

Also included in the mix are Stuart's own narratives. He most certainly developed negative stories about teachers and school in general and perhaps also about the specific teacher with whom he was in conflict. The narratives Stuart holds will probably not take into account the intent of the teacher intervening in the incident. It may be that this teacher genuinely cares about him and wants to help. Unfortunately, years of negative experiences have likely made Stuart mistrustful of any teacher, no matter how well intentioned.

This moment represents a challenge for this teacher. She might feel hurt, believe that Stuart's resentment is unjustified and unfair, and wonder why it is that she must be the only person to change. Why shouldn't Stuart have to change *his* narratives of *her*? While it's tempting to rush in and immediately try to correct his perceptions and defend her actions, negotiators would suggest that during the height of a crisis is neither the time nor the place to do so. Instead, listening and empathy are what's needed. Once a bond of trust has been forged, and we've "earned ourselves a hearing," as international negotiators would say, we will be in better position to assist the student to shift their narratives. As one wise educator noted,

> We can't forget that we're dealing with a kid, so let's not impose adult versions of accountability onto kids. What does accountability mean to kids that are fourteen, fifteen, or sixteen? Not that the kid doesn't understand the concept ... but I think there's a bit of a disconnect with our adult version of accountability.

When students like Stuart are labelled as dysfunctional and blamed for their behaviour, and we see the problem as firmly located within them, we are operating out of a powerful dominant narrative. If we were to condense it, we might use the following two words to describe what we want the student to do: smarten up! This is a narrative of judgment and correction.

Negotiators would likely agree with famous narrative therapist Michael White (n.d.), who once said, "The person isn't the problem; the problem is the problem." This alternative narrative frees us to engage with the student with genuine curiosity. "What's up?" is a narrative of curiosity and empathy.

Ross Greene (2008), in his book *Lost at School*, also talks about the power of this simple question. It very much echoes what negotiators told me was always their first question: "So how'd we get here today?"

An Example

> You've got to have something to eat and a little love in your life before you can sit still long enough for any damn body's sermon on how to behave.
>
> —Billie Holiday

Several years ago my partner, Norm, and I were asked to provide some in-service at an elementary school in the Midwest. This included a school assembly, something Norm often does. After the assembly, as we were walking down the hall toward the library where we would be speaking to teachers, the principal spotted a small boy walking with a teacher in the opposite direction.

"Jorge," she called. "I want you to meet Mr. Norman." Norm reached out to shake the boy's hand. The boy's expression was solemn, and he looked at the ground.

"Now, Jorge," the principal intoned sternly, "you heard what Mr. Norman talked about today. He has a disability, and things weren't always easy for him at school." We cringed a little at this characterization, since that wasn't precisely the point Norm had been trying to make. "And you," she continued, "haven't been doing all that well in school lately, right?"

Jorge nodded.

"So I want you to think about Mr. Norman and what he talked about this morning. You can do better, right?" At this point both the child and Norman were looking uncomfortable. Jorge dutifully nodded, still looking at the floor. We were relieved when the awkward interchange ended.

We made our way to the library, where part of the presentation included an overview of my interviews with hostage negotiators and the need to move from a mind-set of "smarten up" to a one of "what's up?" After the in-service ended, we had a couple of hours before a scheduled community presentation. When we returned and began setting up for our PowerPoint presentation, the principal approached us. I could see she'd been crying.

"I have to tell you something," she said. "After what you said this afternoon, I started thinking about Jorge and the difference between telling a child to 'smarten up' and asking him 'what's up?' So I went and found him and brought him to my office. We sat down together, and I just asked him what was up. Just that. Then I shut up. After a few seconds, he told me. He said his parents had recently separated, and just last week his mother had come back home and told the children she was going away and wouldn't be seeing them anymore. Jorge said, 'Now I just sit and look at the wall and think about how my mommy's not coming back.'" She wiped away a tear.

She paused. "But that's not all. An hour later, a teacher came to me furious about a student she'd been struggling with all year. Given my discussion with Jorge, I suggested that she sit with the student and simply ask him "what's up?" An hour later, she came back, and *she* was crying. This young man told her that life at home was hard. His father was hitting him, and his neighbourhood was tough. She said, "He's growing up where I grew up. He was describing my life!" The principal added,

> What's up is a powerful question. I'm always so busy, and I try to just deal quickly with student behavioural issues. I thought my role was to give advice and tell my students what to do—how to straighten up and fly right. I thought I was listening because I really do care about them, but I guess I wasn't. I wasn't asking the right questions. Actually, I wasn't asking any questions at all! But when you just ask that simple question and wait for the response, everything changes. You hear things that change your perception of the situation. And that gives you so many more options for how to respond.

In Summary

It became increasingly clear through my interviews and research that a shift in narrative from destructive to constructive is the lynchpin upon which modern hostage negotiation rests. There was consensus that without this critical first step—a change of narrative and asking the right questions—what follows will always be ineffective. The process needn't be complex. Simply acknowledging a distraught student as "just a person in a bad place" allows us to relax enough to be able to work empathetically and creatively to find solutions to seemingly intractable problems.

Sometimes all it takes is one person who listens and empathizes to change a life. Suspending judgment and moving from "smarten up" to "what's up?" isn't as difficult as it might seem, and the rewards for doing so are great. Relationships may improve in the short term, and that's obviously wonderful, but even more important, children's lives may be changed and even saved in the long term.

CHAPTER 4

RELATIONSHIP

> One of the most overlooked factors behind the violence and aggression we are experiencing every day, particularly in the western world, is the number of people who are going through losses, have broken bonds, or remain unattached.
>
> —Kohlreiser (2006)

Federal Agents Say the Darnedest Things

I first met Ron Garrison in 1994. My partner Norman and I were scheduled to speak at a conference of special education school administrators in Austin, Texas. They were gathering with a specific concern in mind. In the months preceding the conference, a number of incidents had occurred in Texas schools involving knives, guns, and other forms of violence. The administrators wanted some advice on how to deal with these pressing issues.

Norm and I were first up. We talked about what we usually talk about: the need to create a sense of belonging in schools, to interrogate policies and practices that either contribute to a sense of belonging or detract from it. We suggested that working on issues of belonging and school culture might go a long way to alleviate the disruption and violence they were experiencing. In that context, we talked about the importance of curiosity, listening, empathy, and relationship building.

As we spoke I noticed more than a few looks that could only be interpreted as skeptical. I was guessing based on my experience that the approaches we were suggesting were a little "softer" than what the Texas Council of Administrators of Special Education (TCASE) had in mind, given the events of recent months. However, we carried on with our presentation, and at the end we received a polite round of applause and sat down.

Next up was Mr. Garrison. He cut an imposing figure in his navy suit, white shirt, red tie, and tinted aviator glasses. His impressive CV was part of the introduction. We discovered that he was a teacher and educator who had held administrative positions at the district level and that he had an advanced degree in school safety leadership. He'd also been an expert witness in many court cases involving school violence, had considerable experience with gang violence, was also a field services director for the National School Safety Center, and had received training at the Federal Law Enforcement Training Center in Glencoe, Georgia. In other words, his CV read like the introduction to an Ian Fleming novel, with some educational experience thrown in for good measure. His manner was businesslike and engaging. In short, he exuded credibility and competence.

Schools, he told us, should consider issues of layout whenever possible. For example, it's not a good idea to have tall shrubs, trees, or plants close to windows and doors since they can obscure an incident and even provide cover for assailants. He recommended that new buildings consider washroom construction the way it's done in airports, with semicircular entrances and no closing outer doors. He told us that administrators and staff should check the ceiling tiles in washrooms periodically for contraband and weapons. To illustrate, he'd apparently done just that on a recognizance trip through a few schools in the area earlier in the week. He'd retrieved an empty bottle of gin and a purse dating from 1980.

He went on to advise administrators to get into their vehicles from the passenger side since most drive-by shootings occur on the driver's side. "If you hear a loud pop," he said, "hit the ground! A red face is better than a red chest." It was a hard-hitting presentation that included graphic visuals, sobering research, and a number of newspaper clippings on the topic of school violence.

Although I was just as fascinated with his presentation as the TCASE audience appeared to be, I became equally fascinated with the audience response. The Texas administrators were taking in the information with avid expressions, and many of them were furiously taking notes. I guessed that this was exactly what they'd been looking for.

And then the most interesting thing happened.

In order to fully appreciate what took place, I should tell you something I didn't know then that I do now because it's relevant here. Ron Garrison spent many years working in theatre productions. In other words, he does not lack the dramatic touch.

He finished talking about the pragmatics of school safety and then abruptly stopped, allowing a few seconds to elapse. The audience was attentive, the atmosphere charged.

"Now," he intoned, his voice deepening, "I am going to tell you the three most important things to consider in school safety." The room went even quieter, and the audience leaned forward as if with one body, anticipation palpable in the room. There was a collective intake of breath. Here was the stuff they'd been waiting for.

"It's a lot like real estate," he said. "In real estate there are three crucial considerations, and I'm sure you know what they are." It seemed the administrators did. I could hear mumbled affirmations: "Location, location, location." "Well, in school safety it's the same. Only one thing but important enough to be said three times. I'm going to tell you what that single most important consideration is."

He paused, drawing himself up to his full height, and looked down at the audience through his federal agent aviator glasses. The room was silent.

"It is as follows: relationship, relationship, relationship."

He paused again for what seemed like a full minute but was probably actually closer to fifteen seconds. During the pause I looked around the room, only to be confronted by a perplexed-looking group of administrators. They seemed to have paused with pens halfway to paper.

They looked at Ron, and then at us, and then back to Ron. Finally, they looked at each other, clearly puzzled. I imagined I could hear what they were thinking. Wasn't this that soft, liberal stuff those consultants from the west coast of Canada were talking about earlier. Norman and I looked at each other and smiled. The man the TCASE audience had claimed as theirs only moments before was now clearly ours. We liked him immediately.

But it wasn't over. Then came the truly theatrical moment.

Mr. Garrison wheeled around. Pointing into the audience, he said, "If you think that's soft, if you think that's not pragmatic, go ahead and rely on metal detectors, punishment, and other coercive strategies, and get yourself and your support staff hurt or killed! We think that when a student comes to school upset or disruptive, we need to go into zero tolerance or lock down. We utter threats, we make demands, and we provide ultimatums. At best, we believe we need to fire them off to the principal's office, sit them down forcibly in a chair, and inform them that until they can speak in a civil tone of voice, we will not listen to them. And even when they do, we still make good on threats of detention, suspension, or expulsion."

"Wouldn't it make more sense," he asked the audience, his voice now quiet, "to ask the student, 'Are you OK?' or 'Would you like a glass of water?' or 'Would you like to sit down and talk about it?'

"But we don't do that. We believe that students must be held accountable, and doing either of those things would be 'rewarding bad behaviour.' And we all know what happens we reward bad behaviour. It gets worse, right?"

The Problem with Pop Behaviourism

Is this really true? Are we making a fundamental mistake when we base our approaches on a simplistic idea like this? Garrison believes we are.

In the years since that conference, we've become close friends with Ron and his wife, Lynn (who also spent her career as a teacher, both of middle school students and student teachers). The four of us have had many discussions about classroom disruption and school violence. We've speculated on why it often seems difficult for educators (and the school system itself) to respond to students who are upset or deemed "challenging" without resorting to coercion or the application of rewards and punishments.

Here's our theory. We believe it's because we have been marinated in a culture of pop psychology and behaviourist theory that specifically tells us that being supportive to an angry person will increase the frequency of problem behaviour by reinforcing it. We believe it because that's what the behaviourists have taught us, and it seems to make a kind of circular sense.

But is it really true? Does support during difficult times really encourage bad behaviour? Think about your own life. Imagine coming home after a bad day and feeling irritable. Suppose your spouse or partner said something like, "Gee, honey, sounds like you had a really rough day. Would you like a cup of tea or a beer? Do you want to talk about it?"

Would we really say to ourselves, "Wow, this is great! I think I'll come home in an irritable mood every day!" It's unlikely. What we'd probably do instead is breathe out a long sigh of relief, feel our shoulders drop, and think to ourselves, "Finally someone understands me and wants to listen."

It is simplistic to think that supporting someone when they're upset is simply a "reinforcer", and that reinforcing will lead to further bad behaviour. Human relationships are much more complex than the behaviourists would have us believe. Being supported at a time when we're feeling distressed fosters trust. It de-escalates us. It also has the potential to open up new possibilities for self-reflection and problem solving. Common sense and our own experience tell us that offering support when someone is upset will lead to a decrease in the frequency of the so-called difficult behaviour not an increase. For some students, however, there are few, if any, people in their lives willing to do this.

All across North America, schools are encouraged to wage war on bad behaviour. As mentioned earlier, this war involves everything from zero tolerance policies, metal detectors, high tech security procedures, like facial recognition, mandatory drug testing, detentions, suspension and expulsion up to and including the involvement of law enforcement for even relatively minor infractions—and now even the call for armed teachers. We have been taught to believe that anything short of a hardline approach is tantamount to condoning violence. Ron Garrison's ideas seem to fly in the face of public perception and the policies of many schools.

As a culture we are steeped in these narratives of behaviourism. The self-help industry, child-rearing books, magazines, television shows and commercials, and other mainstream media sources promote approaches based on the assumption that all human beings are motivated primarily by two things: a desire to obtain rewards and a need to avoid punishment. For many, there is also a cynical underlying belief that children are uncivilized, and if we aren't vigilant, they will always behave badly.

When we uncritically take these narratives for granted, we risk making faulty connections based on a simplistic view of cause and effect. When these connections are questioned, many people respond by saying that we all respond to inducements. "It's just human nature" we often hear. They point to programs like Weight Watchers as examples of how providing incentives are effective ways to increase motivation and result in successful behaviour change . However, what is missed is that rewarding ourselves with treats for changing our own behaviour—getting that new dress when we succeed in losing twenty pounds or getting that motorcycle after a year's worth of curbing our spending habits—is not the same thing as offering a student a token for staying in their seats or not speaking out of turn in class. When we extrapolate what we believe to be a universal truth about human nature onto our expectations for our students, we miss a critical difference, namely that when we set goals with rewards for ourselves, we're in charge. It's volitional. No one is imposing such a regime on us, and if we mess up, the stakes are not high. We will not be shamed or ostracized, and we can even decide to have that treat anyway. (And what is not often acknowledged is that even those weight loss programs with their incentive programs find that the rates of recidivism are distressingly high).

We will not be shamed or ostracized, and we can even decide to have that treat anyway. However, when we impose these regimens on students the critical difference is that others – teachers, parents or other adults – are in charge, not the students. When a student does not comply with the established standards, there may well be consequences outside the student's control and externally applied. These may be the loss of privileges or even forcible exclusion. Educators sometimes say that children at the elementary school level love programs with rewards for good behaviour and that rewards are very motivating. This may well be true for some, but again, is it a universal truth? Unfortunately, the promise of a reward is not motivating for the students who never seem to measure up. For those students, watching others who seem to effortlessly glide through school garnering the praise of their teachers is salt in an already present wound. Instead of motivating them to do better, it is a constant, low-grade assault on their self-esteem. We inadvertently teach students to engage in comparison, and for some, they will always be found lacking. As a student who lived with constant exhortations to "do better" and "try harder," I will attest that all the carrots held out for me were never going to be enough. If I could have done better, I would have. But the fact of the matter was that the classroom was a hostile sensory environment for me, and it was all I could do to simply stay in my seat. I am not the only one. In addition, as scholars like Kohn (2018) point out, gains made through the application of rewards are typically shortlived, and promote a culture of "do this and you'll get that" (p. 3) which unfortunately results in students who are extrinsically motivated.

During my interviews with students, I was interested to note that they were unilaterally derisive about programs that rewarded good behaviour just as much as they were about programs that punished bad behaviour. As mentioned, the students found these approaches both patronizing and ineffective.

The Three Rs

Over twenty-five years ago, I found a small, interesting study commissioned by the Canadian Employment and Immigration Commission (CEIC) that unfortunately I have been unable to locate since. The CEIC was interested in learning why students drop out of school. The researchers interviewed over 1500 high school students who'd left school, then collated the information they received.

When they analyzed student responses, they fell neatly into three startlingly consistent categories. Students claimed they didn't feel *respected* by their teachers, they didn't feel they had positive *relationships* with either school personnel or other students, and they didn't feel that the curriculum was *relevant*. The study was later called "the three Rs."

For these students, the need to be respected, the need to engage in relevant work, and above all, the need for positive and reciprocal relationships superseded any desire for extrinsic rewards. Students in this study were prepared to give up graduation and all that academic success promised because they did not feel these important needs were being met. This suggests that what motivates people is much more complex than the behaviourists would have us believe.

These students clearly felt alienated in their schools. By pointing to what they saw as lacking in their school experience, they actually provided clear clues for us about the antidote. Respect and relationships (and of course relevant learning content) can make all the difference to whether students succeed or fail. While teachers don't always have control over the curriculum and the content, they do have the ability to foster positive relationships and model respect.

Most of us have stories about that one (or more, if we're lucky) teacher who really made a difference for us. Mine was a ninth grade English teacher. I'd been failing his English course (and everything else that year), and I was a decidedly disruptive presence in his class. One afternoon after class ended he pulled me aside. I was certain I was in for another stern talking to, something I'd become accustomed to in my other classes. But instead, and much to my surprise, with genuine curiosity he asked me how it was that I was failing a course I could so easily excel in. He said he'd noticed how much I read and called me a gifted writer. All my belligerent resistance melted away in an instant. The next semester my grades went from D to A+. His interest, concern, encouragement, and belief in my abilities made all the difference. I will always remember him.

I recently saw a YouTube video (Pulver, 2018) of a speech given by a young man about his early educational years. Because it was described as a motivational speech, I was concerned that it would be the usual "pull yourself up by your bootstraps," something I am bit wary of, but something in the leader intrigued me, and I decided to watch. I was glad I did.

He talked about how his time at school was characterized most by his absolute inability to sit still and attend class, and how all the excess energy and anxiety coursing through his body would manifest in tapping. The teachers and other students found the tapping both irritating and distracting and were constantly demanding he stop. He talked about how his teachers would reprimand him, and even when they were trying to be helpful, they would offer only suggestions that proved unworkable—things like sitting on his hands. While he dutifully tried to control his runaway energy, it was all in vain.

One day a teacher asked him to stay after class. Head down and disheartened, he walked to the teacher's desk. Like me, he was expecting the usual reprimand. But much to his surprise, the teacher smiled at him and said, "I've seen you tapping, and I have a present for you." He produced a set of drumsticks and placed them in the boy's hands. "I think you're a drummer." The young man giving the speech, it turns out, is now a renowned drummer who has travelled the world playing drums. A simple reframe of something labelled a deficit, something to be eradicated and overcome, turned out to be a talent in disguise and resulted in a wonderful career. Like me with the English teacher, he has never forgotten what was not just an act of kindness but also a deeply relational act with profound and lasting consequences. Teachers have the opportunity to help kids see themselves differently. That opportunity can either be squandered or supported.

Did the English teacher's intervention with me mean I stayed in school? Sadly, no. By then I'd experienced enough negativity that I just didn't feel I could stay. But I carried his view of me inside like a small ember all through my life. Today I do what he said I could do: I write. And when I write, I remember that teacher. Sometimes it just takes one person to believe in us.

The students I interviewed agreed that teachers who made an effort to create relationships with them made the difference both personally and in the classroom experience. They also noticed when it wasn't present. One student said, "I have had teachers before where I want to ask them, 'Do you like working with children?' They seem so grouchy all the time, and like they don't want to be there."

The students became animated as they described a favourite teacher: "He emanates happiness all the time," said one. Another added,

> One thing that amazes me about Mr. S's class is that he would have the weirdest bunch of kids in there, kids . . . that really misbehave, but then everyone in that class is always so well behaved, and we would work so silently for him. I think it's because there was such a big respect for him. Like, he never got mad at kids 'cause it appeared no one ever did anything wrong in his class, which is weird, 'cause there would be those kids that are little brats in all the other classes, and for his class they would be so well behaved. I think it's just everyone had so much respect for him "We don't want to disappoint Mr. S."

When I asked how Mr. S achieved that respect, one student replied, "He actually had interesting things to say, like to tell stories about his life that are fun to listen to and just make everyone laugh." Another agreed: "Yeah, I like it when teachers get personal, not overly personal, but when they give you little insights into their life." As the students shared stories about this teacher, their appreciation and admiration for him showed in their faces, their body language and the tone of their voices:

> He gives off a real aura. Always good vibes from him. You never feel like, "Oh, he's grouchy today." It's regular, constant, so you get into that rhythm. Some teachers, if you keep, like, not doing your work, they might just give up on you. They'll go, "You know what, I'm not going to try, I'm not going to try again for you," but he never gives up on students that won't work. He just keeps on pushing them to try.

> There's a lot of kids in that class who maybe haven't done well in classes before, but then once they get to his class, it's like he'll motivate them to work. At some point, these kids work for him, and it's amazing. Kids that normally wouldn't work end up doing like a ten-page research paper on a classical artist . . . it's because kids know he really cares.

Good teachers, the students agreed, need to be perceptive and observant. "Know [the students'] patterns." This was one way teachers conveyed caring to students:

> When you've had a bad day, they'll take you aside, and like, "Are you feeling OK, would you like to talk?" Part of the thing about that, though, if they show that kind of emotion to one student, they can't put disregard to the other students.

Although the students appreciated direct, effective, and respectful correction, they also observed that many teachers needed to think before speaking: "It's called professionalism. I think the worst thing is when anyone in a position of authority, when they discipline, is like actually angry. Then it isn't discipline, it's just venting." When I asked what the student response to that approach was, one told me, "Students fight back—'You know what? You can stop talking to me like that!" Another said, "Teachers will hold grudges and then it's just a bad association and it lasts all year, and it just becomes such an ordeal."

Interestingly, several of the negotiators also spoke of the need to maintain a professional approach; however, like the students, there were some striking differences between their definitions and those commonly associated with the idea of professionalism. While all agreed that it was important to avoid taking issues personally, to "get tweaked" or allow "buttons to get pushed," and although all noted the need to suspend judgment, they did not suggest that this should be accomplished through a distancing approach. "You have to care. No matter what these people have done, they are still a human being."

But Doesn't Relationship Building Take a Long Time?

There is a strong perception among most people that relationship building is a long and incremental process, involving time spent in intimate proximity. While in some respects this is true, it is not necessarily always so.

For example, when my husband does high school assemblies, he is aware that he has a very short period of time in which to bring his audience (teens aren't always the most receptive audiences) into a relationship with him. To accomplish this, he uses humour and finds ways to relate to their experiences. In the hundreds of assemblies I have witnessed, the vast majority receive a standing ovation and a line-up of kids at the end wanting to ask questions or just say hello. We have received emails and letters from students all over the world who tell us how much they appreciated what he had to say and what reflections and insights it engendered in them. In a single hour, he manages to create a relationship with an entire auditorium full of students.

To the claim that creating bonds takes too much time, negotiators respond by insisting that they must build relationships with unknown subjects within the first fifteen to forty-five minutes of an incident (Dolan & Fusilier, 1989). To further complicate matters, in many instances negotiators must develop these trusting bonds not directly and face to face but over the phone. Furthermore, these bonds must be created at a time when the person is in crisis, highly distraught, and probably not thinking clearly—perhaps they are suicidal or even homicidal. One negotiator recounted the story of her first negotiation, fresh out of a two-week training program:

> I'd just finished training, and I got a call. My first ever! We were sent to an apartment building where a guy had barricaded himself on one of the upper floors. He was threatening to throw himself off the balcony. He was adamant that I couldn't come in, so I had to conduct the entire negotiation through the intercom system of the building. I just worked on reassuring him and taking my lead from him. We had to establish that bond. Thankfully, he didn't throw himself off the balcony, and he gradually de-escalated. The next day I went to see him, and he let me in. He told me that if we'd tried to gain access to his apartment, he would have jumped.

For most of us, the notion of creating a relationship with an upset person over the phone is already a daunting idea. As to conducting a complicated and sensitive negotiation through an apartment building intercom system? I have trouble with "could you buzz me in!" And yet this is the sort of thing that hostage negotiators routinely do.

If we need more proof that relationships can be built quickly, and strong bonds between people do not necessarily have to take a lot of time, consider the following.

The Two by Ten Study

In one of my internet searches, I ran across something called the two by ten study (Cox, n.d.; Smith & Lambert, 2008). I located and called up the researcher, Dr. Raymond Wlodkowsky, a psychologist and educational theorist. He was surprised at my interest in his work, more than twenty years later.

Wlodkowsky asked a group of teachers to identify one student in their classrooms who had given them the most difficulty during the past few months. Then he asked them to do a simple thing. For two minutes a day, for ten days, he asked them to sit down with this student and have a personal conversation—about anything—and to listen deeply.

At the end of the ten-day period, he went back to the school to see what the results were. What he found was surprising. He expected that the children would enjoy the individualized attention, and they did. In fact, 85 percent of them reported experiencing a better relationship with the teacher. Other students in these classrooms also seemed to have benefited. But what he told me he didn't expect was the effect it had on the adults. Many teachers reported having learned a great deal about the student that dramatically changed the way they viewed them. For many, these children were transformed from the pariahs of the classroom to some of the students the teachers liked best (personal communication, March 2010).

Two minutes a day. This underscores what negotiators told me, and this is the reason I bring this example forward. It proves that empathy, strong relationships, and bonds of trust can be built in short periods of time.

However, I bring this example forward with a caveat. I mentioned this study to an Autistic friend and colleague, Cal Montgomery, an activist and deep thinker. Cal had a difficult life before, during, and after his time at school. He expressed serious reservations about any wholesale implementation of the two by ten study, and I believe his point is critical. Cal worried that students already marginalized and lonely might indeed experience the attention positively, but once the two minutes a day for ten days ended, the results could be catastrophically hurtful unless a genuine and ongoing relationship resulted. It's a sad reality, he reminded me, that many of the students who cause us the most trouble are students who have never experienced empathetic adults, and for that reason engaging one-to-one with a teacher who listens deeply can be a powerful experience. But what happens if those two minute exchanges stop? How confusing might that be to the student who actually believes the teacher cares? For many of the students we see coming to school, the betrayal of finding out that they've been treated as a study subject might be enough to make them cynical forever.

I took Cal's comments to heart. I don't believe this should ever be used prescriptively, as an interesting experiment, or as a quick fix. It can't be used as another way to manipulate students into doing what we want them to do without letting them know we're doing it to them. This is a powerful intervention and as such can be terribly misused. It underscores my concern with approaches built on models rather than genuine relationship building.

Because He's Nice

Much of relationship building in schools is accomplished through reputation. Students know which teachers genuinely care about them, even if they've never been part of that teacher's classroom. In our son's elementary school, Mr. T. was that teacher.

Grade three wasn't a particularly good year for our son. His third grade teacher, Mrs. P., was, by her own admission, more than ready for retirement. She seemed to have lost patience with children in general, but when it came to Evan, she often went overboard.

If it hadn't been for an itinerant hearing teacher who spent time with Evan in Mrs. P.'s classroom periodically, we'd probably never have heard about half of what she did. For example, Mrs. P., we were informed, had written Evan's name on the black board and, next to it, in quotation marks, "space cadet." Evan and one other boy were the targets for an array of humiliations, ranging from simple yelling and detentions to name-calling and isolation.

One day Evan came home with a new addition to his list of grievances. "Mrs. P. won't let us use the bathroom during class time," he complained.

"Why not?" Norm asked.

"She says we do it to get out of work," he replied.

"Do you?" Norm countered.

"No. She says we're supposed to use the washroom during recess, but I never have to go during recess. It's just when I come in and sit down that I have to go."

"Actually," he went on, "she does let us go, but she keeps track of how long it takes, and then we have to stay after school for twice as much time!"

After a moment in which the three of us silently contemplated the evil Mrs. P. and her Machiavellian ways, we innocently asked, "Do all the teachers do that?"

"No," he said. "Mr. T. lets his class go to the washroom whenever they want."

Norm, attempting to apply the Socratic method for eight-year-olds, asked, "Do kids in Mr. T.'s class go to the washroom to get out of work?" It seemed like a simple question. Evan looked at Norm incredulously.

"No," he said, a scornful edge to his voice.

"Why not?" asked Norm.

Evan rolled his eyes. Clearly the question was another example of how obtuse adults can be. "Be-cause," he said, drawing the word out into two long syllables, "Mr. T. is a NICE teacher."

Nice? What on earth does that most banal of all words have to do with education?

Vivian Gussin Paley (1993), a teacher in the laboratory schools in Chicago, wrote that her goal at the beginning of every year was to make the children like her. She cultivated their trust and worked hard to win their approval. This idea stands in sharp contrast to the attitude that many teachers and even some parents have: "I'm not here to make students like me. "I'm here to teach. Kids need limits. They need to know who's in charge, and they need to respect their elders."

This attitude doesn't exactly come from outer space. Many of us would agree. We suspect that teachers who are well liked are dupes who get taken advantage of. They have chaotic classrooms where the children run rampant and call the shots. Many of us remember teachers who sacrificed order and control in order to be liked. While we may have liked them, we didn't respect them.

Many adults assume that students like teachers who have lax classroom rules, but this wasn't borne out in my interviews. The students felt that passivity was just as problematic as holding grudges and yelling. They emphatically did not conflate likeability and a high degree of relational closeness with passivity. One student said, "I think what makes it worse is when they just sit there and watch. And then the whole class gets crazy, and they [the teachers] don't do anything. They just sit there. They don't care at all, and that's the problem."

Another concurred, "Yeah, you can't be weak, have no backbone. Kids like structure, as much as they say they don't." The students wanted clarity, but "it shouldn't be mean, not abusing the control."

Isn't it a false dichotomy to assume that teachers like Gussin Paley who work to obtain student regard are going to be ineffective? Haven't all of us had a few teachers whom we both liked and respected? Why should being liked necessarily go hand in hand with a loss of respect? Don't we all work harder when we feel valued and appreciated? We might argue that people will work hard when they are driven to do so by unpleasant and tyrannical bosses, but we also know that those same workers will stop working the minute the boss turns away. There's no commitment to do your best work for someone who makes you unhappy. Most people in those situations spend at least half their working hours trying to figure out where to find another job.

Why should it be any different for kids? In classrooms characterized by conflict and mistrust, students will also spend their time trying to find ways to avoid the distress. Sometimes those attempts to escape get characterized as bad behaviour or even escalate into crisis events. Escalation that results in a student being forced out of the classroom is often put down to another attempt to avoid work. But is it? Perhaps it is actually an attempt to leave an untenable situation.

Support and Expectations

There is another false dichotomy in education and in the mainstream view, namely that support and expectations are mutually exclusive. There is a pervasive view that young people today are selfish, coddled and over supported and that the only antidote to this trend is to place higher expectations on them. However, perhaps it is important to remember that support without expectations is protection, but expectations without support is tyranny.

One negotiator stressed the importance of tempering support with strength.

> It's true that you can't appear weak-willed. You can't let a person push you all over the place. However, timing is everything. You do need to be decisive—but maybe not at that moment. Asking kids if you can help won't make you look weak to other students. You have to have empathy. Unfortunately, some educators are like some law enforcement—they want to just say, 'Sit down and shut up.' Those aren't good negotiators, there has to be a level of mediation.

Even though providing support can seem as though we aren't doing anything that helps students take responsibility and learn how to manage their lives going forward, how and when and with what motivation we take those actions is critical. Negotiators suggest that we should separate the issues of support and expectation. We can deal with both, but we should not conflate them. During times of escalation is not the time to remind people of their civic and moral responsibilities or to remind them of their shortcomings. Later, when the situation has cooled, is a better time to talk about what other options might be possible and even optimal.

An Example: "Fill the Bucket"

Several years ago, we met a woman in Alaska who told us this story over lunch.

She'd come to the school initially as a substitute, asked to teach fifth grade in a school widely considered rough. She wasn't a new teacher, but she'd been out of the classroom working at the district level for some time. When she discovered that a substitute was needed for a teacher who was going on maternity leave, she jumped at the chance to get back into the classroom.

Within a very short time, she'd gained a reputation for being able to deal with conflicts in the schoolyard more effectively than any of the other teachers. If a fight broke out, she would walk up to the children who were fighting and, simply by calling their names, could get their attention and stop the fight.

The other teachers were amazed and impressed. Whenever they tried to intervene, they told her the kids simply ignored them. Then they'd have to ratchet up their responses. Even then, threats and punishment weren't always effective. What, they asked, was her secret?

"You haven't filled the bucket," she said enigmatically. The other teachers looked puzzled.

"Here's what I mean. When I first got to the school, I spent some time figuring out which kids were getting reputations as troublesome. I intentionally spent a lot of time getting to know these kids—what they're interested in, how they like to spend their time. For example, I know that Bill likes hockey cards and that Jason rides BMX bikes. So when they're fighting, and I walk into that fight and call their names, we already have a relationship. They know I care about them. You can't expect kids to respond to you if you've never made an effort to get to know them. That is what I call filling the bucket.

"What matters is not what you do when the fight occurs; what matters is what you do before the fight or a crisis occurs. It might be a day before or a week before. Every time I stop to talk to them in the hall, it's like putting water in the bucket. It's creating and maintaining that critical relationship. That gives me something to draw on when there's a fight. The problem isn't that you've done something wrong; the problem is that you haven't put enough water in the bucket."

How do hostage negotiators go about building trust and creating authentic bonds when they don't have a previous relationship with the subject – when they haven't had the time and the luxury of "filling the bucket?"

Unfortunately, there isn't much research available regarding exactly how relationships are built during negotiation. Ironically, we know much more about how relationships are damaged. Womack and Walsh, for example, cautioned negotiators to avoid the use of threats or coercion. Weaver (1997) went further and pointed out that "the threat of punishment often causes the same psychological reactions as actual punishment . . . our perception of reality, not reality itself, determines behavior" (p. 123).

While it is understandable that we want to bring crisis situations to a close quickly and decisively, the desire for quick resolution may undermine our goal. Under threat, many of us will utilize strategies that, even if not intended, may be easily perceived by the other person as coercion. For example, it is widely believed and taught in many crisis prevention programs that clear directives are our best bet in accomplishing de-escalation. Negotiators strongly disagree and say that we risk damaging and even permanently destroying relationships with hard-line directness and demands. They suggest we approach the situation with finesse and care. As several succinctly noted,

> Most people think that when someone's in the middle of a crisis the best thing is to get directive. You hear this in some crisis training programs [not in hostage negotiation training]. They say to give people orders and keep the phrases short. "Sit down. Do this." This goes with a kind of misunderstanding of brain science, I think. It's true that people under duress can't take in as much information, but this approach, I think, is misguided and dangerous. What we do is the exact opposite. We ask questions. And we allow for silence. We slow the process down. And we never tell the person what to do.
>
> I'm not going to be nasty. I'm not going to be condescending. I'm not going to be bossy. I'm going to be real careful with my voice. I don't want to be a nag. I don't want to [act] quickly, miss rungs in the ladder, jump to the next phase, ask the person to do something when I don't have any bond developed. And not be like the authoritarian cop. You don't do that as a negotiator. We're used to giving orders all the time on the road. "Go over there, do that." You can't do that when you're . . . with a person in crisis.
>
> You want to be a sensitive person. You can't have, for lack of a better term, a hard-ass guy being a negotiator. [If] you're going to start talking like a bully, that's not going to work for you.
>
> Nice voice is really important, and you've got to be calm, and you can't be argumentative, and you've really got to listen.

Negotiators know that successful resolution in the absence of an authentic relational bond is highly unlikely: "The most important thing is—and I repeat it all the time—is the respect issue. You have to develop some kind of relationship with your subject." Another added, "You want to build that trust, [and] if you break that trust, then it is all over."

I asked exactly how negotiators go about developing those trusting relationship bonds in difficult circumstances. I heard that creating a feeling of safety is the crucial first step. "It's got nothing to do with anything verbal, it's just showing that we're not there to attack you," one negotiator said. Another told me,

> Traditionally, they're going to be yelling. It's going to be short sentences, but we're just going to keep working that. We're going to say, "Look, I want to help you in there, but I'm not going to be able to do that unless I can get a handle on what's happened. I promise you, nobody's coming in to get you; we're here to make sure no one's hurt, and that means you, too. Why don't you tell me what's going on? I'm here to listen, and then we're going to figure out a way that we can get you out of this with no one being hurt."
>
> In the process of letting off steam, nine times out of ten he's going to tell you what the problem is—information that is very useful! Because he'll usually tell you what the solution is, too.

In this context, the most important consideration is to work intentionally to create a non-adversarial atmosphere of mutual cooperation. One negotiator said, "What we want to do is, ultimately, on a good day (which happens most of the times), we want to get this feeling going that you and I are working together to solve this whole thing nonviolently."

Pared down to its essence, hostage negotiators believe that trusting relationships are built by honouring basic human needs. They take great pains never to violate the need for dignity, respect, autonomy, security, or hope. As Mike Webster noted, "The theory of social influence tells us that people are more likely to cooperate with us if they see us as: willing to listen, understanding, worthy of respect and non-threatening" (p. 9).

In Summary

Some important lessons come from the field of hostage negotiation that apply directly to education. Relationship, rapport, and empathy are critical components of an effective approach, and it would seem that the best teachers understand that this is also true in their classrooms. Students agree. As one negotiator said,

> Rapport is a huge part of what we do . . . when I teach, I tell people I don't think there's many rules. In fact, there's next to no behaviour rules that are 100 percent. But the only one that I believe strongly is 100 percent is that if a person does not like or respect you on some level, they won't act productively or cooperatively with you because they won't give you the satisfaction. I really can't think of an exception to it.

CHAPTER FIVE

EMPATHY

> This is the communication warrior's real service: staying calm in the middle of conflict, deflecting verbal abuse, and offering empathy in the face of antagonism. If you cannot empathize with people, you don't stand a chance of getting them to listen to you, much less accepting your attempts to help—sincere as you may be.
>
> —Thompson & Jenkins (1993, 2004)

Mark Gerzon (2010) recounted a story about UN diplomat and negotiator Giandomenico Picco, sent to negotiate the freedom of several hostages kidnapped by a Muslim extremist group in 1991. Blindfolded, he was brought to the group's headquarters. Interestingly, he did not begin with negotiation. Instead, Picco asked a series of questions that began with a statement:

> "You may know something about me," Giandomenico Picco said, after a period of silence. "But I know nothing about you."
>
> "What do you want to know?" the masked leader asked Picco.
>
> "Do you have children?" Picco asked.

"Yes," the man replied.

"So do I," Picco replied. "And are you doing this because you want to give your children a better world?"

"Of course."

"Well, I am, too. So it turns out that we are both fathers who want to give our children a better world." (Gerzon, pp. 17–18)

At that moment the dynamic between the two men shifted, and despite their obvious differences, Picco was able to successfully negotiate the release of the hostages.

This story illustrates that empathy is not necessarily a passive flood of "fellow feeling" but is something negotiators develop intentionally. Picco was able to de-escalate a potentially lethal situation by creating a bond between himself and the other man. Through the course of the conversation, he carefully and deliberately built a bridge of connection, understanding, and mutuality between them.

What Is Empathy?

The word *empathy* has roots in Latin and Greek and means "to see through the eye of the other" (Thompson & Jenkins, 2004, p. 63) or to "feel into" (Thompson & Jenkins, 2004; see also Goleman, 1995). According to Michele Le Baron (2002), empathy is "essentially relational" (p. 226) and is "the capacity to think, imagine, and feel with another" (p. 227). Seeing a person as they see themselves, according to Thompson and Jenkins, is the "true essence of empathy" (p. 22).

Frans de Waal is a primatologist. In his book *The Age of Empathy* (2009), de Waal makes the case that human beings are hard-wired for empathy. Empathy, he tells us, operates viscerally, emotionally, and intellectually and allows us insight into not only what a person does but also why. In other words, empathy gains us entry into an individual's view of themselves.

How exactly is empathy created, and is it really possible to be empathetic to people you don't approve of?

Whenever I read a good novel, I typically develop a sense of empathy toward the protagonist and sometimes even the antagonist. A central skill in a talented author is their ability to evoke empathy in readers. This is accomplished through providing backstory and context, and helping us to appreciate the person's humanity and struggle.

It is essentially through listening to each other's stories that empathy is built. Michelle Le Baron (2002) used a surprising story to illustrate the power of this idea. She recounted the experience of a member of the Truth and Reconciliation Commission in South Africa. While interviewing a white leader of the apartheid movement in jail about the murders of three black men, this black anti-apartheid activist shocked herself by instinctively responding to his emotional story by reaching out to touch his right hand. "In the moment they touched," wrote Le Baron, "her heart acknowledged his humanity, despite the blood of others on his hands" (p. 226). Empathy, it seems, may be invoked involuntarily as people enter into each other's stories. For negotiators, however, empathy is also something they must create consciously.

In the course of my research and interviews, I became increasingly interested in how genuine empathy is developed during crisis events. How are negotiators able to forge authentic bonds with individuals they have never met and may not necessarily like or approve of? While most of us believe that true empathy under these conditions is all but impossible or is at most a contrived communication strategy, negotiators tell us it is not, and that without genuine empathy, no negotiation is possible. Kohlrieser (2009) agreed:

> It is a myth that bonding occurs only with people we like. In fact, it is crucial that we learn to form and maintain bonds in ways that allow a relationship to exist even in the face of profound differences or serious conflict. Hostage negotiators are able to negotiate with desperate people because they are able to form bonds with them, irrespective of the acts that such individuals may have committed. (pp. 43–44)

Intellectually understanding the importance of empathy is one thing; developing empathy and staying empathetic under threat is another. This can be challenging, to say the least. Thompson and Jenkins (1993, 2004) noted, "Deflecting verbal abuse and offering empathy in the face of antagonism" (p. 67) represents the ultimate communication challenge. It isn't easy to make this shift, especially if we still hold the view that difficult behaviour should be punished—that those who engage in it must be held accountable. Kenneth Cloke (2006), an international negotiator and mediator, observed that "The purpose of empathy is not to excuse destructive behavior, but to separate the person from the problem, disarm judgments, and consider what might lead them to do the same" (p. 26).

Mayer (2000) noted that, although sometimes difficult, "maintaining the essential humanity of the person with whom one is in deep conflict . . . is one of the keys to productive communication in disputes" (p. 131).

Empathy Isn't Always Involuntary: It's a Decision and a Discipline

When we hear the word *empathy*, most of us associate it with warm, fuzzy feelings. However, what became evident in my conversations is that empathy is often first developed as a conscious and intentional choice to override judgment. Empathy, then, is an act of self-discipline. Negotiators put what they know they must do over what they may want to do. I heard much from negotiators about how they were able gradually, through listening, to enter into the story of the person's dilemma and even their life itself and how that changed their views and led them to experience an emotional bond. One negotiator told me,

> I was listening to the guy tell me about how he'd been homeless and hungry for a couple of weeks, and he didn't have anywhere to go. No friends, no family other than the woman he was splitting with and his kid who she wasn't letting him see. He'd been roughed up out on the street. I thought, "That shouldn't happen to a dog!"

Another said,

> OK, sure. I'm probably not going to be best friends with the guy, but when he asked me to come downstairs and meet him at the police car and go with him to the station, I agreed. Because the things he told me about his situation—well, it was real bad. I felt for the guy.

"Yeah, you get frustrated sometimes," another negotiator told me. "You go round and round trying to get a foothold, something to help end the situation. But at the same time, you gotta feel some empathy. If I'm frustrated and not sure about where this is all gonna end, what must he be feeling like?"

An Example

Empathy requires a voluntary release of judgment, good listening skills, and genuine curiosity. My partner Norm told me a story about an incident that happened before we met that illustrates how empathy can be built and how it can begin with a conscious decision to be responsive and proactive rather than reactive.

> As a person with disabilities who spent the first seven years of my education in a segregated school, then went on to a regular high school and university, I am passionate about the benefits of inclusive schooling. I was asked to provide an in-service for the staff of a high school attempting to

include disabled students into regular classes. I had given an hour-long presentation about the benefits of inclusion. All through my presentation, I'd been observing a staff member in the back row. She did not seem particularly happy about what I was saying. In fact, I noticed her because she was frowning and furiously taking notes after each point I made. I could see that she was pressing so hard that as she wrote, the paper in her notebook was tearing.

During the question-and-answer period, her hand was the first to shoot up. She told me she was a math teacher and began peppering me with questions that challenged much of what I'd said. "What about math?" she asked. "How am I supposed to deal with behaviour? How the heck do I deal with a wide range of abilities and still meet the curriculum goals in a limited amount of time?"

Meanwhile, the special education teachers in the front row—all passionate proponents of inclusive education—had turned around and were glaring at her. I knew I had to hold them back because they looked like they were going to attack her!

I don't exactly know why, but for some reason her interrogation wasn't really bothering me that day. Maybe it was because I'd slept well and drank a lot of water beforehand; I'm not sure. But when I looked at her, I saw a person for whom teaching was like a puzzle in which all the pieces neatly fit together. And in my presentation I'd taken her puzzle apart, thrown the pieces into the air, and gone, "Whee!" That visual image helped me stay patient and curious. I addressed each of her points respectfully, acknowledging their credibility. But the most important thing that happened was that I honestly began to empathize with her. I realized that I'd been asking her to call into question all of the practices she'd developed over many years—practices she'd developed with the best of intentions—and rethink everything. I'm sure she felt that not only had her competence been questioned but so had her ethics. She was understandably upset and confused.

When our interchange ended (and it really only took a few minutes), it was clear that she'd de-escalated. She looked up at me and said in what felt like genuine bewilderment, "I did my practicum in a segregated school. I thought I was doing good work, and the students were happy there. Was I just fooling myself?" It was a sincere question, and I had to treat it gently and respectfully. When I talked with her, I told her she wasn't wrong. In some ways I had enjoyed my time in the segregated school. But I also pointed out that had I remained there, a host of opportunities would have been denied me. We talked a little more before I had to move onto other questions.

Three months later one of the special education teachers from that school contacted me to let me know that this math teacher had become one of the strongest proponents of inclusion in her school. This is one of the times maybe I got it right and didn't let what I wanted to say supersede what I suspected would be most helpful.

I was aware that my response to her was a pivotal moment. If I'd attacked or diminished what she was saying in any way, I would have lost her and probably a lot of other teachers, too. Taking the time to hear her story allowed me to feel genuine empathy for her. After all, none of us do well when our worldviews are challenged. Very few of us change our opinions during an hour's presentation. We often go through a process of rethinking our assumptions; it doesn't always happen right away. Knowing this allowed me to engage with her and systematically work through her concerns. On my worst day, I might have seen her response as defensiveness, and I likely would have gotten defensive, too. I'm glad I didn't.

The hostage negotiation literature supports what Norm said. In order to reduce defensiveness and facilitate de-escalation, Goulston (2010) suggested that it was far more helpful to move into and empathetically explore what might initially be interpreted as a negative mind-set rather than attempt to argue the person out of it.

As the stories about Picco and Norm illustrate, it is not only the negative mind-set that we might need to explore—although that can be important since we want to take concerns seriously—but also the places of intersection and connection. Even when they don't seem apparent, it is critical to look for and be open to finding common ground.

Unfortunately, the search for common ground has often been mistaken as a search for compromise. This is a misunderstanding of what is meant by common ground in this context, and I would argue that understanding it as compromise seldom results in an effective outcome. Although compromise is often viewed as a good goal in resolving a dispute, it frequently results in one party or another feeling that their issues have been inadequately addressed. Common ground, on the other hand, can be as complex as shared identity or cultural background, or as basic (and tenuous) as shared humanity. In either instance, it is only through genuine empathy and engagement that common ground can be found and built upon.

As mentioned, the prerequisite for empathy in a difficult situation is the conscious adoption of a constructive narrative. To be empathetic to a person we agree with is easy. The challenge is to be empathetic when we disagree or disapprove of someone. It is here that it becomes critical for us to challenge our assumptions and judgments, since without first changing our view of the person, it won't be possible to become empathetic, and without empathy, it's unlikely that they will change their views, either. An effective negotiator has to put their own feelings, perceptions, and judgments aside and enter the perspective of the person with whom they are negotiating.

Norm utilized a mental image of a scattered puzzle to help him reframe what might have been interpreted as a personal attack. Several negotiators I talked with underscored the importance of reframing the situation to "just a person in a bad place." Whatever the process, it's clear that a flip in perspective must precede the development of genuine empathy. A negotiator framed it in this way,

> You've always got to remember that anybody can find themselves in a bad place in their lives. Whoever you're communicating with, you've got to look at it like, "There but for the grace of God." That's somebody's father, mother, brother, uncle. They have to be treated with compassion. The thing I usually close out with [in my training sessions] is I throw one slide up and that's the golden rule. I tell people, "If I had four to five minutes, this is the only slide I'd show you. If you can keep this central in your thoughts, you're going to be operating ethically and probably well in accordance with the law or policy." I really believe it's just a matter of trying to put yourself in that person's position.

Self-awareness and self-management (which I discuss later in the book) are something that one negotiator described as crucial in the development of empathy: "The key to establishing empathy is we won't react to these guys whether they're yelling or insulting, or nasty, we're just going to let that roll off."

We know through brain research that intense anger can be sustained for only brief periods of time. Anger is physically and emotionally exhausting. Interventions are much more successful when they come after an episode is over, not during the time when people have downshifted into a more primitive and reactive state. As Ron Garrison pointed out to the Texas Council of Special Education Administrators, we are likely to get ourselves hurt or killed if we try to intervene at the wrong time. It is a case of enlightened self-interest to be supportive and empathetic long before we become prescriptive.

We Have the Best Professional Development Sitting Right Here in our Classrooms!

It isn't just negotiators who understand this. So do the best educators. Like negotiators, the administrators and educators I talked with identified the need for empathy and good communication skills. Three of them told me:

> Being empathic, that's really important with difficult kids. An understanding of the unique needs of the student. Being a good communicator. I have had staff say to me that they find it refreshing that someone with a counselling background has come into this role. They see this background as very useful in this job.

> And you have to like people. You have to really enjoy kids and be curious and passionate . . . and [offer] an interest that you want to share. There's the academic part.

> I want the kids to know me. And I must know them. That's not just saying, "Oh, Mr. G. is nice." I try to give them many opportunities to read me.

Norm and I were asked to give a keynote at an international schools conference in Bangkok for the Near East Schools Association in 2018. A highlight of the conference for us was another keynote by educator, parent, and author Pernille Ripp. Ripp made a thoughtful, engaging, and even self-deprecating presentation in which her empathy for both students and teachers was clear. Her ability to be self-reflective and actively question her own practices was equally clear. "Would I want to be a student in my own classroom?" she asked. It is a question she believes all educators should ask themselves. "May we never be the reason a child hates school," she added.

A story she told involved a student who'd written in a teacher evaluation form that Ripp was the worst teacher they'd ever had. After a night of self-doubt and tears, rather than becoming defensive, she decided to find out more. What she learned changed the way she organized her classroom and related with her students. "I would rather have students dare tell me the truth than have students who don't dare to speak out," she said. "We have the best professional development sitting right in our classrooms!" she added. She put up a PowerPoint slide with a quote from one of her seventh grade students, Carrie: "My hope is for all teachers that they should look at everything as if they were the student."

The Limits of the Golden Rule: A Caveat

As the negotiator and the student mentioned above stated, empathetically putting ourselves into the shoes of another person is an ethical and important thing to do. However, there is a caveat. When we ask ourselves, "What would it mean if I were doing x behaviour?" we run the risk of making faulty assumptions. For example, if I assume that if I were the student leaving my seat without permission or refusing to take part in an activity, I'd be doing it out of malice or spite or as a way of thumbing my nose at authority, my reactions might be quite different than if I understood these actions as motor-driven or out of the student's control. Trying to walk a mile in someone else's shoes has inherent limitations. Perhaps it would be more effective to engage in what might be called respectful hunches, then to check those out with the student or their family and others who know them well.

In Summary

Empathy is a vital part of the de-escalation process and is often a much more intentional act than we might think it is. It is a mind-set we can consciously cultivate, and it requires the commitment to remain open-minded under challenge and to ask a different set of questions. As narrative mediators Winslade and Monk (2001) noted, perhaps empathy on its own is not enough:

> One of the first things we need to bring to this task is an attitude of wonder, or curiosity. Empathy is not enough because, although it helps us enter into the experience

of another, it does not achieve the space for thinking about how this could be different. We are not speaking against empathy which is still important in understanding problematic experiences, but we are suggesting that we need to value curiosity more highly than has been the case (p. 125).

This leads me straight into the next chapter.

CHAPTER SIX

CURIOSITY

> A storyteller, above all, likes suspense. It is the not knowing about characters that makes them interesting. In a good story we watch for the unanticipated turn in the plot, and we presuppose that we are not seeing the entire picture.
>
> —Gussin Paley & Coles (1991)

> I do not have any particular talent, I am just passionately curious.
>
> —Einstein

For many years I worked in the field of human services, providing support for people with disabilities and their families. Like many people in this field, and like many educators, I'd assumed that my role was to solve problems and come up with viable answers to the dilemmas we faced. Many of us are hired to be problem-solvers, and we do our best to live up to that expectation, even though we often feel like it's an impossible task. That was certainly true for me.

About midpoint in my career I decided to begin mediation and negotiation training. To my absolute amazement and delight, one of the first things I learned was that I was not expected to have answers. Instead, I was told it was much more important for me to have questions. This was a liberating revelation since the pressure to have all the answers is intense, and many times I felt like I just didn't have them. My training catapulted me into a deep exploration of the role that curiosity and questions play not only in the de-escalation process but also in every aspect of life.

The next thing I learned was that not all questions are created equal. Some just don't work as well as others. For example, closed or leading questions aren't always very effective, and using the word *why* can get the asker into trouble. You may know that closed-ended questions are questions that leave the person answering them with only two options: yes or no. In some instances, that may be all we need to know, but in many other situations we miss the opportunity to learn important and sometimes crucial details. Open-ended questions are generally more effective since they elicit more information, details, and even rationales for behaviour. Asking why might initially appear to be an effective approach to gaining information, but unfortunately it often leads to defensiveness. For some reason the word *why* can sound like a challenge. "Why did you do that?" can sound suspiciously like "Why on *earth* did you do *that*?" even if it isn't your intent to sound incredulous or judgmental.

Another important thing I learned during my training was about something called powerful questions. When I first heard this phrase, I'll admit I was intimidated. What, I wondered, was a powerful question? It sounded complex and difficult to master. While I learned it is true that there's real skill and finesse involved in asking good questions, I also learned that some of the most powerful questions are really quite simple, and the finesse is more about learning when to ask them.

A few years ago, I heard a radio interview with noted celebrity television host Larry King, who had just written a book. The interviewer said, "There are people in your book who know you well and say that you ask ridiculously simple questions when you are interviewing people on your show. What do you make of that?"

King laughed. "They're right!" he said. "When I first started out in journalism, I used to watch TV hosts who would ask a question, and before the person had a chance to answer, they would launch into twenty minutes of their own opinion. Finally, when there was only a moment or two of airtime left, they'd turn to the person and say, 'So what do you think?' I always vowed that I wouldn't be that kind of interviewer. Now I just ask simple questions like, 'Say more' or 'And then what happened?' and people tell me all kinds of interesting things!"

Powerful questions, then, are often the short, open-ended questions that elicit more information and show the speaker that we are listening and interested in hearing what they have to say. They can be deceptively simple.

The hostage negotiators I interviewed confirmed the importance of powerful (and short) questions. They reminded me that when people are under duress, long and complicated questions simply won't register. They also warned against compound questions—the kind of question that contains several questions. At the best of times, even when people are calm, layering a series of questions can be confusing and difficult to take apart and decipher. It's hard to know which question to answer first, if we remember them at all! Particularly when people are upset, deconstructing a compound question is almost impossible. It is therefore critically important to limit our questions to one at a time, and then let a little silence fall.

The Importance of Silence

During my interview with Robin Burcell, a former hostage negotiator and now best-selling crime writer – on her own and with Clive Cussler –she told me that "the biggest thing they teach you in negotiation is silence. [It's] really hard for someone not to fill in the silence." She promptly stopped talking, and sure enough (to her amusement) I found something to say. "See?" she said. "I did it to you, and you filled the silence! You even knew I was doing it, and you *still* filled the silence." We both laughed.

Silence gives people the space they need to gather their thoughts and fits very well within the overall crisis negotiation philosophy of "go slow to go fast." As one educator I spoke with eloquently (and poetically) said,

> One of the important pieces of this is space, lag time, or quiet time. And after the person says something, being silent and just doing the minimal encouragers, so that people have time to reflect. That silence that asks to be filled. Dig a little deeper. It's almost like pouring water on sand, you need time for the water to filter through.

When we feel we've heard everything someone has to say, listened well, and asked important questions, and the person seems to be de-escalating, that's precisely the moment to make sure we've heard everything. In many instances there may be things left unsaid—sometimes the most important things. The person may have been afraid to bring the issues up, or they may not have developed enough trust in us to make a sensitive disclosure. One of my favourite questions at the end of any mediation, coupled with silence, is deceptively simple and deceptively powerful.

"Is There Anything Else?"

Let me give you an example. On one occasion I was co-mediating a session with a couple who were splitting up. We'd been working for several hours, and overall the mediation was smooth, and many issues like custody, child support, and the division of assets had been amicably agreed on. When it seemed that the mediation was coming to an end, my co-mediator and I asked what we thought might be the last question of the day. "Is there anything else?" And then we let some silence fall.

After what felt like an interminable amount of time and an oddly uncomfortable silence, the young woman looked up and said, "Um, we haven't talked about his drinking yet." It was a startling moment since this was the first we'd heard about a potential drinking problem. The mediation went on for another hour, and both parties seemed satisfied with the resolution at the end. After it was over, my co-mediator and I expressed mutual relief that the issue had indeed come up since there would have been little chance that the rest of the agreement would have held up without addressing that issue.

Hold onto Your Dreams!

Although I've talked about the need for broad and open-ended questions—and they are important—there actually is such a thing as a question that is *too* broad or open-ended – at least at first.. For example, in human services and in education, particularly in transition or IEP meetings with disabled students, we often start with big, impossible questions like "What would like to do when you grow up?" This is a huge question and probably hard for many of us to answer without a lot of thought and enough time. This is particularly true for children or teens. A complicating factor is that many young people have been conditioned to believe they need to tell us what we want to hear. We have to counter that tendency first by building trust, then by staying persistent and asking deeper questions. Sometimes we need to break the question down into smaller components. Here's an example that comes from the work that Norman and I are sometimes asked to do.

Years ago, we were doing a workshop on self-advocacy for a group of adults with intellectual disabilities. One of the participants was a middle-aged woman who volunteered to be interviewed by us in front of the group. We began by asking her what her dream for herself was (there's that broad, unanswerable question again), and to our dismay, she replied, "I don't have a dream." Concerned, we probed a little, hoping this assertion wasn't true. She was adamant. "I don't have dreams because when you have dreams, you just get your heart broken." We were shocked and saddened to hear this, and it was hard to know how to proceed with the conversation. Despite being taken aback by this comment, we continued on with the interview.

In the course of the conversation, she casually mentioned her husband. We were surprised. She hadn't mentioned a husband before, so we asked about him. She told us she'd been happily married for ten years. We learned where she'd met her husband (at a dance) and how they came to fall in love and decide to get married. "He's a good dancer," she said proudly. As she talked, her face changed. She began to smile as she told us about her wedding and their life together. Noting the change in tone, we doubled back to a variation of the first question but this time with a bit more specificity. We asked if it had been a dream of hers to get married. "Well, yeah! I guess it was! I'd dreamed about my wedding since I was a little girl," she said, looking just a bit surprised.

We asked how she liked to spend her days. "Well," she said, "I work, of course! I have a job at the thrift store." It turned out that she really loved her job and the people she worked with. "I knew somebody who worked there, and they helped me to get that job." It wasn't a big stretch at that point to ask if being employed was a dream she'd had for her life, and she confirmed that yes, it had been a big dream to earn her own money, do work she loved, and also do something valuable for the community.

At the beginning of this interview, when we asked about her dreams and heard that she didn't have any because "your heart gets broken," we honestly weren't sure what to ask next. The tragedy contained in that statement all but knocked the breath out of us. That was the point at which we had to relax, take a deep breath, and make a conscious decision to stay curious and probe a little further. The last question we asked her was one we often like to ask in self-advocacy workshops since it tends to elicit gold nuggets of useful information that we then impart to participants in other workshops.

"What advice would you give to other people in a situation like yours?"

"Hold onto your dream!" she said. "Never let go."

There's a saying that people will start out telling you what they know and end up telling you what they didn't know they knew. Curiosity is an effective way to help a person access what they didn't know they knew.

It's a Process

One of the things I've learned about curiosity is that it is a process. We don't always arrive at the heart of the matter by asking a single question. Sometimes we need to be persistent and ask more than once. Sometimes it means we have to rephrase the question. I've learned a lot about the value of rephrasing a question from my son, Evan. Evan is hard of hearing. When he doesn't hear something, he'll ask the speaker to repeat what they've just said. The tendency for most people is to repeat what they said verbatim, just louder. Unfortunately, if Evan still doesn't understand, people will continue to ratchet up the volume, and this is often coupled with irritation and facial contortions that aren't lost on him. Early in his life I learned that repeating myself was usually ineffective; simply rephrasing what I'd said was often enough to help him understand.

Skating on the Surface

In this age of technology and speed and increased expectations for quick productivity, we seem to have developed a universal tendency to "skate on the surface" of issues and try to arrive at solutions quickly. It isn't uncommon to find employees of large corporations engaged in standing-only meetings. This tactic is designed to keep people uncomfortable and focused on finding solutions quickly. The obvious risk is that rather than looking for creative ideas, they will make snap decisions just to end the discomfort.

We don't always delve very deeply. When it comes to asking questions, we will generally ask only one, then move on to the next topic. This is often a mistake. For several years I coached mediation and negotiation students at the Justice Institute of British Columbia, and the thing I coached them on the most was the tendency to ask one question and quickly move on to the next, often unrelated concept. I encouraged them to ask more than one question—dig a little deeper. Narrative therapist Michael White called this process "hovering." I watched a video interview with a family he was counselling and saw this process in action. He asked what seemed to me to be the same question several times. I expected that the family would have found his repetition frustrating (you already asked me that!), but surprisingly, they did not. Each time he asked, they gave him more information and added rich detail.

Asking a series of good questions that elicit more information is a bit like opening a set of Russian dolls. When we are handed a Russian doll, the first thing we want to do is open it. And then open the next one and the next one until we come to the tiny doll in the centre. I like this as a metaphor for curiosity. Each time we ask a question, it's like opening up another Russian doll and finding out what's inside.

Sometimes people complain that they don't have time to dig deeper. My experience tells me that spending the time building trust and gaining more details pays off in the end. It's what negotiators call "front-end loaded." The work we do in the beginning makes the work we do later when it comes time to find solutions much quicker. The other payoff is that doing the exploratory work helps us to adequately define the situation so that we don't find ourselves solving the wrong problem. What I've learned echoes what negotiators told me repeatedly. It is that universally accepted negotiation mantra I mentioned earlier, and is worth repeating: "Go slow to go fast."

What Would You Say If You Did Know?

There are times when we feel like we're asking all the right questions, but especially with children and teens, we are met with silence or those implacable three words we've all heard many times: "I don't know." When confronted with this response, it is helpful to remember that most adult-to-child interactions contain an inherent power differential. We may be doing our best to minimize that power difference, but kids know that adults retain the authority to override them and dismiss their concerns, so they may not always feel safe enough to tell us what they need. Perhaps they also feel like our questions call for the "right" answer, and they are reluctant to be wrong. Part of the process is about building the kind of trust that allows for more disclosure, but this can be difficult if we are repeatedly met with shrugs and "I don't know." However, overcoming this communication snag can be easier than we might think.

A response I've found helpful during this kind of stalemate is "What would you say if you did know?" This question tends to surprise people, and it often elicits more information. I suspect that it works well because it gives permission for the person to speculate, give their opinions, offer their perspective, and not worry about getting it right.

Specificity

What I learned about curiosity in mediation training I brought back to my work in human services, and I found that it made a huge difference in how I interacted with others. Rather than imposing my "answers" onto them, I simply became curious. Not only did I find that it is important to be curious, but also that it is necessary to be specific. When I was preparing for certification in mediation and negotiation, I was lucky enough to have a wonderful mentor, Donna Soules. During a coaching session just before my certification exam, Donna said something that stuck with me: "If there are only two things you can remember, remember these: be very, very curious and be very, very specific." Asking for specific details helps us avoid the pitfall of making assumptions.

Listening for euphemisms and globalized statements and then asking about them can help us deconstruct the conversation in useful ways. For example, use of words like *always* or *never* inevitably send up a flag for me during the mediation process. Simply asking for an example ("tell me about when this happened") can focus the scope of the conversation and perhaps even result in a re-evaluation of the assertion's veracity. Likewise, when people use "motherhood" terms like *respect*, *safety*, or *doing what's best,* those are opportunities to inquire further. After all, in a room of ten people, we are likely to get ten different definitions for each of these words. "When you say you feel disrespected, what does that sound like or look like?" can yield a lot of useful information! Conversely, failing to ask the question and merely assuming we know what it means can result in substantial misunderstanding.

Negotiators also talked about this process, reminding me that the first question they ask is short and simple. It is always a variation on "So how did we get here today?" – an open-ended question designed to begin the negotiation while leaving space for the individual to explain the situation. The word *today* is specific, and quickly begins to focus the conversation.

What Part of "No" Don't You Understand?

When students are disruptive, they may resist our attempts to calm the situation and regain control by refusing all our efforts. It's as if they are giving us a resounding *no* to everything we suggest. This can be a source of frustration, since a globalized no isn't an easy wall to penetrate.

Perhaps a visual representation might help. All of us are familiar with this picture of an iceberg submerged in water (see Figure 6.1).

Figure 6.1

We know that most of an iceberg is under the water; a relatively small part of it shows above. I've often thought that the small part of the iceberg represents the disruptive incident or the refusal—it's the "no" that students present us with. Bearing in mind that most of the iceberg is under water—in other words, the rationale for that "no" is hidden from us—can help us figure out how to proceed.

Figure 6.2

Asking questions can be helpful in bringing the underlying reasons why the person is doing whatever they're doing to the surface (see Figure 6.2). It's easy to make assumptions about why someone is refusing to cooperate, but the problem is that those assumptions are often incorrect. If we stay curious, we may be able to get to the real heart of the matter.

There might be any number of reasons or rationales underneath a no. "I don't trust you," "Not now," "I'm not feeling well," "I don't know how to do what you're asking me to do," "What if I fail?" or "Someone is bullying me" are all plausible.

If we simply assume that a student is doing things only for attention, to manipulate us, or to get out of work, we may miss important information that might help us support that student more effectively. Delving into the underlying reasons for the behaviour might seem overly time consuming, and even like we're coddling the student, but failing to do so can result in fruitless time spent trying to solve the wrong problem. After all, ignoring what's underneath the water is what got the *Titanic* into trouble!

My Favourite Role Model

I have a role model from whom I have learned much about curiosity. He's probably not someone you'd expect; he isn't a well-known presenter, author, or public figure. In fact, I've never even met the man. I only know him by reputation, hearsay, and through the written words of others, since he never actually wrote anything down himself. To the best of my knowledge, computers weren't even around in 429 BC.

Who is this mystery man? My role model is Socrates. Surprised? Let me explain. In order to do so, I will have to do a brief synopsis of what Plato claimed Socrates did. I'm sure scholars of Plato's *Republic* and the Socratic dialogue will cringe as I do Socrates what is likely a great disservice, but here goes.

As you probably know, Socrates was a Greek philosopher. When Socrates engaged his contemporaries in debate, he did so through what later (not surprisingly) was called "the Socratic method." He would walk around the Agora (market) and engage people in discussions about truth, government, and other important topics. Socrates would pose questions like "What is justice?," "What is knowledge?," or "What is truth?"—important philosophical questions that we continue to struggle to define today.

Socrates would send the debaters away to wrestle with these big questions. Sometimes the process of arriving at a definition would take days. When they returned, having arrived at consensus and satisfied with their definition, Socrates would listen intently. He would then engage in a process of asking questions and forcing them to define their terms, particularly their ethical terms of reference. After they were finished, he would begin systematically to undermine each of their arguments. The way in which he did this was invariably the same. He would say, "I don't think so, and here's why" and then proceed to question their rationale and poke holes in all of their arguments.

I've always had a visual image of those poor adversaries of Socrates lying on the floor in demoralized puddles once he was through repudiating their hard-won theories. Then I imagine them doing what I would probably have done—standing up, putting their hands on their hips, and saying "OK, then. If you're so smart, what is justice? What is truth?" And apparently, that's exactly what they did.

Socrates would respond to these challenges with the same answer. I've always imagined him shrugging his shoulders as he replied.

"I don't know," he'd say. Then he'd add the crucial second part of that sentence: *"But at least I know that I don't know."*

Socrates believed that the only infallible thing is, in fact, fallibility. To know that we don't know is crucial if we want to avoid doing harm. It's also the first step in genuine curiosity. When it comes to interpreting other people's behaviour, Socrates' response is perhaps as good as it ever gets. We often don't know what leads a person to do a particular thing. But as long as we can acknowledge that we don't know and become curious, we will never do harm. Making assumptions not only often leads us to faulty conclusions but also can result in fractured relationships and escalated exchanges.

As mentioned, these are the moments when the notion of the golden rule—and attempting to walk a mile in someone else's shoes—has some serious problems. However, if we can proceed on the assumption that we do not have all the information we need, we can avoid exacerbating a difficult situation. Hostage negotiators often told me versions of the same idea with their much-repeated motto. "Go slow to go fast." The key to going slow is curiosity.

In conclusion, I'd like to offer you a few vignettes that illustrate the importance of maintaining a stance of curiosity.

"Mom, What's a Spaz?"

There are a lot of good reasons to stay curious, but one of the more humorous was illustrated to me in the following story. As you will see, staying curious may have a point of enlightened self-interest for us!

Our friend Tim was the special education director in a large urban area for many years. He and his wife, Bambi, have two children, the eldest of which at the time of this story was seven-year-old William.

One day Bambi was driving down the road with the kids in the car. "Mom," William asked from the back seat, "what's a spaz?"

It's easy to imagine her distress at this question. Sighing, she prepared for the lecture on teasing and name-calling that seemed to be required.

"Well, William," she said, "that's a name that people sometimes call someone who has cerebral palsy and has spasms. It's not a very nice thing to say."

She went on to explain what spasms were and what caused them. A few minutes later, her disability 101 lesson for seven-year-olds finished, she added, "I sure hope you never say that, William!"

"No, Mom," William answered, suitably chastened.

"By the way," she said, suddenly curious, "where did you hear that word? Was it at school?"

"No. It was on that sign back there. It said 'Pools, hot tubs, and spas.'"

The moral of that story is obvious: save yourself some time, effort, and embarrassment and ask the question first. I remember telling this memorable story at a conference once. A parent emerged from the audience and said ruefully, "I made that same mistake once. My six-year-old son came home from school with a form one day and said asked, 'Mom, what's sex?'"

"So," she said, "I told him. After a few minutes of confused silence, he pointed at the paper. 'I'm supposed to check off one of these boxes. M or F." (Now, we won't get into the troublesome and important issue of gender binaries here, but the moral of this story is obvious: ask the question first, and save yourself the embarrassment.)

Now, Class, Say 'Em

Our friend Tom Osbeck was involved with a university project for inclusion. One of the students he was helping to include into a regular second-grade classroom was a little boy named Sam. Sam had recently moved north to Michigan from North Carolina. Although he didn't speak, he'd been successfully included in his first-grade class, and Tom didn't foresee any problems for second grade.

About two weeks into the school year, Tom got a distress call from Sam's teacher. "Get this kid out of my class!" she said. "He yells and screams. He throws himself on the floor. I don't know what he wants. I've tried everything! He's just too disruptive."

Tom tried to extract more details about the situation from the teacher, but she was too upset to talk. He asked if he could visit the class to observe Sam. She agreed reluctantly but added a warning. "If you can't fix it, he has to go."

Tom arrived just in time for a lesson on vowels. The teacher was using a somewhat dated teaching strategy that relies on a kind of call and response between teacher and class. "A E I O U and sometimes Y," she began. "Now, class, say 'em." The whole class—except Sam—dutifully began reciting the vowels. Sam, on the other hand, immediately dropped to the ground and began kicking and screaming. Tom watched in amazement.

Several minutes and a lot of chaos and confusion later, Sam seemed settled again. The teacher began another unit that involved the same call and response strategy. Once again, as if on cue, Sam dropped kicking and screaming to the floor in a flurry of books, papers, and pens.

It is a very good thing that Tom also hails from North Carolina, or he probably wouldn't have been able to solve this mystery. My friend Cyndi is also from North Carolina. She thinks I have the funny accent, but I know she does. Actually, I love to hear Cyndi talk. She, too, has a son named Sam, and when she calls him, it sounds like his name is "Say 'em."

Think about it. AEIOU and sometimes Y. Now, class. Say 'em.

In an instant Tom understood the problem. Each time the teacher asked the class to repeat what she'd said (she did this often in the course of the day), what Sam was hearing wasn't a request to repeat a lesson. What he heard was the teacher calling his name! "Say 'em."

We can only imagine what Sam might have been thinking. "She's calling my name. She's not looking at me! I don't know what she wants!" Fortunately, it was literally that easy to sort out.

Behaviour is often a normal response to an aberrant environment. Just because the environment doesn't look aberrant to us doesn't mean it doesn't look that way to someone else.

The Million-Word Essay

Many schools are recommending greater opportunities for student and parent input. It is important to remain curious as we elicit this input, and as we know, sometimes this can take effort and ingenuity.

Some years ago I met Josh, a doctoral student at the University of Madison, Wisconsin, who was a tenth-grade teacher. He told a group of educators in a conference workshop about a brilliant strategy he'd come up with designed to elicit important information and input. At the beginning of the first week of school, he would tease his students by telling them that he planned to assign a "million-word essay" at the end of the week. On Friday afternoon, he would tell the students (much to their relief) that the assignment wasn't for them but actually for their parents. This inevitably resulted in relieved laughter. The paper he sent home with his students read, "In a million words (or less), tell me what I need to know about your son or daughter." He said the information he got back was invaluable, and even when he didn't get anything back, that proved to be useful information he could follow up on, as well.

In Summary

Curiosity may be the most important and profound gift we can offer our students. If we can shift from blame and judgment to curiosity, we are in a far better position to solve difficult problems and even to shift the course of a student's life. We know that many students arrive at school unprepared to meet the challenges of education. Maybe home life is difficult; maybe they are being bullied; or maybe they are coping with learning disabilities or sensory issues. We may be one of the only people in a student's life to care enough to take the time to figure out what's going on and really help. Our friend and colleague David Pitonyak once said something that has stuck with me over the years: "Trying to understand someone's behaviour outside the context of their life is fundamentally disrespectful." I always try to remember this when I am involved in a difficult interchange. A line from the classic movie *The Philadelphia Story* sums it up perfectly. "The best time to make up your mind about a person is never."

CHAPTER SEVEN

LISTENING

> A riot is the language of the unheard.
>
> —Dr. Martin Luther King Jr.
>
> We all want, above all, to be heard, but not merely to be heard. We want to be understood—heard for what we think we are saying, for what we know we meant.
>
> —Deborah Tannen (1990)

In 2018 in Silver Lake, California, twenty-eight-year-old Gene Atkins crashed his vehicle into a Trader Joe's market following a domestic altercation with his girlfriend. After exiting the car, he ran into the market with a gun in hand. The resulting stand-off between Atkins and police lasted three hours and involved an exchange of gunfire that injured a police officer. In the process, an innocent woman in the market was accidentally shot and killed by police. More than twenty hostages were present, including MaryLinda Moss, a local artist. In a remarkable show of cool-headedness and bravery, Moss managed to negotiate with the distraught gunman and bring resolution to the situation.

Although Moss took an active role in the negotiation—repeatedly intervening between Atkins and the police—her primary process was empathic listening. Toward the end of the incident, as he was surrendering peacefully, Atkins told Moss he wished he'd met her earlier because all he'd really wanted was someone to talk to.

This is precisely what I heard over and over again from the negotiators I interviewed: "People just want to talk. They just want someone to listen to their story. In almost every situation, I can guarantee you that's what's going on. People just want to be heard."

When we think about high-stakes negotiations like this one, it's tempting to believe that the only people who can broker a serious stand-down will be highly trained professionals. MaryLinda Moss shows that this simply isn't true. Any of us with the right mind-set and a will to suspend judgment and listen empathically can do the same. Many of us are familiar with the stories of teachers who successfully intervened with school shooters and resolved the situations they were in. For example, in 2018, Kelly McManus-Panasuk from Florida spent three minutes she claimed felt like an eternity talking with shooter Sky Bouche and convincing him to disarm. In August 2013 in Georgia, Antoinette Tuff, a school bookkeeper, talked to Michael Brandon Hill for twenty-five minutes while she stayed on the phone with a 911 operator. Hill surrendered his weapon, and there were no injuries or loss of life. In 2014 in Roswell, New Mexico, teacher John Masterson talked a twelve-year-old gunman down.

Dominick Misino, former head of the New York City Hostage Negotiation team, stressed the importance of listening during high-stakes incidents. "It's the biggest thing we do in negotiation," he told me.

> I've negotiated with hostage takers, hijackers and murderers. No matter who we're negotiating with, it's always the same. You've got to listen. Sit back and listen without interrupting them! That's critical. You can't interrupt. What you'll hear is every instance of when he's been badly treated or how no one cares about him. And you know what? A lot of times that's true. In any case, all of its true to him, and that's what really matters.

The Physiology of Listening

Although comparatively little research on the precise nature of listening exists, what we do know is that it is both a cognitive and a physical process. In a book called *Hostage at the Table*, (2006) George Kohlrieser cited James Lynch, a co-director of the Psychophysiological Clinic and Laboratories at the University of Maryland School of Medicine, and noted that Lynch drew "a connection between human communication and the cardiovascular system" (p. 5). Through the use of sophisticated computer technology, and by hooking volunteers up to monitors, Lynch found that when human beings speak, blood pressure increases, heart rate speeds up, and blood vessels are altered. "Conversely, when one listens to others speak or truly attends to the external environment in a relaxed manner, then blood pressure usually falls and heart rate slows, frequently below its normal resting levels" (p. 5).

This research has important implications for those of us who are trying to understand the process of de-escalation. Listening is clearly a key factor. However, it is interesting to note that the teachers who intervened with school shooters in the above examples didn't seem to spend much of their time listening. Instead, they apparently spent most of their time talking. This seems counterintuitive, given what negotiators like Misino have said about the importance of listening. However, in light of Lynch's work, their success in resolving these difficult situations begins to make more sense since it isn't only the negotiator who needs to listen. It is helpful to assist the person in crisis to listen as well.

Unfortunately, the mistake many people make when confronted with a person in crisis is to resort to directives, not questions. As negotiators make very clear, not only are directives ineffective, they are also most likely to cause further escalation. Distraught individuals—and any of us during a personal crisis—do not respond well to being told what to do. These interveners were not directive. Instead, they were supportive, and calm - despite the level of stress they must have been experiencing.

Listening is often the first casualty of crisis. Under duress, few of us are able to listen well. Knowing that listening is a powerful way to lower physiological stressors and bring about de-escalation, how can we influence and assist someone to listen without causing them to feel unheard and re-escalating them in the process?

Kohlrieser's extrapolation of what Lynch found into his own work as a trainer of hostage negotiators might give us some important clues;

> So when a hostage negotiator asks a question requiring the hostage taker to listen, if the hostage taker does listen, he begins to lower his blood pressure and heart rate . . . the hostage negotiator uses questions to focus . . . and to lower the states of arousal, blood pressure, and heart rate by helping to regulate listening. (p. 145)

Interestingly, and perhaps pivotal in this discussion, he noted that even though someone may be speaking, "answering a question is a form of listening" and is, therefore, useful in the de-escalation process. It's also been suggested that causing a person to listen by asking them a question causes a shift from subcortical to cortical (or more rational) thinking (Goleman, 1995; Goulston, 2010). Understanding how this works gives us more options for intervening well during a crisis.

Does this mean listening is less important? Not at all. It is still one of the most critically important aspects of hostage negotiation. This research suggests we can best assist a person to make this cortical shift by asking open-ended questions based in genuine curiosity. As we listen supportively, and encourage an exchange, we can think about listening as a way to de-escalate not only the person we are negotiating with but also ourselves.

Active Listening

Active listening is a commonly taught set of skills found in counselling and conflict resolution courses, and books on communication. It also figures prominently in the training programs hostage negotiators take part in. Negotiators learn specific skills and practice them through role play and simulation. In both conflict resolution programs and in the negotiator literature I reviewed, active listening is held up as a critical skill essential to good communication.

International mediator Bernard Mayer (2004) provided a helpful working definition of active listening: "Communication needs to be interactive to be effective . . . this means we have to listen as we deliver a message, and deliver feedback as we listen" (p. 123). Purdy and Borisoff (1997) defined listening more broadly as, "The active and dynamic process of attending, perceiving, interpreting, remembering and responding to the expressed (verbal and nonverbal) needs, concerns and other information offered by other human beings" (p. 8). According to Purdy (1997), an understanding of the nature of listening must include five basic premises. First, listening is a learned and teachable skill; second, it is a dynamic process; third, it is an active process; fourth, it must involve body and mind working together through both verbal and nonverbal processes; and fifth, listening facilitates receptivity to "the needs, concerns and information of others, as well as the environment around us" (p. 7).

The term *active listening* typically describes a series of skills contained within the broader lexicon of listening and consists of a combination of "listening . . . sharing . . . [and] action" (Slatkin, 2005, p. 24). The specific skills that comprise active listening were initially identified by Carl Rogers (Rogers & Farson, 1957) and typically include paraphrasing, reflecting, summarizing, probing, confronting, information-giving, self-disclosure, minimal encouragers, and immediacy. Each of these can help foster mutual understanding, the development of empathy, and the creation of rapport, and can lay the groundwork for mutual problem solving.

Mike Webster (2005), a hostage negotiator and trainer from British Columbia, elaborated the skills most necessary in active listening: minimal encouragers (I see, hmm), paraphrasing (restating what someone said in your own words), emotion labelling (tentatively identifying the emotion displayed), mirroring (restating the last words of what the individual said), summarizing (periodically encapsulating the speaker's main points and the emotional content), effective pauses (using silence to elicit more disclosure), open-ended questions (questions that encourage the exchange of more information), "I" messages (avoiding blame and helping to personalize the negotiator through self-disclosure), confrontation (pointing to discrepancies between behaviour and words), and reframing (restating negative communication in positive terms). The negotiators I spoke with all had training and used active listening skills during negotiations. They said,

> Active listening is absolutely huge!

> The very act of listening is empathic!

> Being a hostage negotiator is 95 percent about listening 'cause most people just want to tell you what's going on in their lives.

> You have to be able to hear the unspoken message as well as the spoken message.

Greenstone (2005) considered active listening "basic to successful communication" (p. 131). Skilful listening, he added, allows the negotiator to learn more about the subject, build relational trust, and avoid making dangerous assumptions. However, he cautioned that learning to listen well requires practise and is not necessarily a simple process. Many people would agree. For example, at the Justice Institute of British Columbia, certification in mediation or negotiation takes many, many hours of instruction, theory, role play, and practice. However, it's interesting to note that Thomlison (1991) cited a study that found that teaching active listening skills to a group of nurses for "as little as six hours . . . resulted in significant increases in skill levels" (p. 3), which suggests the process is not as arduous as some believe.

A Cautionary Note

Active listening skills are unquestionably an important part of good communication. However, it is also an approach that can be misused.

While it is undeniable that we can all use help in learning to listen more effectively, it's how we apply these skills that is most important. Rote listening skills can actually accomplish the opposite of what we intend. It can feel fake and manipulative. Maybe someone you know has gone to a workshop on communication. I'll bet you can tell right away. These are the people who follow up anything we say with "so what I hear you saying is . . ." and then repeat whatever we just said. Even beyond eliciting eye rolls, this response can make us feel frustrated and angry. We know we're not really being heard, and we suspect we're being patronized. We know when pat skills are being used on us, and we don't like it.

Does this mean active listening skills aren't important and shouldn't be learned? Not at all. These skills are useful. It is how and when we use them that is important. My husband studied family therapy in grad school. One of his teachers offered a kinaesthetic metaphor that I've found helpful. "You can always tell," he said, "when someone is using skills on you to try to gain your compliance. It feels manipulative but also like a barrier. It's as if their skills are in front of them. What we aim for instead is to have our skills behind us. It's our authentic engagement with the other person, our empathy and concern for them that is paramount. The skills are secondary." Interestingly, this is a sentiment I heard over and over again from the negotiators I spoke with and read about. Although each of them clearly articulated the need for specific skill development and practise, they also cautioned against the application of rote skills and emphasized the need for a natural approach: "You can't be condescending. Pretend you're talking to a friend. You're going to talk . . . like a normal human being."

Mitchell Hammer (2007), former hostage negotiator and professor emeritus at American University, worried that an overemphasis on active listening skills might lead us to believe that they are "magic bullets" that will work in every situation (p. 103). He offered an important caveat, noting that active listening was not always the preferred method of interacting and under some circumstances could be counterproductive. As an example, he suggested that someone making substantive demands might escalate when asked a question about their emotional state. Madrigal et al. (2007) agreed. "Immediate application of active listening techniques may not be appropriate or may elicit a mistrustful or angry response from the hostage taker" (p. 129). They suggest it might sometimes be more effective to attempt to establish rapport through exploration of more neutral topics first.

Another potential problem with active listening techniques is the possibility that someone will paraphrase a distorted or inaccurate interpretation of the situation and risk validating "that interpretation and facilitate[ing] the development of maladaptive affective states" (Nugent & Halvorson (1995, p. 153). For example, responding to a comment like "No one understands me" by paraphrasing it verbatim—"So you're saying you are misunderstood"—is likely to result in further entrenchment. "Darn right!"

Michelle Le Baron (2002) also warned against a globalized use of active listening, but her concern was that negotiators could become reliant on a set of pat skills rather than a genuine desire to connect with the individual. Mayer (2004) agreed: "Good communication stems from intention, not technique" (p. 120).

Brendtro, Brokenleg, and Van Bockern, in their 1998 book, *Reclaiming Youth at Risk: Our Hope for the Future*, provide a heartbreaking example of how contemporary active listening skills when misused can be not only counterproductive but also highly alienating and dangerous.

In a tape made just before his suicide, a young man expressed anger and disappointment at the way his counsellors had responded to him. He acutely felt their lack of emotional involvement and noted that their "skills"—something he called parroting—were false and distancing. He felt betrayed and manipulated, complaining that the skills had been used *on* him rather than as a way to engage *with* him (p. 83). His mother, furious and also feeling betrayed, reminded the counsellors that kids are smart and see through such subterfuge. Brendtro et al. agreed: "Human service professionals have a long history of patronizing, infantilizing, or dehumanizing the very persons they are pledged to serve. While they may be unaware of their basic disrespect, young persons are not" (p. 85).

Although research clearly identifies the essential nature of listening in the negotiation process and further supports the skilful use of active listening, the discussion and example above suggest the need to carefully consider issues of timing, intent, authenticity, and context. Active listening, when misapplied, can be experienced as manipulative and trite, and may even impede the de-escalation process.

Although all the negotiators I talked to enthusiastically endorsed active listening, there was recognition that different situations called for different approaches. One negotiator explained,

> There were times [during the prison riot] when there was very little active listening because he was speaking on behalf of the gangsters, I was speaking on behalf of the police. These aren't warm, fuzzy guys. I knew I wasn't going to get anywhere by saying, "Tell me about yourself. Tell me this. Tell me that." I thought very early on, "I'm going to probably do a lot of talking," and I did. Active listening is not going to work if you've got an antisocial person who's out to rule . . . You're going to have to stand up to him, hopefully without polarizing or arguing a lot.

So what's an educator to do? Yes, it's helpful to learn skills. And it's unhelpful to use them wholesale. As a wise friend of mine once said, nothing works all the time. In the end it's intent and authenticity that make the difference. If we're simply using skills to bring a quick end to a situation in support of a problematic status quo, we may risk being ineffective and doing real harm.

A Few Stories

Remember Stuart? I talked about him in an earlier chapter. I met Stuart at the end of a weeklong summer institute sponsored by the local university. He was part of a panel of six young adults who had recently graduated from an inclusive high school. The panel was there to speak about their experiences with inclusion.

Stuart introduced himself in no-nonsense fashion. He told the audience that up until a year earlier, he'd been failing high school. Though he'd managed to muddle his way through elementary and middle school, he'd always been considered a "serious behaviour problem," and as he progressed onward, more than one school had considered expelling him.

He was about to quit school, Stuart told us, when the director of special education, our friend and colleague Rich Villa, approached him. "How can we help you?" he asked.

"It sounded like another setup. Teachers had asked me that question before, but nobody really meant it. I didn't believe this guy did, either. I kept on refusing, but he just kept asking. Finally, I agreed to come to a meeting." (This is an important point. When the question is asked, Villa will tell you, we need to ask as many times as necessary. A person won't always answer on the first try. Continuing to ask a supportive question builds trust. The person knows you are sincere and in for the longer haul with them.)

Stuart came to the meeting prepared. When Villa asked the question again, he was ready with an answer. "I need you to know something first," he said. "I really hate it when I lose it. I feel something boiling around inside me, and it kind of floods up from my belly to my head, and then it just sort of explodes. It feels awful, and then afterward I'm really embarrassed." He paused.

"So what I need is this. When I feel that feeling bubble up inside me, I need to be able to leave the classroom and go down the hall to an empty room. I need to be able to sit there for a while, maybe alone or maybe with someone I trust. Close, but not too close." Another pause. "That's what I need."

Villa, surprised at the simplicity of Stuart's request, readily agreed. He went back to Stuart's teachers to share what he'd learned. But when he told them what Stuart had asked for, the teachers balked.

"How do we know that he isn't just doing that to get out of work?" they asked. "What happens if all the other kids want to do that, too?"

"I know we're frustrated with this kid's behaviour, but maybe we have to make that a separate issue," Villa said. "We have to ask ourselves: What is our goal here? Do we want this boy to succeed?"

To their credit, the teachers agreed, and for the rest of Stuart's senior year, they followed his plan.

The summer we met Stuart, he'd graduated from high school and had a job in a garage, something he was interested in and proud of. Standing in front of the audience, he looked confident and together. He said, "You know, I still lose it sometimes. But these days it's like I know what to do about it."

It was a riveting comment.

Knowing what to do about it clearly represents the kind of shift we hope people will make. We often talk about the problems of operating from an external locus of control—in other words, doing something to either avoid punishment or please someone else and we encourage people to move to an internal locus of control—in other words, learn to self-manage from the inside out.

This was the shift Stuart was making. Because he'd been asked and was included in the discussion and planning about how to organize his own supports, he was not only able to give valuable advice and insight to his teachers but also began to develop important strategies for self-regulation. In the past everything had been done *to* him, and very few people had ever taken the time to listen to his perspective. As far as Stuart was concerned, those were behaviour plans developed for the convenience of others, not to help him. Sometimes they looked a lot more like retribution than genuine help. For the first time, he'd been able to participate in the development of a plan for support that was truly helpful.

Put yourself into the following scenario. Imagine you and your significant other are having relationship trouble, and the two of you decide to visit a therapist. The therapist begins by asking your partner how they see the situation. Your partner leans forward, points at you, and launches into a list of complaints that make you sound like the domestic version of a terrorist. After about ten minutes, the therapist leans back. "I think I get the general drift," she says. "So let's begin."

In one possible scenario, you live up to your new reputation and either commit double homicide or storm out of the session. In another, more likely scenario, you are speechless with disbelief. After all, you haven't been given an opportunity to present your side of things. This isn't fair!

Have you ever noticed we do this all the time? In our schools and even in our families, we confront people with our interpretation of their behaviour without asking for their interpretations or perceptions. Then we wonder why they seem less than enthusiastic about acknowledging what we're saying or cooperating with us.

I've often wondered why we don't ask—and particularly why we don't ask kids. Are we insensitive people? Or is it because we believe the only thing we'll hear will be excuses?

Our unwillingness to listen creates a cycle of pressure and resistance. The less we listen, the more the child protests. The more the child protests, the more we take it as further evidence of their unwillingness to take responsibility. This in turn causes us to become reactive and to apply even greater sanctions. If the child continues to resist and doesn't capitulate, we apply even more sanctions. The vicious cycle repeats.

Some autistic people will tell you they sometimes do things that are involuntary and out of their control. This doesn't mean they can't participate in finding solutions that work for them. Once again, as it was for Stuart, the key is listening. My friend and colleague Pat Amos tells a story about her daughter that describes this perfectly.

> There was an experience that I had with my daughter, and I think that was another big turning point in my life. She

wound up with a diagnosis on the autism spectrum, and when she was in second grade, we were having a difficult time with getting her school services, getting things right, getting people to understand her and her to understand them. One of the things that she started to do in her second-grade class was to just get up and leave.

It surprised me the way in which people reacted to this because they really acted as if they were afraid of her. What would happen is she would just all of a sudden jump up and run out of the room and down the hallway, all upset. Then the teacher would run after her to stop her, grab her, and bring her back. But she was very, very quick, quicker than the teacher, so then the assistant principal would come and follow the teacher, and then the principal would follow the assistant principal, and then the janitor would follow . . . There would be this long procession running through the halls of the school, and she would head unerringly to the cafeteria because there were those great big long tables, and as a little tiny person, she only had to duck a little bit to get under them, and she could then spend hours shifting from table to table to table while the big adults came in and tried to grab her and run after her.

Eventually, of course, someone would corner her and get hold of her. They'd haul her out, hold her up, and she'd be dirty and tear-stained and upset, and at that point they would call me to come to the school and say, "Is this yours? Did you leave this here? Want to come and claim it?" I would take her home and clean her up.

Of course, this led to behaviour analyses being done and behavioural assessment. They didn't call it that in those days, but a team had to come and meet with her and diagnose her and so forth, and among the team's recommendations were that maybe she needed to be in a special segregated school because, you know, we really just couldn't be doing this every day!

When I tell this story, I always ask people, especially if they're teachers or teachers-in-training, "What would you typically do in this situation?" I ask, "Why do you think the child would be leaving the room?"

They'll tell me two things: first, that the child is leaving the room to get attention; that all of this activity is about attention. I will point out to them that she seemed to be crying. She seemed to be upset, but then they'll tell me that bad attention for "kids like these" is the same as good attention. They want either kind, and either kind is motivating. That fits into this little system they've been taught. This fits the belief system. And then the second thing they'll tell me is that she's avoiding tasks. By leaving the classroom, she's not having to do the work, so it must be task avoidance and attention-seeking behaviour.

Then I will ask them, "What would you typically do to deal with this situation?" and what we get are these reward systems, point-and-level systems. Every fifteen minutes they would give her a star if she stays in her desk in the classroom, and if she gets a certain number of stars, she will get a reward, various kinds of elaborate systems of rewards and consequences they thought they could implement to keep her in the classroom.

We sat down, and we had a little meeting, and first of all, I said to the teachers, "Call her in! Ask her!" See, you know, we never ask! We just have meetings about people, but we don't have meetings with people. I don't care if it's only second grade. Ask her! They called her into the room and asked, "Well, you know, honey, why do you get up and run?"

She says, "My brain doesn't tell my legs what to do. My legs tell my brain what to do."

She knew! This is a perfect example of motor-driven behaviour, and she was telling them, "It's not under my control!"

Then they still wanted to do the point system and the reward system so that she could learn self-control. We had a long discussion about how people learn self-control. How do any of us get the personal, emotional, and social space to learn something? We asked them to do something very daring that had never, apparently, been done before, in the history of the earth, and that was to let her leave the room! To simply write up a system whereby when she wanted to, when she felt she needed to, when her anxiety was so great that she needed to go, she should just do what we would do for our own selves: we would go! No one would ask her; no one would remark on it or draw any attention whatsoever, and she would be told, "You can go see the school nurse, secretary, or librarian," three fine upstanding women who would give her a book to read or something to do. And then, when she's calm, and she's ready, she can go back to the classroom. But also when she went back, the teacher was not to say anything. No one was to draw any attention; this would go unremarked.

Well, of course, the initial objections were all about the domino effect. "If SHE gets to do it, EVERYONE will want to do it, too!" But honestly, you have to give kids credit. Kids have much more sense than that. Everyone is not going to want to jump up and go. Kids understand that different people need different things. They have a lot more common sense than we tend to give them credit for. So we said, "Look, let's just try it."

She comes back into the room, and we say, "Look, we've figured out what we can do. With your consent, if you want to do this, this is what your new system will be. If you need to leave the room, you're just going to leave, and this is where you can go, and this what you do. Do you understand that?"

And she goes, "Mm-hmm!"

She goes back to the classroom, and the system is now in place, We would definitely expect to see improvement, and we'd expect to see it somewhat gradual, but in her case, this was so powerful, it was so effective that she never needed to leave her seat again!

People were just astonished. But of course the answer was that this was anxiety-driven behaviour. Once she was given control and the power to play around with how her body felt, she was learning about her body. She was learning how it worked, and she was doing that in an environment where she was not afraid. She could sit there and say, "I feel like I gotta leave, I gotta leave, I gotta leave. Oh, wait, I can leave! OK then, I'll give it another five minutes!" And she was learning to do that very, very effectively.

We had given her the power. If there's anything going on there that we can talk about, that's valid, it's about a lot of anxiety and some issues about needing to be in control. I think our kids, and a lot of kids, whether they have a label or not, feel like they're not in control of their destiny. And the anxiety gets so high that they can't function at all, and I think what we need to be doing is not taking power and control away from them and husbanding it to ourselves, but giving it to them, and I think that's the essence of good pedagogy. It's good education. It's good learning. And it's probably the last thing that we think of to do! And so autism then becomes another repository in our society of what we do when we have bad pedagogy and bad educational practices, where we're always taking power and control away from people and never finding a way to give it to them.

Pat's story illustrates a change in focus from coercion to collaboration, and it involves listening carefully to what students are trying to tell us.

Listening requires more than hearing the words, though, because unfortunately people won't always tell us what's upsetting them in conventional ways. Children especially may not always tell us what's going on in a straightforward manner. Lack of language skills or concepts, lack of perceived power, or even fear can impede them. Some, like Pat's daughter, may express themselves through action. We must learn to look for clues in unusual places and resist assuming we know what the problem is. Two things we can do are to first ask, "How does the person explain their actions?" and really listen. Second, we can resist the temptation to make assumptions and think we already know what's going on and why. The following two stories illustrate how circuitous what we hear from children can be.

Hearing Aids and Flying Fathers

Our son, Evan, is hard of hearing. When he was in second grade, the school fitted him up with an FM system. He wore a receiver around his neck, and the teacher wore a transmitter around hers. The receiver plugged into Evan's hearing aids. Both items were large boxes, but on a second grader, the box that Evan wore seemed particularly huge. It was heavy, cumbersome, and obvious, so the other kids teased him. He hated it.

We encouraged him to try the system for a few weeks since he'd been having some trouble hearing and following the teacher's verbal instructions. He begged to have it removed, but we insisted. Reluctantly, he agreed to try.

After the first week, the calls began.

"Evan came to school without his hearing aids," the teacher would complain. "He took the batteries out of his hearing aids." The next week we were told, "Evan turns the FM system off. He takes the batteries out of it." "Please do something!"Trying to be good parents, we'd sit down and talk with Evan. We'd make sure he always had his hearing aids with him and was stocked up with spare batteries. "Just try it for a little while longer," we pleaded.

But every second day or so we'd get the same call. Nothing we said to Evan made any difference.

Then one day Evan came home from school upset. "Mrs. J. is always yelling!" he said. I found this puzzling, since I'd spent time in Mrs. J.'s classroom, and she'd always struck me as soft spoken. I asked him, "What does that sound like, honey?"

"She says, 'Class, it's time to come to the center for story time!'"His voice went up several decibels as he imitated her. It was instantly, head-slappingly obvious. For the first time, I understood the problem. When the teacher raised her voice in the normal course of classroom events, it traveled through her transmitter, into the receiver Evan wore around his neck, and from there went straight into his hearing aids and through his head like a bullet. It hurt! No wonder he'd been turning the thing off.

Perhaps Evan didn't think he had the power to influence what was happening to him, or maybe he lacked the language to tell us, but I think the real issue is that we weren't very perceptive. He'd tried in the only way he could to let us know about his distress. But we never thought to ask why he'd been sabotaging the FM system.

In the end, the cumbersome and stigmatizing FM system was abandoned, and Evan successfully finished his education without it. The lesson I learned has lasted. People—especially kids—will try to tell us what's going on with them in any way they can. It is up to us to listen carefully and not assume we already know what they're saying or why.

A few years later, the lesson was reinforced.

A friend of ours was employed as an itinerant artist in the school system. One day she was working in a second-grade classroom and noticed a small boy making a very dark and disturbing picture. He'd drawn a house and coloured it a dense, waxy black. At the top was a chimney, and above was a cloud of equally black smoke. Coming out of the chimney with the smoke he'd drawn the figure of a man flying through the air.

She asked him about the picture. "My father just blew up," he said.

Both our friend and the teacher were alarmed. It wasn't just the dark picture but his comment that raised red flags for them. Was there abuse going on in this boy's home?

A little detective work revealed that this little boy's father had recently left the family, and no one had explained why to the children. The picture was this boy's attempt to communicate his distress.

Listening at School and at Home

Linguist and author Deborah Tannen (1991) notes that most people, when asked, will say they are good listeners. However, when asked to talk about their biggest complaints about bosses, co-workers, and family members, these same people will claim that they don't feel heard or listened to. Tannen dryly encourages us to do the math; most of us think we're good listeners, yet most of us don't feel listened to. It just doesn't add up. How is it that we think we know how to listen, and yet it seems that we don't?

We all know that there are essentially four communication skills: reading, writing, speaking, and listening. In schools, which ones do we give precedence to? The first three. If we pay any attention to listening as a teachable skill, it is often interpreted as being quiet. Unfortunately, being quiet has little to do with listening. It is clear that listening is not a passive process. It is, instead, much more active than we might think. Learning to listen well opens up space for us not only to deal well in crisis but also to make better decisions and work collaboratively with students, many of whom are dying to give their perspectives and could offer us invaluable insights into how best to support them. As educator/author Bernard Gassaway noted,

> Students have a lot to say. They want to express themselves. While they want to share with adults how they perceive the world, adults are busy trying to interpret the world for them.
>
> Students think adults talk too much. It is difficult for students to listen to adults unless what is being said is relevant to them (personal communication, 2010).

This is especially true during crisis events. Nowhere is it more important for us to listen well than during difficult interactions.

In Summary

Listening is more than just passively hearing something; it is an interactive process.

CHAPTER EIGHT

SELF-MANAGEMENT

> He's not yelling at me, he's yelling for himself.
>
> —Jewish Proverb

Self-management is usually thought of as the process of controlling or suppressing negative reactions toward events or persons. While there may be times when negotiators must do this, everyone I spoke to and all the literature I read noted that a deeper process is necessary and that this process involves self-awareness as a necessary precursor to self-management. Several negotiators spoke adamantly to this issue.

> If you don't know what's going on inside of you, believe me, the other person will! Other people's sensitivity to your biases is extraordinary! Particularly in a crisis situation.

> Know your triggers. Know what your buttons are. Do you get tweaked when someone is speaking disrespectfully, yelling, or swearing? Or do you have a hard time with people who seem overly passive and seem to play the victim? Know what gets to you before you're in the situation, or it will take you over and that never ends well!

Another suggested the importance of understanding the influence of stress.

You either have it or you don't [the ability to negotiate]. I interviewed people who were interested in coming on [as hostage negotiators], I used to ask them—it's a standard interview thing—"I want you to think of a time when you [were under] what you may consider to be extreme stress, job related or even family, but identify your situation and tell me what got you through it." This is no job for a person who shows that they've behaved badly under a stressful situation.

As mentioned, Fisher and Brown (1989) of the Harvard Negotiation Project believe it is essential for negotiators to be "unconditionally constructive" (p. 24) —in other words, do what is good for you *and* for the relationship. Part of this process is the ability to use self-talk and self-management processes. Negotiators I spoke with noted that the ability to maintain a state of mental and emotional equilibrium during difficult exchanges could be partially achieved by remembering the overall goal: saving lives. One said, "You have to realize what your goal is as a hostage negotiator. It's resolution through negotiation, that's the motto we use. You may not like that person, the person may be a criminal or whatever, but you have to realize what your goal and what your job is."

Bohl (1997) elaborated,

> To succeed as a negotiator, the individual needs to maintain a balance between two opposing forces inherent in crisis situations. On the one hand, it is important to be able to establish some emotional distance from the situation, to exist in a state of "detached concern." Otherwise, the negotiator can lose control of the situation. On the other hand, the individual needs to be psychologically open and personally involved to establish a trusting relationship with a hostage taker who may be upset and irrational. (p. 45)

Admittedly, this is not an easy dichotomy to resolve, and negotiators must work consciously and continuously to manage their own emotions in order to remain in a state of detached concern and to simultaneously promote the development of a genuine bond. It requires commitment.

As discussed earlier, by suspending judgment and listening carefully to the subject's story, the negotiator is able to effectively change their own narratives and perception of the individual. From that vantage point they can begin to see the coherence of the person's actions and understand the rationale for the behaviour. Only then, once a bond of trust is built, can the negotiator move forward to try to resolve the issue. None of this can take place if negotiators allow themselves to become triggered and reactive.

Be Prepared

In addition to being aware of triggers and developing effective self-talk, negotiators also stressed the importance of preparation. Prior to arriving at a callout, they take steps to mentally prepare. "The first part of the call is always the hardest: what're you going to say? I prepare myself by getting information and by breathing. You train yourself not to react to certain things," one said.

The need for preparation went beyond the moments just prior to a specific call, and this is an important idea for educators, who seldom get prior warning about a crisis situation unless it is an ongoing interaction with a particular student. Preparation is clearly a larger, continuing process for all the negotiators, involving both formalized and informal practise:

> It's a tool that you got to practise all the time when you're dealing with people. You've got to hone your skills.

> To me it's always preparing for that call that you think is looming on the horizon. When you hear about them in the news, you think, "What would I have said? What were the keys? What were the hooks? What were the triggers? Where would you have been able to communicate with a guy from this background, this life?" And maybe being

honest with yourself, too, saying, "Is [this a] situation that you just don't think you can face up to?" . . . You'd have to say, "Look, I can't do this." Know yourself that way.

In this context, the negotiators agreed that one of the prerequisites for the job was the ability to deal well with stress. All participants claimed to have a high personal stress tolerance:

[I'm] a melodrama junkie. I love the calls with lights and sirens. I love that stuff.

Generally, I would like to think that I thrive in stressful situations. I may not always necessarily be thinking at that very moment that I'm having the time of my life, but when I hear something is going on, I want to be in the middle of it.

When people act out violently, they're like a pot of water on the stove. Sooner or later it boils, but take it off the heat, and you restore a state of balance, equilibrium. Whether it's a developmental crisis or an acute crisis, when they act out in this manner, by the time we get to them, they are all overflowing or overboiling. But we're prepared, and as long as they're venting, we don't care if they're cursing or if they're yelling, if they're screaming. The question we'll ask is, "What happened today?" with *today* being a key word. Once we've let them bleed off all that emotion or despair or whatever, now hopefully we're going to start doing a bit more. We may self-disclose a bit about ourselves. We're generally going to communicate. At that point that we're going to begin to offer up alternatives to the course of action they've embarked on.

While not all educators may be adrenaline junkies, it's undeniable that teaching will inevitably involve a certain amount of stress. Particularly when there are disruptive exchanges, the ability to successfully manage personal stress is a critical skill for an educator to cultivate and develop. Managing personal frustration is essential.

A film made by A&E and Bill Kurtis (1999) about the New York City Police Department's hostage negotiation team features a real-time incident between Maureen Burke, a detective and negotiator, and George, a man who is barricaded inside an apartment with his young nephew as hostage. Detective Burke calls for a short break in the negotiation (which is being conducted over the telephone) and asks George to take five minutes to think about the situation before they call him back. George agrees. Prior to the break, negotiations had been proceeding excruciatingly slowly, and each time it seemed that George was prepared to come out of the apartment and surrender, the situation would devolve back into a repetitive litany of fear and equivocation. "He goes right to the edge (of surrendering) and then comes back!" Detective Burke complains to her co-workers. "I feel like strangling him. That's the hard part!"

The team share a rueful laugh and commiserate with her for a moment. "He's just a man, Maureen, just a man," says Hugh McGowan, the commanding officer of the team.

"That's what I keep in mind" she quips back. They both laugh. Sometimes a little well-placed humour is the antidote to frustration. It's interesting to note that although the viewer gets a sneak peek into Detective Burke's frustration and fatigue, we never see her allow that frustration to show or leak into her tone while she's speaking to George. It is a stellar example of self-management, and we know, despite her comments, that she is empathizing with him.

Lessons from Labour Negotiations

The ability to self-manage is not necessarily something that a person arrives at naturally. Instead, like empathy, it involves a series of conscious and intentional decisions to remain responsive and avoid reactivity. I learned a great deal about this during my time in labour relations while drafting and updating collective agreements. During heated negotiations, the issues brought to the table didn't always arrive neatly packaged and politely stated. When people are passionate about their concerns, they have a tendency to couch them in accusatory ways. Children and teens are no different. During times of duress, it's unlikely that what students have to say will come to us in "palatable" ways. Sometimes those accusations and even personal slurs are hard to hear. What I learned at the negotiating table was that two minutes of reactivity and defensiveness could undo two weeks of relationship and trust building. It may be tempting to lash back, but it is not only potentially damaging and perhaps even dangerous but it is also not pragmatic.

Does this mean we won't get frustrated? Of course we will. It's what we do with that frustration that is critical. Developing a way to talk *ourselves* off the ledge during crisis situations is just as important, or maybe even more important, than trying to talk someone else off their ledge. The more we know about our own potential triggers, the more prepared we are to respond non-reactively. The way I ensured I would not get triggered was to use a simple self-talk mantra: "Don't take this personally. This is not about me. Everything in the world is not about me." It helped.

Self-talk can be an effective way to mitigate stress and reactivity. Finding a short phrase (short is good, since it is more difficult to remember complex ideas while under duress) can be a powerful way to stay responsive to the situation. Some people I know simply remind themselves to breathe.

Does any of this mean we have to put up with all manner of disrespectful behaviour? This is a question I often hear from educators. Of course it doesn't. At least, not in the long term. But again, it's how we respond in the moment that matters. If we give in to our first knee-jerk reaction and hotly respond with something like "You can't talk to me like that!" it is unlikely to help calm the situation. There may be time later, when the tension has abated, that we can have conversations about mutual respect. If we try to have them during the heat of an exchange, it's certain that we'll only make things worse.

That said, there can be effective in-the-moment interventions. During labour negotiations that became highly charged, there were times I could address difficult behaviour directly. For example, during one particularly contentious moment the union rep repeatedly jabbed his finger in my face, and his tone was elevated. I was able to say, "Dan, I really want to hear what you have to say. But it makes it hard for me to hear you when you're yelling and pointing at me." In negotiation, this is called immediacy, and essentially it means momentarily backing away from *what* we're talking about in order to talk about *how* we're talking. It's a respectful way to ask for an alternative communication style. Of course how we say it is critical, since an accusatory tone or a demand will undermine the request and probably escalate the other person even further. It's also important to note that a person in crisis may not have the resources to make the shift at that moment. In that case it's up to us to model what we want rather than insisting on it from the other person. As Fisher and Brown (1988) of the Harvard Negotiation Project point out, it is critical to do what is good for yourself and the relationship, *regardless of reciprocation* (p. 31).

An important consideration when asking for a different kind of communication is to preface it as I did with an expression of intent: "I really want to hear what you have to say." This is a critical step, as without it we will be perceived as simply making demands, which will be likely to aggravate the situation. The first part of the exchange reassures the person that a change in communication style is in service of better understanding. Again, it's always about how we say what we say that matters. As Ani di Franco noted, any tool is a weapon if you hold it right. An irritated or demanding tone can undermine the most innocuous of requests. Thompson and Jenkins (2004) wrote about recent studies that show that police work, like education, is 97 to 98 percent about speaking. The words and message are only 7 to 10 percent. The rest is voice, at 33–40 percent, and other non-verbals like body language and tone, at 50–60 percent (p. 58). According to Thompson and Jenkins, "if there is conflict between your role and your voice, people will always believe your voice" (p. 131).

Another valuable thing I learned from my experience in labour negotiations is that just because people may sound irrational and their concerns may initially appear petty, it does not necessarily mean that their concerns actually *are* irrational or petty. It may be just the way they are being brought forward; it's the tone and manner that sometimes cause us to discount the issues. If we immediately take offense to the tone, we shut off any opportunity we might have to learn about the situation, much less try to resolve or deal with it.

When I was able to manage myself and remain calm and curious, I often discovered (sometimes to my surprise) real and substantive issues in desperate need of solutions. While it was true that initially they often came couched in adversarial language, as time went on and bonds of trust were forged, concerns were raised in ways that were easier to hear, and solution-finding became more collaborative. Staff and their union representatives needed first to know that their concerns were taken seriously. Once they had seen evidence of our team's intention to follow through and deal with those concerns, subsequent issues became easier to address, and the way they were brought forward became more collegial. In other words, the ability to respond non defensively was "front end loaded:" by not responding in kind, we were able to forge the necessary relationships and open space for a resolution of future issues.

People Will Try to Make You Feel the Way They Feel

> The greatest single cause of dissonance is the fact that people behave their worst when they feel most powerless. The person who's yelling doesn't feel intimidating and scary (although that's what the other person perceives). Instead, the yeller feels powerless and small. This is dissonance at its most extreme, and it always ends badly. (Goulston, 2010, p. 80)

A Story

Jason was working in a segregated school for children labelled behaviourally disordered. He recounted a time he was called by a particularly distraught teacher who told him that one of the students had become upset, somehow gotten his hands on a hammer, and tried to hurt several other students. The staff had managed to corral him in a time-out room and lock the door, but they hadn't been able to get close enough to retrieve the hammer safely. They could still hear him yelling and banging on the walls. They were worried that he might hurt himself and had no idea how to intervene without endangering themselves. There was talk of calling the police and more talk about the need for serious psychotropic medications.

I immediately had a mental image of the staff group calling the counsellor and, given his role as problem-solver and peacemaker, probably thinking, "OK, you think you're so smart? You deal with this!" Jason, however, had no such illusions about himself or his abilities. He got to the door, could hear the boy slamming around the room, and realized he had absolutely no idea what to do. And he was afraid.

At that moment he remembered a similar situation he'd read about in a book. The author said, "People will try to make you feel the way they are feeling." As soon as he remembered this comment, Jason knew what to do. He stood by the door and began talking to the distraught student. He said, "I'm feeling scared. I'm scared for you, and I'm scared for me. I have a feeling you might be scared, too." Almost immediately, the boy seemed to quiet and stop hitting the walls with the hammer. In a short period of time, Jason was able to find out what had brought the situation on and brought the boy to safety—without police intervention, restraints, or medication.

In almost any interaction, understanding this deeply ingrained tendency in ourselves and the people we are negotiating with is a powerful tool to assist in de-escalation. If we know that our own feelings are often a pretty reliable clue to the emotional state of the other person, we have important information to work with. It gives us some indication of how best to proceed. Feelings of powerlessness, for example, almost always accompany an outburst. While anger, sadness, fear, and shame may also be present, a sense of powerlessness often drives a confrontation. On some level the person who is acting out is likely feeling backed into a corner. This is seldom more obvious than in the case of a hostage taker or barricaded person, but even a student throwing a desk is likely acting out of a sense of entrapment.

Motor Mimicry and Emotional Contagion

Have you ever noticed that humans have a tendency to copy one another's movements? Maybe you've caught yourself replicating a friend's body language across the lunch table. As your friend leans forward and smiles, so do you. If her hand goes to her chin, your hand goes to your chin. This is called motor mimicry, and while we might not do it all the time, and some of us do it more than others, we all do it. Once we become aware that we're copying another person's movements, we might feel self-conscious and try to stop. We worry that what we're doing is obvious and maybe will even appear disrespectful. If the other person notices, they might think we're making fun of them. Trying to stop is difficult because as primatologists like Frans de Waal (2009) tell us this tendency is deeply ingrained at a cellular level.

Emotional contagion operates much like motor mimicry. We are susceptible to taking on the moods and emotional states of others. For example, have you ever walked into the staff room at school and been confronted with someone who's in a bad mood? Within a short period of time, the atmosphere is heavy. While a few intrepid souls may attempt to engage with the disgruntled co-worker and inquire about their apparent distress, if those overtures are unsuccessful, most of us will quickly try to remove ourselves from the discomfort of the situation. Positive social contagion works in the same way. I remember my mother coming home one day after having received some particularly good news, saying, "Everyone seemed so happy and upbeat today! Even perfect strangers were smiling at me!" Her initial thought was that everyone else was just as happy as she was, but in fact it was likely her mood and demeanour that elicited those smiles—without her even knowing she was doing it.

Neuroscientists talk about these phenomena as "mirroring." Although still a controversial subject (Hickock, 2014), some scientists believe they have identified parts of the brain that fire and light up in response to the emotional states of others. They call these "mirror neurons." Scientists like de Waal (2009) believe we are hard-wired to respond to each other, and this is a very old part of our brains. We respond to each other's emotional states, and we also try to influence them, whether consciously or unconsciously. In other words, we try to make others feel the way we feel.

Our own feelings during a crisis situation give us a powerful clue about what's going on with the other person, and this gives us an opportunity to open up more options for constructive responses and help us avoid doing something counterproductive. For example, when someone is upset and seems threatening, rather than assuming that this show of bravado and intimidation is an overt power play and responding with a power play of our own, it might be more important to first question our perceptions. Is this really a bid for power, or might it be just the opposite? Taking a step back to notice our own emotional state, we may find that, like Jason, we are actually feeling powerless and maybe even afraid. This, in turn, gives us the important information we need to guide us as we decide how best to respond. It's likely that responses based on this insight will be quite different than the more reactive actions we might first have been tempted to take. One of the educator/administrators I interviewed described her process in this way:

> If the kid is escalated, I have to first manage myself before I am able to help them manage their emotions. Then I can help them de-escalate and breathe. It's really important to understand anger management. Match body language, do breathing, match intensity level and tone, and that kind of stuff. Sometimes, especially with the boys, we'll just head out the back for a walk, and if they want to start talking they can while we are walking. Sometimes we'll just sit for a while, both just slumped in our chairs. And then take a deep breath and figure [it] out.
>
> Most of the time what looks like anger is something else. It can take time to figure out what. But what's certain is that responding to anger with more anger isn't going to help.

Other educators identified how important self-awareness and self-management are in dealing well with disruption. They mentioned the need to maintain a calm demeanour and refuse to engage in power struggles:

> I think that being aware of ourselves is the most important.
>
> Coolness, and by that I mean temperament. They can't be taking things, particularly with disruptive and disrespectful behaviour, personally.

Despite the empathic support the administrators I interviewed felt for the teachers they supervised, and their deep recognition of the difficulties teachers face when confronted by escalated students, concerns about the nature of student–teacher relationships surfaced repeatedly. One administrator said,

> Most of the issues I deal with are about power. The teacher isn't going to give; the student doesn't want to give. But we are the adults in the relationship, so [we need to figure out] how can we back off a bit. Some teachers are not at that point.

The students I spoke with agreed. They had stories, both positive and negative, about their teachers. One told me,

> Teachers need to be able to control their emotions. If they can have a calm head, and sort of see it from a different perspective . . . if the teacher's really involved in the conflict, and getting their emotions up, then it's going to get messy.

The students were unanimous in stating that hard-line approaches were counterproductive. According to one student,

> One of the teachers, when people do something wrong, he doesn't talk to them, [he] gives you flak, he's just screaming, he just yells, he will not talk to you! He gets so angry.

When I asked what response students had to this, this boy replied, "Then the student gets angry! Haranguing is not helpful."

You Can't Take It Personally! Or "I Just Love It When a Kid Tells Me to F$%# Off!"

I once met a school counsellor working closely with a number of challenging students in a very difficult school in a large urban centre. He told me many of the students he saw came from poverty and unstable home situations, and his goal was to help them stay in school and succeed. This was, he admitted, a daunting task, since many of them showed up at school hungry, tired, and feeling hopeless. Several admitted to living with their families in shelters and cars. He noted that many were perennially angry and easily triggered, sometimes by what seemed to be the smallest of slights, and more than a few students had developed gang affiliations. He talked about how important it was for him to stay clear-headed and observant and, above all, avoid taking confrontations and apparent disrespect personally:

> If I allow my buttons to get pushed, I am useless as a counsellor. I absolutely cannot take the situation personally! I'm no help to the student when we're both escalated. For another thing, once I let my buttons get pushed, I'm going to stop noticing what's going on around me—and in the environment I work in, I have to be hyperaware. It's a safety issue. There've been kids who've come to school with weapons, and teachers have been threatened.
>
> So here's the thing; I've learned to love it when a kid tells me to f#@ off.

I'm sure I looked puzzled. He laughed and went on, "That's how I know he doesn't have a gun or a knife!"

A Cautionary Tale

The front page of a prominent newspaper in British Columbia many years ago featured a blurry, indistinct picture of a small boy with his face on his desk. The headline read "Teacher Duct-Tapes Child to Desk," followed by a second headline: "Boy Reports—'I was so

Scared!' In the two column article that followed, it was reported that the teacher had become so frustrated with this boy for repeatedly leaving his seat that she decided that duct-taping him to his desk was the only solution. The child had ADHD and experienced difficulty staying still. Needless to say, once reported, the teacher was suspended and ultimately lost her job. It was a shocking expose of a clearly abusive situation, but even though I was appalled by what she'd done, I couldn't help but wonder how it was that this teacher came to a point of such frustration that she found it acceptable to do what she did. I also wondered what might have helped her cope with the situation more humanely.

The article was a cautionary tale, and for many years I used the picture in presentations to illustrate the importance of self-awareness. If we are not sufficiently aware of our triggers, we risk "losing it" and doing lasting damage—not only to our students but also ourselves. For this teacher, the inability to cope not only traumatized a child, but also lost her the job and the respect of her community

In Summary

Self-awareness must precede self-management. Once we know and acknowledge our triggers, we can create self-talk and other strategies that will help us resist becoming reactive when situations become difficult. Self-management, then, can be defined as a conscious and intentional decision to remain responsive and not take things personally. The more we can prepare and practice, the easier it will be to stay balanced during crisis situations.

Knowing that we are "hard-wired" to make others feel like we feel can be important and helpful information that can help us make good decisions under pressure.

CHAPTER NINE

DYNAMIC INACTIVITY

> There is always that constant pressure—I must do something, I must take action . . . sometimes doing nothing is better than doing something . . . we call it dynamic inactivity.
>
> —Harvey Schlossberg

Don't Just Do Something, Stand There!

More than forty years after Schlossberg developed the New York Plan, something called *dynamic inactivity* is still one of the key components of modern hostage negotiation. It stands in counterintuitive opposition to what is commonly called the action imperative of law enforcement. In dynamic inactivity, according to Schlossberg, the negotiator takes their cues from the person they are negotiating with. He noted, "You deal only with what is happening in front of you, nothing more. You don't read into it, and you don't add to it" (p. 210).

Dynamic inactivity allows the negotiator to slow the process down, or, as mentioned earlier, "go slow to go fast"—a phrase I heard often during interviews and frequently found in the literature. Slowing the process down allows negotiators to avoid becoming reactive and instead to engage the hostage taker in effective communication. It allows the time and space to choose a constructive narrative, then to assess the situation calmly before taking action.

I was lucky to have Alfie Kohn, a friend and colleague and also the author of many books on education and parenting, as the advisor for my master's thesis. When he heard about dynamic inactivity, he said, "Hey, that sounds like what I just read on a bumper sticker! 'Don't just do something, stand there!'"

It's important to note that dynamic inactivity is not the same as doing nothing. The dynamic aspect means that taking the time to become aware of ourselves, observant of the environment and the person we're negotiating with, and begin, through a calm and intentional approach, to foster trust and safety. I was told that

> Dynamic inactivity means you are aware of what's going on. As much as you want to be doing something, you really need to just wait.

But how do we do that when the situation seems to be moving too quickly and the pressure is on us to solve it fast?

I learned the value of dynamic inactivity through a few experiences that became metaphors useful during difficult interchanges. Consider the following examples.

Spilling Wind

My husband, Norman, is an avid sailor. He's been sailing and racing sailboats since he was a teenager in Ontario. We used to live on Vancouver Island, arguably one of the best places in the world to sail, and for a few years we had a sailboat. Although I'd never sailed before I met Norm, I was intrigued with the idea. I'm a strong swimmer, I love the water, and I come from a long line of seafaring folk from the Netherlands. It sounded like fun.

Unfortunately, it wasn't. To my amazement and Norm's consternation, I turned out to be a reluctant sailor. At best, I'd consider myself a fair-weather sailor. Although picnics, wine, and pleasant weather are things Norm and I agree on, the need for calm winds is where we differ drastically. Sailors live for the gale. Personally, I fail to see the appeal.

At least in part, this is because once I began to sail, I discovered I hadn't outgrown motion sickness after all. I'd mastered cars but boats were another matter. The application of anti-nausea drugs was occasionally helpful, but the price was invariably an afternoon spent in a Gravol-induced stupor. But it turned out that even motion sickness wasn't my biggest challenge. My biggest challenge was fear. Given my hereditary background, this was a humiliating surprise.

My anxiety is primarily around a phenomenon that even non-sailors will recognize. Sailboats (all of them) do something called heeling over. This happens when the wind is blowing hard into a tight sail. The boat tips over at an angle of anywhere between five to twenty-five degrees. Sailors love this because the more the boat heels, the faster it goes. Norm usually gets a huge grin on his face at this point. I, on the other hand, can be found attached to some part of the boat limpet-like, looking a little green. Somehow I just can't get used to looking at the horizon from a slanted, almost in the water position. I can't shake the irrational idea that the boat, it contents, (and most importantly *me*) are about to end up in the water.

Norm realized very early on in my sailing career that he was going to have to do something about this fear if he wanted a sailing partner. No amount of reassurance seemed to be working. So instead of trying to talk me out of my fear, one day he simply put a line in my hand. This line runs through a cleat at the bottom of the cockpit of the boat and controls the position of the mainsail.

"I'm going to tell you a secret," he said. "You can always tell when a gust of wind is coming. If you look out at the water, it will begin to ripple. You can't look only at the sail because by the time that gust of wind hits the sail, the boat will heel, and it is too late to do anything. You need to look in front of you and around you to see what might be coming so you're ready to let out the sail the second the wind hits. Now, when you see that, I want you to take this line"—he pointed to the rope in my hand—"and uncleat it."

"Uncleat it?" I asked in disbelief. Every cell in my body was telling me to pull on it, and hard!

"That's right," he said. "Let out the line, and the sail will loosen and do something sailors call 'spilling' wind. That means the wind doesn't meet as much resistance in the sail and is diverted across it, then flows out. As soon as that happens, the boat will automatically right itself, and we'll slow down."

The first time I tried this technique, the boom began to swing, and the sail flapped alarmingly. But to my relief, the boat began to level, and we slowed down. This gave me a sense of control, which helped with the panic, and even better, it gave me a new (and possibly obvious) metaphor for dealing with crisis.

Human beings have a tendency to tense up and pull in hard when confronted with situations that we perceive as threatening. When that metaphorical gust of wind slams into us, everything in us wants to regain control of the situation, as quickly as possible! We think that taking some form of action—often any form of action—will be more productive than what we believe to be the only alternative, namely doing nothing. Negotiators would say this is a false dichotomy. There are more than two options available. When confronted with crisis, intentionally letting out that metaphorical line allows us to become mindful, to stop and take notice of what's going on in and around ourselves and choose our next move. This is an example of dynamic inactivity. Although there is a suspension of activity, it is not passive. It's a deliberate choice.

The first part of dynamic inactivity is observation. It is important to be aware of what's going on around you. Just as Norm suggested I do on the sailboat, look for those telltale ripples on the water. Crisis events are seldom random or sudden. If we're alert and aware, we can often see them coming. For example, we may notice that a student is becoming agitated or seems upset. In that moment we have an opportunity to think proactively and "let out the line" before the gust of wind hits and we are blown backward. Again, this is not the same as doing nothing. Sometimes this will be enough to divert or prevent an incident; other times we may not be that fortunate, but at least we will be in a position to respond non-reactively and to stay light on our feet.

Our tendency when a person is becoming agitated is often to respond with demands for compliance. "Sit down!" "Stop talking!" This is the equivalent to pulling in the line and tightening the mainsail. We're often surprised when our "sailboat" heels over abruptly, and things begin to move quickly and dangerously. Negotiators deliberately resist demands and instead ask questions and provide choices. They recognize that what's most needed is space and calm.

At times in my career I have been asked to consult with organizations experiencing conflict and crisis. Over and over again, I have seen people reflexively reach for policies, procedures, rules, and regulations in an effort to solve problems in much the same way that I wanted to yank on that line in the sailboat. We think that the more rules we make, the safer we'll be. If one overarching rule doesn't seem to accomplish what we want, we write an even more detailed policy with subheadings. And if those don't work, we add even more detail. When we do this, we're operating on the assumption that the more specific and clear our rules and expectations are, the less likely it is that we'll find ourselves in crisis. It seems to make sense. Unfortunately, this approach often has unintended consequences. In our efforts to second-guess everything that could possibly go wrong, we sacrifice flexibility. We find ourselves frustrated at the amount of red tape we have to struggle with and find that we're unable to get anything done without violating some rule or policy. Discretion is the first victim of rule proliferation.

We all know that rigid structures don't respond well during crisis. We know that buildings and bridges without architectural "give" will blow over in hurricanes or collapse in earthquakes. What we forget is that rigidity is also a counterproductive strategy for dealing with conflict. The key is flexibility and mindfulness. But how do we stay calm when everything around us is moving quickly and we are expected to solve problems promptly? Consider the following example that shows dynamic inactivity may be less time consuming than we might think, and although it's more a mind-set than a strategy, there are specific actions we can take that can help during crisis.

Breathing Lessons

We have a friend on Vancouver Island who provides crisis prevention workshops for teachers. He starts his training by demonstrating a very simple breathing technique. He notes that when faced with a crisis situation, our tendency is to breathe in sharply. The first thing he teaches his students is simply to become aware of this tendency. The next step is to replace it consciously with a better response. Breathe out instead, he says. It will change the way you respond to crisis.

If you try this yourself, note the difference between the sharp, panicky "in" breath and the relaxing effect of the "out" breath. Breathing in can actually escalate the tension we feel. Exhaling, however, does the opposite. It is a physiological de-escalator, and as a happy side effect, simply taking the time to breathe out also gives us a moment to take stock of what's going on around us and inside ourselves and then to consciously decide what our response will be. Rather than reacting, we can opt to respond. We have given ourselves, quite literally, some breathing space.

Once again, this may feel counterintuitive. Most of us already know that breathing is the antidote to panic, but what we might not know is that breathing out is far more calming than breathing in. Obviously, we must do both. However, when we begin by pulling our breath in sharply, we often forget to breathe out! Holding our breath is part of the same reflex that causes us to pull in the line or participate in the development of restrictive rules and regulations. Although it is part of a self-protective instinct, it often works against us and causes even more anxiety. Let out the line, and the boat rights itself. Breathe out, and we become calmer. Counterintuitive? Maybe. Effective? Negotiators tell us—absolutely!

Make the Room Bigger

Some years ago I watched a television documentary on hostage negotiation. One story in particular stuck with me. The negotiator described an incident where a man was holding his estranged wife at gunpoint in her bedroom. The negotiator had managed to work his way inside the apartment, and from where he was standing, he could see into the bedroom. He was immediately struck with a sense of claustrophobia. There was barely enough space for the bed, let alone the hostage and her husband. To make it even worse, the day was hot and the room was stifling.

He told the audience that his goal was to make the room bigger. I was puzzled by this comment. Obviously, that's a physical impossibility. What on earth did he mean?

Making the room "bigger," he explained, is about creating psychological space. He went on to say that this could be accomplished by offering choices, helping people to feel safe, reassuring them of our good intentions, ensuring that our body language is unthreatening and that we aren't blocking an exit.

This example perfectly illustrates the concept of dynamic inactivity. Negotiators understand the danger of moving in on people when they are upset. They understand that their actions, even if well-intentioned, will be perceived as threat and may not only be counterproductive but also potentially lethal. Moving in physically, particularly with people who have been traumatized, is almost certain to reactivate that sense of trauma and result in dangerous escalation.

Before I talk about the implications of this idea for classroom teachers, let me give you an example that illustrates this concept in more concrete terms. Ruth Seigfried runs an organization in Pennsylvania called InVision. It supports adults with developmental and intellectual disabilities. According to Ruth, InVision has a history of taking the people no one else wants to serve—individuals who have been incarcerated, institutionalized, and are considered dangerous to themselves and others. She has a strong ethical stance about providing individualized supports, and as a result, the staff at InVision provide support without resorting to coercion, restraint, or seclusion. This story illustrates another way of "making the room bigger" in a different but relevant context.

> Over the years, we have really focused our attention on people who have both intellectual disabilities and significant psychiatric complications in their lives. Many have a history of very, very physically assaultive behaviour. They become very aggressive, and we see that as an understandable defence mechanism because of what they've been through in the past—physical, emotional and/or sexual abuse. We serve the folks whose alternatives would be institutional care and environments where they would be subjected to a significant amount of physical and mechanical restraint, as well as chemical restraints.

> There's no formula that we can give you, A, B, C, and then the outcome is, there's perfect behaviour and there's no aggression. That would be nice, of course. It's actually much more complicated than that, and it really starts well before you're involved with the behaviour. It starts with getting to know the person and developing a relationship with them, and understanding their history, and where the behaviour comes from. What I always say is that if we start with trying to change or fix and eliminate the behaviour, we're always going to fail. We always have to start with: What does that person need? Why is that behaviour there? And really trying to focus on helping the person meet their needs. What is the underlying need behind that behaviour? If we can focus on helping the person there, then that behaviour naturally begins to dissipate.

Let me give you an example. Mike was a young man we supported, and he really provided a lot of inspiration for me to start InVision back in the early 1990s. I met Mike because he lived at a state institution and he desperately wanted to leave, but he was also extraordinarily fearful of what would happen if he left. He didn't want to end up in jail. He didn't want to end up hurting someone so badly that he had to live the rest of his life with a severe injury or their death on his conscience. While he had an intellectual disability, and many, many psychiatric diagnoses, he was also a very insightful person, and he was able to express those concerns as I got to know him over several years.

I sat with a large group of people at the state institution before he left, and I sat right next to Mike. People around the table were saying, "Ruth, do you realize that when we restrain Mike, it takes, like, eight football-player-sized guys to hold him down? What are you going to do when he loses his ability to control himself?" I reached over and put my hand on Mike's arm, and I said, "Mike, I think you know this, but I think we need to tell them so they understand also. We have no intention of holding you down."

I used to say to people, "You know, we typically think personal space is an arm's length." And it might be to us, say in a normal meeting environment. But to Mike, when post-traumatic stress was affecting him, when his anxieties were affecting him, when other mental health issues were at play, Mike's personal space could expand beyond the whole house. It could be the whole neighbourhood! If the staff involved with him didn't recognize his need for that personal space, then they would be physically endangered. We had to consider that his personal space needs might vary from one time to another, depending on how much . . . how much he was struggling at that point in time. But we also knew that if we didn't respect that, then someone was going to get hurt, and that Mike's future was in great jeopardy if that happened. So a lot of what we did . . . was to learn to anticipate what was going on with him, to recognize the changes in his facial features when he was experiencing enormous stress, and to recognize it early on, not late in the game when he could not contain it any longer. Never once, in the years that Mike lived with us before he died, did we attempt to hold him down.

What we did was join with him in partnership to figure out how he was going to deal with the issues before they became problems. We also had to learn how we were going to respond in such a way that staff and other people in the environment were safe. We had to figure that out. That's part of what we have to do for every single person because I can't take Mike's situation and say, "Oh, if you have a person who has PTSD, then you need to use this technique in order to deal with them." Because with Mike, we learned a certain set of things that would really work to help him control himself and things that we could do to help him do that. But I couldn't put that same set of practices for any other of the 130 people we serve in our residential programs today.

This is a concrete and powerful example of how we can make the room bigger. For Ruth and her staff, working *with* Mike instead of working *on* him was the key. Not only did it ensure that everyone stayed safe, but also in the process they were helping Mike learn to self-manage. In this context, it's important to note that self-management is not an individualistic activity. It is relational. Mike's staff needed to work with him as he figured out effective ways to cope with anxiety and other issues.

Obviously Ruth's example doesn't completely relate to what happens in a classroom, – it is perhaps more extreme than what teachers might face – but what is relevant and ties her experience with Mike to the negotiator in the story above and to the classroom is recognition of the need for space. This may be physical or psychological space. It might be a moment of downtime, a walk on the school grounds, or some non-punitive time spent in another space (like the library or an empty classroom). It might be developing a shared signal for times when the student feels a loss of control looming. Making the room bigger relates to the creation of options. As Edison once said, "Any idea is dangerous if you only have one."

Unfortunately, this is the opposite of what happens in far too many situations. Ron Garrison, during the course of his time as a school safety expert witness in cases involving restraint and seclusion, recounts example after example of educators who left no space but instead moved in to restrain students, trapping them in four-point restraint or in seclusion rooms. In one tragic instance, two adults knelt on the chest of a prone student, resulting in broken ribs and asphyxiation that led to his death. In their efforts to control and end the crisis, they were making the room smaller, limiting both their own and the student's options. Confrontation invariably leads to violence, and in this case the tragic result was death.

Ron offered some alternatives based on his extensive knowledge of crisis prevention and personal safety strategies. These apply whether a weapon is involved or not. He said, "First, do not stand between the person and the door. Second, stand sideways so your shoulder is facing the person. But most importantly, take two or three steps backward. All of these are ways that we can make the room bigger for a distressed individual and keep ourselves and others safe at the same time."

I Don't Have Time for Dynamic Inactivity!

Concerns that often arise about this approach are about time and the impact a crisis has on the whole classroom. "How am I going to teach all the things I need to teach if this one kid is constantly in my face? What about the other kids? It isn't fair to them if I have to keep interrupting the class to deal with the disruptive student?" These are indeed legitimate concerns. However, the logic may be misplaced. Remember the idea of "going slow to go fast"? What does that really mean?

Negotiators know that a successful negotiation is front-end loaded. In other words, if we manage the situation well, especially in those first few minutes, and if we respond empathetically and not reactively, we are more likely to defuse the situation quickly, and it is less likely that incidents will be recurrent. This, in the longer term, will save time. Dealing well with an incident builds trust between ourselves and the student in crisis and is also reassuring for the other students as well. Consider this story as a cautionary tale:

A friend and colleague recounted an episode that took place in her daughter's third grade elementary school classroom. Three classrooms had convened in the library to listen to an author read from a book. One of the students became distraught during the reading and began crying loudly. The principal and the instructional assistant attempted to deal with the situation without success. He continued crying loudly. Finally, in desperation, they moved in on him and began to physically restrain him. Once they had him on the floor, they proceeded to drag him by his feet into a nearby book closet. They closed the door and locked it behind them.

The author was unable to continue her presentation since the student was kicking the door and yelling, "Let me out!" All the students were upset.

Over dinner that night, our friend's daughter asked, "If I was crying, would they lock me in the book closet?" Not knowing anything about the incident, her mother was nonplussed. "Why would you ask that, honey?" Her daughter told her what happened that day in the library.

Our friend, who also happens to be the executive director of an organization that supports the families of children and adults with disabilities, has worked tirelessly over the years to intervene in incidents of restraint and seclusion. She was appalled to hear of this incident and immediately called the principal of her daughter's school. She told the principal she was calling because she was dismayed both on behalf of her daughter and of her organization. She expressed concern for the young man in question and for the rest of the class who witnessed the event.

The principal promised to take some time to explain the situation to the other students. "I'll let them know that it won't happen to them," she said. Our friend pointed out what had taken place should not happen to anyone.

The next day, as promised, the principal arrived in the classroom. She explained that the boy's behaviour could not be tolerated in the school. She said the student had not paid attention to something she called the "zones of regulation," and although regretful about the way the situation was resolved, she claimed it had been inevitable and that they had had little choice under the circumstances. She then asked the students if they had any questions. Our friend's daughter was the first to put up her hand, palpably angry. "How does it make you feel," she asked, "to know you've done something illegal and unfair?"

Incidents we respond to with fear and anger don't affect only the child who experiences them firsthand. They affect all the students, and they negatively affect our reputation as well. Over and over again, I heard and read about the effects of witnessing restraint and seclusion on bystanders. It is sobering to realize these affects are far-reaching and damaging. In Appendix A I have included an interview with Ron Garrison. As I have mentioned, he is an international expert on school safety and an expert witness in more than eighty-five court cases involving restraint and seclusion. Mr. Garrison is clear about the serious and significantly deleterious effects of interventions like these on all students and on teachers and support staff as well.

This does not, of course, minimize the need to find solutions. In chapter 12 I deal specifically with what I learned about effective problem-solving. Negotiators told me it's more about timing than anything else. The short version is that the urge to move quickly to problem solving—whether an attempt to broker a quick deal, a threat to remove the student from the classroom or even the school—will almost always be a mistake.

Schools that deal with violence, bullying, and gang activities often try to solve these problems with a combination of punitive measures and technology in hopes of solving them quickly. The appeal of these approaches is that they are quick and decisive. However, they rely on the same action imperative that negotiators consciously resist in their work. At first glance, the action imperative seems to provide a sure-fire way to manage a frightening situation. Unfortunately, as many schools have discovered, it does not.

In Summary

Find useful metaphors for yourself. Mine is "let out the line, and the boat will right itself." Some of these can translate into helpful self-talk strategies. Remember to breathe, and train yourself to take a moment to breathe out before you breathe in. Buddhist monk Pema Chodrin offers a meditation technique that involves breathing out to the count of seven and breathing in to the count of three—in other words, spending twice as long breathing out than we do breathing in.

Resisting the urge to rush to resolution and simply committing to remaining present with the person in crisis is often the most effective thing we can do.

Make the room bigger by offering choices and creating both physical and psychological space.

CHAPTER TEN

FACE SAVING

> There's nothing quite so grand a feeling as helping one another out of a trap.
>
> —Gussin Paley& Coles (1993, p.141)

In this chapter we look at why negotiators believe it's important to assist people in crisis to save face. In order to understand what it means to help someone save face, I begin with a short description of "face," then look at what it means to lose face.

What Exactly Is "Face"?

Folger et al. believe that face is probably best and most succinctly defined as "the communicator's claim to be seen as a certain kind of person" (p. 145). In other words, we all want others to see us as we see ourselves and to understand our concerns and values as we understand them. We want to be taken seriously and seen as competent and worthy of respect. Face is primarily an issue of identity.

Although the concept and the importance of face is more commonly associated with Asian cultures, it is a cross-cultural phenomenon and present in all human interaction. Whether we are consciously aware of it or not, we all are constantly in the process of attempting to influence how we are perceived by others. Even the assertion that we don't care how others see us is evidence that it does matter, since this is an identity claim that fits into a long-standing Western tradition of individualism and self-sufficiency and as such is an effort to be seen as a certain kind of person.

Isn't Face Saving Just Placation?

While directness is a strongly held value in Western culture, it is not valued in the same way in many other places. In parts of Southeast Asia, China, and Japan, and in many indigenous communities, politeness and face-saving are paramount, making confrontation of any sort both rude and offensive. In these societies, if I confront you directly or criticize you, I have caused you to lose face. In the process I lose face myself. These are serious issues, and many an international trade negotiation has been derailed because Western negotiators have not adequately understood the importance of face.

The idea of allowing someone to save face is a concept not easily embraced or well understood in Western culture. Many of us believe that direct communication is the best way to solve problems, deal with difficult interactions, and ultimately clear the air. We believe people should be held accountable for their actions and worry that if we allow someone to save face, it automatically means we are condoning what they've done and letting them off the hook. Face-saving is often conflated with placation and excuse-making. For many of us, the idea of helping someone to save face during an interpersonal conflict is distasteful; we feel that we are letting people get away with bad behaviour and actually reinforcing it. We also worry that, in doing so, we have weakened ourselves and lost power. However, negotiators understand that many interactions we characterize as power struggles may not actually be about power at all but instead about the need to have our issues and concerns taken seriously—in other words, to save face.

Losing Face

In order to fully understand why saving face is so important, we must first understand what it means to lose face. Simply put, losing face is about being embarrassed, humiliated, disrespected, or feeling devalued in front of others. We've all had these moments, from the minor to the major—a clothing mishap, tripping over our own feet, an athletic blunder, or, more seriously, failing an important test. An example that appeared on social media a few years ago showed a young woman walking on a city sidewalk while texting on her cell phone. Oblivious to her surroundings, she walked directly into the concrete ledge of a fountain, spectacularly tripped over the ledge, and fell headfirst into the water, cell phone and all. Her mishap was compounded when a spectator recorded the incident on a smartphone and posted the video online. Overnight, the video went viral. Incidents like this one, however humiliating, are still relatively benign. We are all aware of more serious and devastating examples: cyberbullying and compromising pictures posted and widely shared online. In some tragic instances, this kind of public shaming and humiliation have led victims to chronic depression and even suicide.

We Don't Lose Face When We're Alone

It's true. We don't lose face when we are alone; it is always a relational event. Rogan and Hammer (1994) point out that face is "a socially created affect; one that is wholly dependent on interaction" (p. 39). No matter how introverted some of us may be, we are all social creatures, highly attuned to the perceptions, scrutiny, and criticism of others. The way we are seen matters. We notice the covert eyeroll or the derisive snort. Being shunned, segregated, or ostracized can be intensely painful and have a lasting impact on self-image.

We all lose it sometimes. Luckily, these instances don't usually take place in public. When they do, we feel the consequences intensely. For example, maybe you thought you hit the mute button but didn't during a frustrating phone call. While you thought you were off the air, maybe you said some things that were not intended for an audience. Venting that felt justified, harmless, and even cathartic in a private exchange changes instantly as the realization that others have heard sinks in. Now damage control becomes essential—first of all managing that hot flush of embarrassment and self-recrimination, then the obvious need to restore social standing and apologize for the outburst. Even years later, remembering an event like this can make us cringe.

Research indicates that public shaming has a very real and pronounced physiological and psychological influence. Muller Pinzler et al. (2015) believe our brains are hard-wired for embarrassment and that ignominy and shame result in very strong paralimbic responses. Although the part of the brain that lights up under public duress is the same part that lights up when we are successful and receive praise, the effects are much stronger when we are experiencing emotional distress. Interestingly, this suggests that moments of public disgrace have a far greater impact on our self-esteem than do achievement and accolade. Perhaps this explains why public speaking is widely considered more terrifying than illness or death. It's failure and potential loss of face that scares us.

"PE Doesn't Stand for Physical Education. It Stands for Public Embarrassment."

Unfortunately, school is often a place rife with opportunity for humiliation. For many students, the school experience by its very definition is demoralizing, particularly for those who experience learning difficulties or have disabilities. Students are often asked to "out" their areas of incompetence at school. Dyslexic students tell stories about being asked to read aloud in class and being unable to do so, and uncoordinated and clumsy students describe being picked last for the team. What we sometimes miss when students publicly fail is the constant low-grade (and sometimes excruciatingly high grade) humiliation they suffer. They not only have to struggle with mastering the content of what they're supposed to be doing, but also with the embarrassment of failure. Casey, Hill, and Goodyear (2014) conducted an interesting study looking at why so many girls are disengaged with physical education. They describe the phenomenon as epidemic. The title of their journal article is telling: "PE doesn't stand for physical education. It stands for public embarrassment." As a student who struggled mightily with spatial issues, the title resonated loudly for me.

While dunce caps, donkey ears, and other means of inducing public shame are no longer used (or at least seldom used, with the possible exception of one Florida teacher who made tardy students wear a kind of dog collar she called "the cone of shame"), other more subtle and often unintentional forms of public indignity still take place. Negotiators assert that these incidents have a deleterious effect on self-image and are often the precursors to a crisis incident. Whether the incident seems relatively minor, what's important is how the student perceives it and what that student's history with failure and embarrassment has been. It's critical to remember that these events are cumulative, which may explain why sometimes a minor event will trigger a major crisis.

"She's a Sweet Lady, But It's Not Professional What She Does"

Dignity and respect emerged repeatedly in my research and discussions as a critical component of good teacher–student relationships. When it was absent or violated in some way, the students I spoke with noticed. One student worried that the classroom management tactics employed by one of her teachers, while not overtly hostile, undermined relationships anyway:

> Her version of disciplining them is pretty much talking down to them all the time, and I think if I was that kid I would come in expecting to behave poorly because that's what she expects. That kid will walk in and she'll look up, and like, she's a sweet lady, but it's not professional what she does. They'll walk in and she'll be like, "Oh, it's going to be a long day today, look who's here," and then like that kid is expecting another bad day. Her version of discipline is sarcastic comments toward them in front of the class, and that doesn't work. You're not gaining respect.

> Essentially, like, discipline comes down to they have abused your respect, and it's not respectful what she does to them, so obviously they're not respectful in turn.

It isn't only the difficult students who lose respect for teachers. Another student told me,

> I'm just a little bystander, but when I hear them say certain things I'm like, why would you say that? And the whole class kind of goes on edge, and a lot of people don't like her not because of what she's done to them necessarily but what she's done to other kids, and then in the long run no one really respects her because she doesn't respect those two boys or whatever.

This student's perception is consistent with research reviewed by Woolfolk Hoy and Weinstein (2006): "When teachers embarrass, insult or demean students publicly, they may actually engender sympathy for the misbehaving student" (p. 190). This is an interesting finding because it points out that in the process of humiliating a student in front of his peers and causing him to lose face, the teacher also loses face. While she may not immediately recognize the consequences of her approach, her reputation among all her students has been damaged and may be difficult to restore. Of course, this also means that her scope of influence has been reduced. In other research, Spaulding (2005) found that although respect is expected and demanded from students by their teachers, it is not always reciprocated. Negotiators also stressed the need for respect. "Again, I keep going back to it—having the respect for the individual that you're communicating with, that's by far the most important."

Another negotiator said,

> If a student's upset, now's the time to get to know them. Like negotiators, you've got a controlled environment, and you have authority figures. But it can't be a dictatorship. If you've got a student who's upset, first you have to make sure you're not taking away their dignity. Whatever you do you

can't do it in front of the class. You may win temporarily but you'll lose long term.

"If You Go in Blazing Guns with Kids, They Just Don't Buy It"

The school administrators I spoke with noted that the pervasive misunderstanding about accountability and the purpose of face-saving sometimes interferes with teachers' ability to work proactively during crisis. Specifically, the desire to hold students accountable often resulted in instances of humiliation and public embarrassment that proved counterproductive. Despite their empathic support and recognition of the difficulties teachers face, they repeatedly voiced concerns and frustration about the nature of student–teacher relationships. Two administrators told me,

> As much as things have changed, some things have remained the same . . . if you go in blazing guns with kids, they just don't buy it. The authoritarian approach doesn't cut it. In most cases you will find that there will be a lot of resistance.

> I don't want to say it's necessarily an old-school approach, but I think that people . . . will do things to inflame the situation. It's not their intention, but they aggravate it with the way they approach [it]. Maybe they are stuck in their way of looking, or just don't examine their own practice.

Personal Face Is Always a Fighting Issue

What makes it hard to resist the temptation to react to a challenge by pointing out the irrationality and wrong-headedness of the person we're in conflict with? It is likely because we feel that our own face needs are under threat. Especially when we are challenged by another person's behaviour, it is important to be aware of how our own need for respect and to be perceived as competent arises. When the challenge feels personal or unfair, we aren't dealing only with the other person's identity and face claims, we're dealing with our own. Particularly if the attack is direct—if someone says something undermining and disrespectful—we become most vulnerable to responding reactively. Unfortunately, as noted above in the students' perception of a particular teacher, the very act of trying to preserve face for ourselves at the expense of the other person produces the opposite result: we lose face.

Goffman (1955) points out that all interactions between people at any time have the capacity to be face-threatening. This is never more true than it is in conflict and crisis situations. In this context, Thompson and Jenkins (2004) point out that "personal face is always a fighting issue" (p.33) because it is a fundamental human need to protect and maintain reputation, respect, and autonomy.

Unfortunately, once a person has initiated a full-blown public crisis, they will often do whatever it takes to maintain a positive sense of self. This may manifest in defensiveness and verbal lashing out, or worse, escalate into violence or self-injurious behaviour: "Research shows that people are willing to retaliate and sacrifice rewards at great costs when they perceive the threat of humiliation" (Brown, 2005).

Face needs, as Hammer (2007) points out, "are not bargainable. That is, a subject cannot 'trade' 50 percent of his or her self-image for 50 percent of something else" (p. 94). This implies that despite a common belief that offering rewards or making threats of punishment are the most effective ways to influence behaviour and de-escalate a charged situation, they are not. International negotiators have long understood this. They recognize that identity is not negotiable, and both individuals and groups are sometimes even prepared to die in an effort to maintain identity claims. While our students might not be prepared to die, they may be prepared to respond in drastic and sometimes violent ways when they feel their self-image has been challenged.

Negotiators know that ignoring the face needs of distraught individuals not only risks escalating the situation but also can result in tragedy. For example, Hammer (2007) analyzed the transcript of a negotiation involving a subject who made repeated attempts to engage the negotiator in face restoration. Because the negotiator did not adequately acknowledge the need, the subject continued in a downward spiral and ultimately committed suicide.

"I Have Never Seen a Hostage Situation or Any Act of Violence that Was Not Preceded by Some Loss"

In a comprehensive study of face-work issues as they relate to hostage negotiation, Rogan and Hammer (1994) found that the way most subjects try to save face is primarily by telling their stories. Therefore, negotiators spend the majority of their time listening and actively helping the person to regain face. Folger et al. (2005) suggested that negotiators can assist subjects to save face by offering explanations for the incident, apologizing, suspending judgment, or correcting misperceptions and miscommunications in ways that allow subjects to retain dignity.

In addition, interveners must recognize that the notion of face goes beyond what is happening during the presenting conflict and can include less obvious but equally important cultural and familial roles and considerations, and even in-group and gang affiliations (Hammer, 1997, 2004; Le Baron, 2002; Ting-Toomey & Takai, 2006). The role of loss is also a critical consideration. As Kohlreiser (2006) points out

> I have never seen a hostage situation or any act of violence that was not preceded by some loss—a person, territory, a pet, money, an object, a self-image, a goal, freedom, and so on. And I have seen countless examples of violence prevented by having a secure base—a grandparent, teacher, friend, therapist, police officer—who walked the violence-prone person through the rages about life's losses successfully. (p. 105)

Folger (2006) says, "People who are convinced that they have little influence and who are threatened with loss of a particularly valued goal or possession may feel pressure to commit acts of desperation" (p. 135).

"He Had to Get Out with Dignity"

Hostage negotiators deal with individuals who have in some way made a personal crisis public. It's the public nature of the event that brings about loss of face; therefore, becoming intentional about counteracting the embarrassment is paramount. Consider the following vignette told to me by negotiator Dominick Misino.

> There's this guy, and we went into a section of the city to violate him—that's what they call arresting someone who's violated parole—and there were about 400 people on the streets. It's Spanish Harlem. It's 3:00 a.m. This is the most exciting thing they've seen in ages. He's inside and he's barricaded. He's got a gun. We're talking, and he says, "Look, I want to come out, but I can't just do that with all those guys watching. They're going to think I'm weak." So basically he's just told me how to get him out. So I tell him, "Here's what we can do. You let my guys come in there and cuff you, and then I'll come forward and we'll walk out together. As soon as your head hits the air, I want you to come out screaming." And he says, "You'd do that for me?" He agrees. We get to the door, and I raise his cuffed hands up behind his back a little too high, and he yells, "Ouch," and I say, "Oh, sorry, man I didn't mean to hurt you," and he says, "No, that's OK. It's got to look real."
>
> We walk out, and he starts yelling and cursing, and that whole crowd starts up a chant. They go, "Jose, we're with you. Jose we're with you." As soon as we get in the car, he ducks down. We drive a couple blocks and I say, "You can sit up now." He says, "Hey, thanks, man, I appreciate that." He had to get out with dignity. It was about saving face in front of his peers.

This story illustrates that in every crisis situation, the person in crisis is in danger of losing face. Misino was able to successfully resolve this situation because he was aware and attuned to this dynamic and worked actively to counter it. One of the school administrators I spoke with routinely uses a similar approach to good effect:

> Saving face is certainly something I think in working with teenagers is important. It removes the situation off their shoulders. They can deflect it [to] someone else. I think it works well with kids because you just say, "Look, I'm telling you, you can't do something, but I know that your friends are going to make some difficulty for you. So you make me the bad guy." It's an opportunity for the kid to see that, "OK, I have a way out."

Interestingly, another educator I spoke with indicated that face-saving was useful in assisting several of her students to separate from gang affiliations: "You need to be able to communicate before you can shift behaviour. You need to connect. Then the face-saving, working with the person rather than trying to use power to shift them back into the shape that you think is the shape they should be. I think that's very powerful."

Saving Face: An Active Process

There are two specific aspects of face that interveners need to be aware of: positive and negative face. These two categories are not binary. Positive doesn't represent good, nor negative bad. Instead, positive face arises from a need for belonging, respect, and approval; we all want to be liked and approved of, whether or not our actions make us look like that's what we want. Negative face arises from the need for autonomy and freedom from the interference of others; we all want to feel we have some agency in our lives. Young people in particular often feel they lack control over their lives and are subject to what in many instances feel like arbitrary rules and regulations. In a crisis situation, positive face can be supported by reassurance and support and negative face by acknowledging strength and capacity in authentic ways. Consider the following true story:

A high school principal found himself struggling regularly with a student who was not only acting out but also encouraging others to follow his lead. Having exhausted all of the usual approaches, the principal decided to take a different tack. He called the student into his office and said, "I admire you." When the young man looked surprised, he continued. "You are a leader. You don't always lead where I wish you would, but you are definitely a leader." The student looked nonplussed but seemed pleased by this assessment and open to hearing more. "Given your leadership ability," the principal went on, "I'm wondering if you could use your influence with the other students to help me.

"I'm having some difficulty managing the back corner of the sports field. A lot of things go on there that are dangerous, and some are even illegal. Could I ask you to monitor that area for me?" It's hard to imagine what the student was thinking, but clearly he felt that the request was sincere and not an attempt to patronize or manipulate him. He agreed and within a short period of time managed to make the back field a safer place. The student and the principal continued to work together until graduation a couple of years later.

This story illustrates how authentic acknowledgement can be a powerful way of engaging with a person during a difficult situation. While the young man in question was not in the middle of a crisis, the situation had been escalating for some time, and following the usual protocols would probably have devolved into suspension or even expulsion. By attending to face issues, the principal turned an adversary into an ally. We might also surmise that the principal's sincere esteem and invitation to adopt a partnership role with this student might potentially have had long-term positive effects after graduation.

It's more than just *allowing* someone to save face. Interveners must actively *assist* the person to save face. However, it's important to note the difference between reassurance and cheerleading. Take this as an example: A student in crisis says something like "I can't do anything right. Nobody likes me." These are moments we might be tempted to tell her to stop feeling sorry for herself and buck up. Hopefully we resist this temptation since it's an obviously unhelpful response.

Instead, we might try to contradict this perception and say something like "That's not true! Lots of people like you! I like you!" Although the second response is well-meaning and intended to be supportive, it is no more effective than the first one.

What's the problem with the second response? First of all, it's unlikely that the student will believe us. It's more likely to come across as invalidating and dismissive. Very few people respond well to either cheerleading or contradiction when we're upset. In addition, although a comment like this appears supportive and positive at first glance, it is actually argumentative. Pointing out positives and trying to convince a person that their assessment of the situation is faulty will not be perceived as supportive. Instead, it can be highly alienating and result in re-escalation. Negotiators note that arguing with a person in crisis—even if our comments seem logical and rational—is dangerous and counterproductive. One negotiator emphatically responded with a colourful set of mixed metaphors.

> You can't argue! The minute you start arguing, your bubble's burst or your ship's gone down. You cannot argue!

What we really want when we're feeling upset or hopeless about our situation is someone who will listen empathetically without agreeing or disagreeing. Face can be restored by gently exploring the comment and reframing it. "It sounds like you're feeling pretty lonely" is an empathic response that encourages the person to say more. Listening seriously to people as they tell their stories and explain their actions helps them to restore their reputations. Once that shift has begun to take place, gentle reframes are possible. For example, "Fairness is pretty important to you" or "Sounds like you'd like to . . ." These reframes can help the person re-assess the situation.

In the A&E production Talk to Me (1999), Detective Maureen Burke is negotiating with George, a man barricaded in a walk-up apartment with his nephew Jose as hostage. George tells Maureen how afraid he is—afraid of getting shot, afraid of going to jail.

"You don't have to be scared," she says. "You're in this situation because you're under pressure and you're upset. You're not a criminal, you're just someone who has reached the end of his rope and needs help coming back, and everyone knows that. I really want to help you with this—I want to help you to get out of here . . . to be safe."

She neatly paraphrases what other negotiators have said—"just a person in a bad place"—and reassures him of her intentions. What is also implicit in this exchange is her attempt to help him save face.

In Summary: What Can You Do to Help?

1. Try not to take the situation personally.

Admittedly, this isn't easy. In some respects, as Thompson and Jenkins (1993) noted, it is the ultimate communication challenge: "If you can carry this mind-set with you, one that appreciates other people's sense of dignity and self-worth, curiosity and healthy suspicion, you'll never be upset by people who initially challenge your authority" (p. 44).

2. Normalize the situation.

Normalizing the event can be a powerful way of helping someone to save face. Normalizing is a process of "joining with" the individual by showing them we see their distress as understandable and even relatable. As one negotiator told me, "Sometimes I've brought up personal experiences to help them relate to me. Because maybe I've been through the same thing they're going through. When someone decides that they're going to take a hostage or barricade themselves, they've pretty much come to the end of their rope. A lot of times you can see similarities in things that have happened in your life, whether it's financial problems or domestic problems or whatever."

This is not an unfamiliar strategy for most of us. In day to day dealings with friends, family and co-workers, it's likely that you frequently engage in this activity. You may not think of it as face-saving, but in fact it is. For example, if friends make a social gaffe like forgetting an appointment, arriving late or having a speck of spinach on their teeth, we are quick to normalize the situation and protect their self-image with comments like "maybe we weren't clear enough about the time" or "yeah, the traffic's been really bad lately" or "that happens to me all the time." We see these as polite ways to smooth out potential difficulties and help our friends and colleagues avoid embarrassment. What is important to remember is that this is not the same as condoning an action.

It is also wise to consider the possibility that we hold our students to higher standards than we do our friends. The immediate rush to enforcing accountability would be considered rude among friends but is unfortunately often something that occurs between teachers and students.

3. Use inclusive and relational language.

As Paulo Friere (1970) once suggested, language is never neutral. The words we use can either help to defuse a situation or to escalate it. Phrases like "you always" or "you never" or "you should" will invariably engender defensive and escalated responses in all of us. Thompson and Jenkins (1993) recommend using "we" versus "I," "here" versus "there," present tense versus past tense, "this" versus "that," "these" versus "those," and "our" versus "mine" (p. 89). While these may seem like subtle and perhaps even imperceptible linguistic alterations, they are powerful. Our use of words can either draw people close or alienate them. All of these word pairs reflect a move from confrontation and distance to relational closeness and can help the person understand that it's not a matter of *you against me* but rather *us against the problem*.

4. Use questions, not declaratives.

"So how did we get here today?" is a question that negotiators almost invariably start any exchange with. Supportive questions based on genuine curiosity will not only show the person that we are not there to harm but also help us to see the situation from their vantage point. This will give more information to work with when it comes time to solve the problem. Using questions rather than declaratives is a departure from some standard psychology and counselling ideology. Many self-help books encourage us to state our needs and expectations clearly and at times even bluntly. This is a particularly Western mind-set, and while it is certainly useful in some situations, it can be counterproductive when the person we're communicating with is in deep distress. There will be time for more direct communication once trusting relationships have been built and de-escalation has taken place.

5. Don't make demands or use directives.

In a similar vein, Thompson and Jenkins (1993) caution against using the following common phrases under any circumstances: "come here . . . you wouldn't understand . . . because those are the rules . . . it's none of your business . . . calm down . . . what's your problem . . . you never, or you always . . . I'm not going to say this again . . . I'm doing this for your own good . . . why don't you be reasonable" (pp. 47–54). They note that these phrases almost always result in an escalation of conflict. Demands for compliance will rarely result in de-escalation. Even if we can coerce people to do what we want them to do, the result will invariably be resentment and retaliation, not to mention a serious rift in relationships. Success will merely be short-term, and the damage much longer.

Negotiators observed that relationships could be damaged in the following ways: by inappropriately offering advice; judging, patronizing; arguing; interrupting; lecturing; demeaning; criticizing; making assumptions; becoming authoritarian; providing ultimatums, directives, or deadlines; making false promises; lying; saying no; challenging and confronting; using loaded words; being defensive; and attempting to solve problems prematurely.

They know that most people in crisis will feel misunderstood and that they have been treated unfairly in some way. In addition, embarrassment about the incident will likely have had a negative impact on the individual's ability to regain rationality and calmness. A negotiator's primary concern is to mitigate this impact. Face saving, in this way, is pragmatic. It's a crucial first step in de-escalation.

Saving face isn't just about making someone else the bad guy, as Misino and one of the educators I interviewed discussed. This may be an effective strategy in certain circumstances, but since saving face is fundamentally about identity and self-perception, helping someone to save face is a much more nuanced process than simply deflecting blame. Face saving also is also not about finding sophisticated ways to preserve the status quo—by making people do what we want them to do without them knowing we're doing it to them.

Instead, helping someone to save face is, as Vivian Gussin Paley and Robert Coles (1993) state, a fine way to "help each other out of a trap" (p. 141). During crisis, people do feel trapped and constricted, and because they are escalated and not able to think clearly, they see few options for an alternative to the action they've embarked on. What we can do first is help them regain composure by acknowledging their face needs. A mentor of mine once said, "People begin by telling you what they don't want and what isn't working. It's as if they're looking behind themselves. Our task is to gently take their face in our hands and help them turn toward what they do want and what does work." We cannot do the sensitive and difficult work of de-escalation without helping the other person to regain equilibrium and self-regard.

CHAPTER ELEVEN

THOUGHT INTERRUPTION

> Another simple kind of system is when we interrupt the chain of thought.
>
> —Schlossberg(1975)

Although negotiators describe the process of de-escalation as something accomplished primarily through the development of relational bonds, listening, and empathy, some of the ideas that emerged fell into categories not generally considered components of mainstream conflict management processes. An example is thought interruption. This concept is understood in hostage negotiation literature as akin to distraction and redirection but with an added element of counterintuitive surprise.

Folger et al. (2005) noted that there are times when interveners in a conflict situation should consider doing "the opposite of what's expected . . . [since] doing the unexpected can produce surprising results" (p. 289). In the book *Verbal Judo*, Thompson and Jenkins (1993, 2004) provide an example of an innovative intervention in a domestic dispute: unable to interrupt a couple's argument, the negotiator sat down on the sofa, picked up a newspaper, and began using the couple's telephone to follow up on want ads. Shocked and puzzled by the tactical non sequitur, they stopped fighting. Andy DeWeese, one of the negotiators I spoke with shared a similar example:

> I was on a domestic dispute one night, and this man and woman were . . . screaming at each other . . . and anything I'm saying is just not working. So I went over to the refrigerator and began to make myself a [peanut butter] sandwich . . . and all of a sudden they don't even remember what they were fighting about! It was something they weren't expecting to see. We sat down and had coffee, and the next day the woman called to apologize and thank me for helping them. All I did was surprise them!

Bolz and Hershey (1979) recounted an instance where a young man was threatening to jump off the edge of a rooftop of an apartment building in New York City. They'd been negotiating with him for several hours but hadn't made much progress. In fact, they'd become concerned that he was going to make good on his threat since he'd begun doing something negotiators recognize as "suicide by cop" and was offering to give away his belongings. He steadily moved closer to the edge of the building and actually raised one foot up on the ledge. The negotiators were aware that they needed to exercise extreme caution since he wasn't the only one in immediate danger. He had his infant child in his arms.

Although the day was sweltering, the negotiator looked up at the sky and asked the young man if he expected snow. The unrelated question was clearly startling. The man looked up in confusion just long enough to allow the negotiators to move in quickly and gently bring both him and the child to safety. By interrupting the dangerous direction of his thinking, the negotiators created a millisecond of space for safe resolution. That millisecond was all they needed.

Dominic Misino provided another graphic example.

> There's this guy, and he's got his girlfriend on his lap [with] a big knife to her throat. He's threatening to kill her and then kill himself. We've got snipers, and they're set to take him out, but he's not stupid. He's got in behind her. So we're stuck. We can't do nothing. Then one of the snipers says, "Hey, there's blood running down her throat." The carotid

artery isn't far underneath the skin, so it's life and death. So I say—'cause I know this guy has a thirteen-year-old daughter—I say, "Look, you need to let your wife go. I know you don't like her much 'cause she left you, but if you kill her and then we kill you, your daughter won't have anyone, and she'll go into foster care, and you don't want that. If you let her go, I promise we'll take you to the hospital. You can get a shower." The guy had been telling me about his life. He hadn't showered in days. He'd been sleeping in the park, and I'm thinking, "Wow, this guy's life really sucks." So I say, "We'll get you some food and get you cleaned up, then tomorrow if you still want to, you can kill yourself." Now I don't know why I said that last part, but . . . the guy lets her go! And Hugh, my supervisor, he's standing there just shaking his head because we just don't do that! I guess I got him to step back from the edge by being rational. He took a look at it. I knew he loved his daughter, and he stepped back from the edge.

Refocusing and thought interruption appeared well integrated into the practice of all of the negotiators I interviewed. For example, one person told stories about two separate suicide negotiations, one involving a young mother and the other a grandfather. In both instances she was able to save their lives by refocusing them on their children and other family members. "[I tried to] divert their attention away . . . by not being so negative, by trying to get them refocused on something else."

In the film "Talk to Me", George, the hostage taker, believes his former partner and her family are laughing at him. "George," the negotiator says, "she's not laughing. Nobody's laughing! I don't know everything that's gone on between you and Anna, but I do know that her baby's father is in an apartment trying to make a decision about her baby's future. That baby that she wants to grow up with a father. That's what she's thinking of, and you should be thinking about it too." By redirecting George's attention to his infant son, Maureen interrupts the looping trajectory of his thinking. This is also a good example of face-saving since embarrassment was clearly a factor in the incident.

George worries that if he surrenders, he will go to jail because he has a gun, and this is a repetitive loop as well. Maureen responds, "George! You're not going to jail for a gun. Nobody in Brooklyn goes to jail for a gun. It's just an accessory." Sometimes redirection is humour.

Dominic Misino recounted another, albeit unintentional and humorous, example of thought interruption. He was called to a twenty-seven-floor high rise where a man was on the ledge of the seventeenth floor threatening to jump.

> This happened before I was even considered a negotiator. So I was tied onto the ledge out the window beside this guy. He's not your average jumper—nice suit, nice shoes, not typical. And he's not talking to me no matter what I say. All he says is, "Go away." I go back in for a moment, considering my next move, and there's this high ranking guy, some official from the police department in the room, saying, "Why don't we get a psychologist?" I don't get it, and I don't really agree, but he keeps on about it, and he's got the rank.
>
> So someplace in the building they actually find some guy, and honest to god he looks like Sigmund Freud! Long grey hair, a suit he got in 1937. He's not a psychologist; he's a psychiatrist. So he says, "Where's the guy?," and they point at the window. He thinks they're pointing at me. I just shrug and shake my head no. He says, "So, where's the guy then?" We tell him. "He's out on the ledge."
>
> He looks at us like we're nuts. "I don't do ledges," he says. "Bring him in and downstairs. I'll make him feel better. But I don't do ledges!" He leaves, and we're laughing. The guy outside hears us and says, "Are you laughing at me?" He's upset, so I come back out to talk to him. The good news is he's finally talking!
>
> I tell him no and explain about the guy who doesn't do ledges. He starts to laugh too. That gives me my in. I say,

"What the hell are you doing out there, anyway?" He says, "My girlfriend left me." I say, "You've gotta be kidding. You're out there because your girlfriend left you? Really?" He nods.

I look at him. "This is New York, man. Look around. There's a million of them out there. Get your ass off that ledge and come in and talk to me." He says OK and comes in. And that was that.

I'll Have Your Wallet

In a wonderfully creative book about unusual responses to conflict situations called *Sweet Fruit from the Bitter Tree* (Andreas, 2011), chapter contributor Michael Perez recounts an incident that happened to him in Glasgow. Walking home from dinner one evening, he accidentally found himself in a dark and questionable part of town. He was quickly confronted and surrounded by a group of menacing-looking men. The apparent leader of the group put out his hand and said, "I'll have your wallet."

To this day, Perez doesn't know why he did what he did, but it was a brilliant example of thought interruption. He looked up in feigned amazement and said, "You have my wallet?" He began explaining effusively that he'd not only lost the wallet, but that it contained all his important travel information. He told the group how grateful he was that they'd found it. The ring leader – obviously nonplused and confused by the exchange - stuttered that he didn't actually have the wallet. Perez responded with dismay, asking why they'd claimed to have the wallet when they didn't. He then dramatically dropped to his knees and began searching the surrounding area. What ensued was a hilarious exchange, with all of the men on their hands and knees searching the darkened field. After what he thought was a suitable period of time, Perez stood up and sadly told the group it was clear his wallet wasn't there. He thanked them all profusely for their kindness, stating that he'd met so many wonderful kind and helpful people on his trip. He shook each of them by the hand, and walked back to his hotel. One can only wonder what went on in the minds of the would-be wallet thieves.

Remember my friend Tom Osbeck? He told another story that illustrates how thought interruption works. A person Tom was supporting, a very large man named Ronnie, became enraged and began running toward him, obviously intent on violence. Tom stayed where he was and simply looked down at his shoes. "Ronnie, Ronnie!" he said. "Look at my shoes! Just look!"

Ronnie stopped dead and looked down at Tom's shoes in confusion. "Wh-what? Wh-what's going on with your shoes?" he asked.

"I dunno," Tom said. "They just aren't comfortable. Look at them! They don't fit right!" In that moment the interchange was altered, and the violence that was imminent was handily deflected.

In Summary

When a person is upset, it's easy to get into a repetitive loop of thinking. Many counsellors are trained to encourage their clients to vent in order to get whatever is bothering them out of their systems. This confirms a widely held belief that suppressing powerful emotions like anger is unhealthy and can even lead to physical illness. In her book *Anger, the Misunderstood Emotion* Carol Tavris (1982) challenges this notion. She suggests that expressing anger repeatedly can be counterproductive because it can crystallize it in our minds. Going over and over an event can convince us that our version of what happened is the only accurate one and even compromise our ability to entertain other interpretations that might be more helpful or even accurate.

It is interesting that after 9/11, many counsellors began to question the notion of catharsis and the value of reliving and retelling terrible experiences. They found that asking people who'd experienced trauma to recount their experiences repetitively and in detail actually re-traumatized them. It was more helpful, they decided, to look for areas of resilience and ask questions that allow a person to revisit the situation from another perspective—for example, asking someone who has experienced a difficult situation, "How is it that you've managed to continue in your life so far, given what you've experienced?"

One of the assistant principals I spoke with had a story that illustrates this point from a school perspective.

> There was one boy... a young First Nations man who had been avoiding school. He'd show up for [physical education] and a computer class, and those were the only ones. He was not doing anything toward graduating. It's been a real tough haul trying to connect with him. He'd come from an alternate program. I just [asked him] the question, saying, "That's really tough. How do you manage that you even showed up here today?"
>
> He just sat for probably three minutes or so, and he turned to me and said, "You know, I just need to be responsible for myself." He said some amazing things. It was like it almost gave him permission to step into his own power. The tone of voice wasn't like just reciting what the adults have said. "Now, here's Lecture 32A." It sounded authentic. I don't know what his follow-through will be like, but it put it onto a much more equal footing of us talking to each other.

In her book *What Is Narrative Therapy? An Easy-to-Read Introduction* (2000), Alice Morgan says problem stories, told and retold, can become so large and foregrounded that they push the possibility of alternative stories to the margins of consciousness. Thought interruption is one way of stopping such a downward spiral of thinking during a crisis and creating enough space for alternatives to emerge.

Needless to say, this does not negate the need for listening. We never want to minimize or dismiss someone's distress or move on too quickly. People often do need to tell us what's going on in their lives, and as the negotiators told me, when we listen well, people will also likely tell us what they need, which in turn will offer clues that will help to resolve the situation. However, continued repetition can be counter-productive and increase anger and exacerbate the situation. It is at that point that another approach can be useful. Thought interruption and redirection can be helpful, but like active listening techniques, they are not magic bullets and need to be used with discretion. For example, redirection is not recommended as an intervention for a person experiencing a full-blown PTSD flashback. Rather than de-escalating the person, it can make the situation much worse.

I had a very real experience with that phenomenon a number of years ago. A young woman I knew was in the midst of a traumatic flashback, convinced that the people who'd hurt her in the past were in the room and trying to hurt her again. The support worker intervening meant well, but her suggestion that they wash dishes together did not exactly help to de-escalate the situation. (To add a little additional perspective, I'm not sure that dishwashing would be high on many people's list as an appealing alternative.) This seemingly innocuous request re-escalated the young woman dangerously, and she became even more distraught. It wasn't until a second person stepped in to reassure her that she was safe and that the people who had hurt her were not present that she began to become calm and de-escalated.

Thought interruption should not be confused with thought stopping, a technique involving the use of elastic wrist-band snapping, tapping, and other interventions sometimes employed by therapists to help people deal with anxiety and recurrent negative thoughts.

Thought interruption in crisis intervention is simply one way of creating a momentary distraction that can provide a small window of space in which we can reset the interchange. It is an intervention that must be used with caution, since like any intervention, it must be used in context; it can be perceived as disrespectful if misused.

CHAPTER TWELVE

PROBLEM SOLVING

> You've heard of grabbing victory from the jaws of defeat, right? Well, rushing to premature problem solving is just the opposite. It's grabbing defeat from the jaws of victory. You're getting somewhere, and then, bang! You blow it by offering solutions before the person's ready to hear them (negotiator study participant).

Go Slow to Go Fast

As this statement illustrates, the typical mind-set during conflict favours action, but immediate action is not always appropriate. In our action-oriented society, we believe when confronted with a crisis situation, we need to act quickly and decisively. Unfortunately, we often take action before we have even clarified the problem. Einstein famously once said that if he was given sixty minutes to solve a major problem, he would spend fifty-nine of them identifying what the problem was. If we haven't done this critical work, we may end up trying to solve the wrong problem, then becoming discouraged and frustrated when it continues to arise. This is why negotiators stress the need for listening, curiosity, and dynamic activity before moving to problem solving. One negotiator said,

> Listening is more important than talking. Find out what's important to people. When you listen, invariably they'll tell

you what they need. If you really listen, you can probably solve the thing.

Another negotiator worried that the tendency to leap to solution finding could leave important issues unaddressed.

> A lot of conflict management is putting a Band-Aid over what the real issues are. It may be that people are afraid to pull that Band-Aid off for what they are going to find underneath, [so] if they can just settle this quickly, then it's no longer our problem. They only have time to put the Band-Aids back on by jumping ahead to "let's solve this problem, get it out of the way."

What follows are a series of stories and examples to illustrate the need to pause before acting.

Sit In the Snowbank

When my partner, Norm, was doing his master's degree in family therapy, he had lunch with a friend who was studying pastoral counselling. His friend was doing a practicum at CAMH in Toronto, a residence for people with significant mental health issues. During lunch, Norm asked his friend to share the most important thing he'd learned so far.

"It's actually a story one of my supervisors told me," he said. "It goes like this. A parish priest was saying goodbye to his parishioners at the door of the church after service one day. An older woman approached and said, 'Father, when your car breaks down on a lonely road in the middle of winter, why doesn't God fix your car?' The priest paused, then replied. "You know, God could fix your car, but He'd much rather sit with you in the snowbank and wait for the tow truck."

What Norm's friend said he'd learned through this story profoundly changed his response to people experiencing crisis and trauma. He'd learned to resist the urge to offer advice and suggestions, and instead simply stay alongside the person as a supportive and listening presence.

It makes sense. Think about your own experience. Have you ever confided in someone about a difficult problem you were struggling with, only to have that person turn to you and blithely offer a quick solution? The way we feel when this happens runs the gamut from frustration to fury. We feel patronized. All we really want is a sympathetic ear, not a quick fix. We often know how to solve the problem, but being supported to talk it through, being taken seriously and listened to can allow us to access our own problem-solving acumen more effectively. Sitting in the snowbank is a good example of dynamic inactivity, as discussed in Chapter 9, and cannot be stressed enough as the critical precursor to problem solving.

For those of us who consider ourselves good problem solvers, it's often difficult to resist the urge to introduce solutions, especially when we can see what appears to be an obvious answer to the problem the person is facing. However, we may be wrong in our early assessments. Our impatience to get the thing solved can compound the issue, and sometimes dangerously so. Unfortunately, many negotiators have learned this the hard way.

Lessons from Waco: A Cautionary Tale

One of the most infamous failed negotiations in North American history occurred in Waco, Texas, in 1993. David Koresh was the charismatic leader of the Branch Davidians, a breakaway group of the Seventh Day Adventist Church. The group of almost a hundred of his followers were living in a compound at the Mount Carmel Center Ranch just outside Waco. In early 1993, the FBI began covert surveillance of the group after reports that the Branch Davidians had amassed a significant arsenal of weapons and were converting AR-15 rifles into machine guns and making grenades. The FBI were concerned that a fanatic militia group with unknown motives was in the making.

The FBI planned a surprise raid for February 28, 1993, hoping to disempower the group by confiscating their weapons and disarming them. A newspaper reporter who had become lost enroute to the compound inadvertently tipped off the group when he asked a passing stranger for directions to the compound. The stranger happened to be a member of the group and promptly reported his concerns back to David Koresh. The Branch Davidians prepared for the expected arrival of the FBI by barricading and arming themselves. Four federal agents and six Branch Davidians died in the shootout that followed, and that event began a siege at the compound that lasted from February 28 to April 17, 1993, and expanded to include almost 700 members of the Federal Bureau of Alcohol, Tobacco and Firearms, Texas State law enforcement and the US military. The siege ended in a fiery conflagration where seventy-six members of the Branch Davidians, including David Koresh, died. Many of them were children.

What isn't widely known is that in the middle of this chaotic situation, a parallel negotiation process was taking place. Negotiators were strategically housed in a nearby building and were in almost constant contact with Koresh over the phone and through video throughout the standoff. In fact, a total of 754 phone calls took place, and Koresh sent the negotiators hours of video footage showing him with his family and supporters. During the course of these communications, Koresh opened up to the negotiators, explaining his beliefs and confiding that his childhood had been lonely and that he'd been bullied for being dyslexic.

Phillip Arnold, a religious scholar from Houston, offered his assistance to the negotiation team early in the process. After hearing about the standoff, he'd spent a great deal of time analyzing Koresh's work in an effort to understand his beliefs and theology and to get a clear sense of his thinking. Arnold's subsequent view of Koresh and his group contradicted what the FBI believed. Arnold thought that rather than simply being a manipulative cult leader and child abuser hiding behind religious rhetoric, Koresh truly believed he was doing the will of God. Arnold suggested that one way of breaking the impasse and brokering surrender might be to suggest that Koresh write a book outlining his thinking about the Seven Seals, something he was particularly passionate about. Writing a book would allow him to both save face and present his ideology to the world, something Koresh was keen to do. Arnold's and Koresh's attorneys were able to enter the compound to present the idea and broker the deal. Koresh, taken with the notion that his ideas would reach a broader public, responded positively and agreed that once the book was complete he would surrender peacefully.

A mitigating factor that probably contributed to the ultimate tragic outcome of the Waco siege is that David Koresh, as he'd admitted to the negotiators, was dyslexic and had limited literacy skills. This meant he needed help bringing his work into written format, which proved arduous and time consuming. The SWAT and military groups waiting outside the compound became increasingly frustrated with the delay. Further, they did not believe Koresh was negotiating in good faith but was simply using the book as a manipulative stalling tactic.

The two approaches to the Waco siege were in sharp opposition to each other. While the negotiators engaged in conversation with Koresh and his followers and believed they were making important progress, the military, FBI, and law enforcement disagreed with this assessment and began using increasingly inflammatory tactics in an attempt to bring the situation to a head. While both professed to want a peaceful solution, the extreme tactics used by law enforcement belied that commitment. They kept the barricaded Davidians awake and on edge by shining bright lights into the windows of the compound, shouting commands through bullhorns, and blasting loud music at all hours of the day and night.

Impatient and frustrated at their lack of success—and unbeknown to the negotiators—the FBI decided to take matters into their own hands. They went straight to Janet Reno, then US attorney general, and asked for an order allowing them to move in and end the siege. Although Reno reportedly asked several times if there weren't other alternatives to such an aggressive approach, she was told there were not. She was told Koresh was a sociopathic controller and a child abuser, and that he would never come out peacefully. Reno was never told about the agreement Koresh had made with the negotiators. Lacking this information, she issued the order.

Immediately tanks were deployed into the compound to batter the walls. Within a short period of time, observers began to see fire inside the building, and very quickly the small fires escalated into a raging inferno. It remains unclear how the fire started; the remaining Branch Davidians blamed the assault; and the military blamed David Koresh.

Tragically, after the incident was over, it was discovered that Koresh had completed the manuscript of the First Seal. He was working diligently on the second until the last day of the siege and his death. He'd apparently made the agreement with the negotiators in good faith and was attempting to live up to his side of the bargain.

Since that time, many conspiracy theories have been floated about who fired the first shots, how the fire started inside the compound, and whether the actions of the government were deliberately designed to inflame a larger issue. It continues to be widely believed that Waco was the match that lit the fire under the current debate between gun owners and those who want to see firearm regulations. It has been difficult for law enforcement to convince gun enthusiasts that government is not, as many profess, "coming for your guns," given what happened at the compound.

Could this tragedy have been prevented? The military, FBI SWAT team, and ATF continue to assert that it could not. Some of the negotiators, historians, and journalists involved persistently continue to disagree. In their view it was impatience that forced the confrontation. With more time and conversation, they believe a peaceful outcome would have been possible. Even Bill Clinton later admitted he wished they had decided to wait Koresh out instead of moving in.

I wonder if we would be where we are today—with the NRA in the United States fighting gun control and students rallying to protest gun ownership—if Waco had been successfully negotiated? Would the Oklahoma City bombing in 1995 have taken place? This incident been linked directly back to what happened in Waco. Of course these are unanswerable questions. The proliferation of conspiracy theories and paranoia might possibly have been forestalled.

Unfortunately, as the experience at Waco so clearly shows, SWAT responders and negotiators differ widely in their approaches and are sometimes at odds with each other. Sniper training is still firmly based in the action imperative, and in many instances SWAT responses are adrenaline-fueled. Negotiation training, on the other hand, is firmly based in a philosophy that is best expressed in their own words: "go slow to go fast." These two ideologies exist in uneasy juxtaposition, and negotiators describe situations where they are not only required to negotiate with a subject but also simultaneously hold the SWAT team at bay.

Another example of the tension between negotiators and SWAT was graphically evident in the earlier mentioned A&E production "Talk to Me". In this film we see Maureen Burke, the negotiator, making slow but steady progress in her interaction with George, an armed man barricaded with a child hostage in a New York City walk-up building. Part of the team's "go slow to go fast" strategy was a series of planned breaks in the conversation. These breaks (also a good example of dynamic inactivity) had a cooling down effect, allowing the subject time to think and take stock of the situation. During one such break, the SWAT team, unbeknown to the negotiators, stormed the staircase and began pounding on the apartment door, demanding that the man surrender and come out.

When the phone conversation between the negotiators and the subject resumed a couple of minutes later, the shaken and frightened George asked why there were people banging on his door. "They're going to kill me!" he said. The negotiators, confused and upset, scrambled to reassure him that no one was going to hurt or kill him. Hugh McGowan, then leader of the negotiation team, rushed outside to find the SWAT leader and demand he tell the SWAT team to stand down. "Who's in charge here?" he asked. "My track record is just as good as yours!" He asked why the team had acted in the first place. "Because you lost the phone line," the SWAT leader replied. "I didn't lose the phone line!" McGowan retorted. "We hung up to give him time to think!" As a result of this SWAT intervention, Maureen, the negotiator, had to spend a significant amount of time reassuring George and rebuilding trust. Although the trust bond was not broken irrevocably, for a time it was precarious. This conflict of approaches could easily have resulted in tragedy. Luckily, the situation was successfully resolved and both hostage taker and child were brought to safety.

The perception that negotiation is somehow soft and ineffective isn't just an opinion sometimes held by the people holding the perimeter and the guns. It becomes a problem for all of us in a climate where our governments and the general public are increasingly demanding hard-line approaches and "tougher measures." Negotiators I spoke with agreed that these ideas make their work more difficult, and despite statistical success in resolving tough situations, they sometimes have to fight to keep the SWAT team in abeyance. This mind-set among politicians and the public puts the same pressure on schools to implement hard-line measures with students, and like negotiators trying to hold back the SWAT team, educators find themselves having to justify alternatives to punishment. While tough approaches seem to promise safety, negotiators stress that demands for compliance or ultimatums in the absence of a strong relational bond are not only ineffective but also represent a significant danger. I heard a sobering story that illustrates this point:

> This is a case that a man had taken his children hostage. He and his wife were having issues, and they got in a fight; and he is in there with those kids. And, they (the SWAT team) decide it's time to get him out of there, so they tell (the negotiator) to tell the guy he's got thirty minutes or whatever it was. So the negotiator did, and in thirty minutes, "boom" right on deadline, he killed his kids. The big lesson from that is you don't do deadlines. The lessons you learn are always from horrible tragedies.
>
> Never, never, never back someone into a corner! A metaphorical corner is just as bad as a physical corner. We never do that. It won't end well.

In Appendix A, Ron Garrison talks about the issue of restraint and seclusion and reminds us that incidents like these seldom, if ever, occur without a substantial amount of anger. They are adrenaline-fuelled. He tells us that the physical confrontations he's consulted on are always evidence of a fight and not done with calmness and deliberation as some would believe. Adrenaline is a dangerous addition to a fraught conflict situation.

The desire to end situations quickly is almost always attempted through the use of demands. The following is a situation that hung on a thread because the negotiator made a demand that nearly broke the bond of trust he'd been developing with the subject. The situation was saved when he backed down and apologized.

> One of my longest negotiations was about seven hours. This guy is holding an eighty-four-year-old woman hostage, and he's armed. We're talking and I'm trying to humanize this woman—that's what we do—but it's just dragging on. At one point he says to me, "You're making me feel bad." (We call this the Stockholm syndrome in reverse. You know how the Stockholm syndrome is when the hostage supposedly identifies with the hostage taker? That never happens, by the way, that I've ever seen.) Well, this is the opposite. I guess he was starting to see her differently, like a person. I kept telling him things I'd learned about her life and her family and all.
>
> Then all of a sudden he says, "Look, if you get me three cigarettes, I'll let her go." I said, "Three cigarettes? Is that it?" and he says, "Yeah." So I turn to my boss, and my boss says, "No way. He has to let her out first, and then we'll give him the cigarettes." Well my response is "You're kidding, right?" But no, I guess they were scared he'd get the cigarettes and still keep her. So I tell the guy, "You've got to let her go first," and he gets angry. Now he doesn't trust me anymore. I go back to my boss and convince him to give the guy his cigarettes. I apologize for not trusting him, and I make him promise he'll let her go (not just "Yeah," but say the words out loud: "I promise. "That's important). We give him the cigarettes, and he lets her go.

> Three cigarettes! That was a first. But it was a close call. You can really piss someone off if you try to horse trade at the wrong moment or make a demand.

Apology is not always easy for many of us. In reading this vignette, we might ask, "Why should the negotiator apologize? He's not the one who caused the situation!" However, negotiators repeatedly noted the importance of apology:

> I'm going to use his language. I'm going to shoot from the hip. If I say something that offends him, I'll just backtrack and apologize for it.

> I train people not to be afraid of conflict. I teach them to expect conflict and learn how to get out of it. If you hit a land mine, apologize! What you're saying is, "I respect you. And I won't do it again." That builds trust.

In assessing these incidents, I am reminded again of one of the most important lessons I took from negotiators and the literature, namely that impatience during crisis is counterproductive. As the negotiator quoted at the top of this chapter framed it: when we rush in with metaphorical guns blazing, we are likely to "seize defeat from the jaws of victory".

Daniel

Daniel was one of my best teachers. I met him when he moved from his family home into a group home. He was a bit of an obsessive, but being one myself, I couldn't be too critical. After all, one person's perseveration is another person's tenacity.

I liked Daniel a lot. He was probably one of the most colourful people I'd ever met, with a quirky view of the world and an interesting sense of humour. He could also annoy people to the ends of their coping ropes.

It's an understatement to say that Daniel loved food. But because he was diabetic and considered overweight, and he had a diagnosis of Prader Willie syndrome, which carries with it an eating disorder, food was an area that was being heavily policed by his support workers and family. Support staff were expected to restrict his access to the kitchen and ration his food at all times. Since logic and rationale didn't have much effect on Daniel's single-minded pursuit of food, staff responses soon degenerated into padlocked fridges and double-locked cupboards. I'm sure you can appreciate the effect this had on Daniel.

Food, or the unavailability of it, became the focus of every discussion. As the weeks passed, the interchanges between Daniel and the staff became more and more intense. His pleas for food were met with implacable denial. Things were thrown. Sanctions were implemented.

One evening senior staff were called to Daniel's home because violence had erupted. He'd broken a plate glass window in the living room and was in a corner shrieking uncontrollably. The staff, shaken and upset, were in their own corners. The police had been called.

Just before they arrived, it seemed that Daniel had become calmer. One of the braver staff members, noting that he seemed tired and quieter, thought it might be a good time to process the incident with him. From what we could gather, this was a combination of mild rebuke and advice. While I'm sure it was a well-intentioned attempt, it was badly timed and therefore predictably backfired. Daniel picked up the coffee table and threw it through the window, launching himself at the staff person. The police arrived at precisely that moment, and in seconds, Daniel was on the floor in four-point restraint, weeping uncontrollably. They put him in handcuffs and began taking statements from the staff.

It wasn't until sometime later that I understood what had happened that night. Why did Daniel explode again when it seemed he was calming down? What hadn't the people who supposedly knew him best noticed? Bill Page, a colleague, friend, and thirty-five-year veteran teacher and consultant to schools, provided a metaphor and some insight that might help us understand why Daniel re-escalated:

As educators, or support staff, or even parents, we have two roles. We are swimming instructors, and we are lifeguards. When things are going well, and students are learning what we're teaching them, we're swimming instructors. But when conflict breaks out and there's a crisis, we need to put aside our lessons and be the lifeguards.

Page believes that a disruptive person is metaphorically drowning:

> When someone is drowning, it makes little sense to stand at the edge of the pool and shout at them to kick their legs. When people are upset, they can't hear us. And yet that's what we do in education. We keep on talking, telling them what's wrong with what they're doing and how we want them to change and what we're going to do to them if they don't. What we really need to do is get into the pool and help them back to shallow water where they feel safe. Later on, when they're back on solid ground, that's when we can slowly move back into our role as the swimming instructor! That's when we can work with them to figure out how to solve the problem. It's only when people are feeling safe that they can hear us. (personal communication, 2010)

This Is Your Brain on Stress Hormones

A brief look at the area of neuroscience gives big clues about why Daniel exploded and why the staff response was problematic. It also explains why giving swimming lessons while someone is drowning is an exercise in futility and can further exacerbate the situation. Neuroscientists say that when we are in crisis and upset, we down-shift to a more primitive part of our brains. This is the moment we feel like the room is getting smaller or when we "see red." This is not a good time to ask people to think logically, since their rational brain has been hijacked by a potent cocktail of stress hormones.

When our brains down-shift in this way, we are unable to relate to others or even physically hear very well. This means that no matter how logical and persuasive we may be, the upset person simply can't take in what we're saying. In order to hear, we first need to shed some of the stress hormones that have flooded our bodies. This takes reassurance, support, and time—probably a lot more time than we might expect. Interventions that focus on reprimand or even advice before these hormones have dissipated will invariably cause immediate re-escalation of the situation. This can be a repetitive cycle of explosion, followed by calm, followed by yet another explosion.

Unfortunately, in many classrooms, these simple neurological facts are either not known or are ignored. Too often this results in situations that re-escalate just they seem to be abating.

A Personal Story

One weekend, when our son Evan was about six years old, my husband decided to clean the basement of our home. Evan wanted to help. Pleased and surprised by this offer, Norm gave him a few fetch-and-carry tasks suitable for his age and size.

Then Evan spotted a large sledgehammer in a corner of the basement. Intrigued, he picked it up and began to walk across the basement floor with it. It was very heavy, and the effort it took to lift and carry it turned his face bright red. Alarmed, Norm suggested he put it down. "That's too big for you, Evan," he said. "You might hurt yourself."

"No, I won't," Evan responded with typical little-boy bravado. He continued to heft the thing across the room. Suddenly, as predicted, it slipped from his hand and landed squarely on his toe. He burst into tears and collapsed to the floor holding onto his foot.

By the time I got there, summoned from the main floor by the sounds of distress, Norm had things under control. He was sitting on the basement floor holding Evan and commiserating with him. "Oh, Evan," he said, "that must have hurt so much. Let me see it." Evan was already calming down, sniffling a little, and removing his shoe and sock to examine the poor toe.

The two of them went upstairs to minister to the wounds, and I went back to what I was doing. Soon Evan was outside playing with his friend Andrew, having decided that the basement wasn't as much fun as he thought it would be. Norm and I sat down for coffee.

"Well," he said, "I finally figured out what Bill Page meant." I probably looked confused. "When Evan picked up that mallet, I told him not to. I knew it was too heavy and that he could get hurt. But he wouldn't listen. So when he dropped it on his foot, guess what every cell in my body wanted my mouth to do?"

I smiled. "Say 'I told you so?'" I asked.

"Absolutely. But, hey, I'm learning. I didn't do it. I remembered to be the lifeguard."

The next weekend Norm resumed cleaning the basement. Again, Evan volunteered to help. This time, when he went toward the sledgehammer, Norm was able to gently remind him of what had happened the previous week.

"Look, Evan," he said. "If you hurt your other foot, you'll have trouble walking. Just think, if you and I go to the mall together, everyone's going to think cerebral palsy is hereditary!" (My husband has cerebral palsy.)

Evan laughed and put the sledgehammer down.

Some people might call what happened to Evan a natural consequence. I suppose it was, but how or even whether people learn from natural consequences wasn't what interested us about this scenario. The most useful lesson was probably ours, not Evan's. We learned that support is the most effective response during an incident where people are upset. Later, when everyone is calm, it's easier to be rational and talk about what to do differently next time.

What Should We Do When We're the Ones Drowning?

But what if the person who is drowning is you? What do you do when both you and the student feel like you're drowning?

This is when we need each other. Remember Margaret Wheatley's suggestion? When you're stuck, bring in more people. Negotiators stressed the need for teamwork. As most negotiations are conducted over the phone, the negotiator will almost always have a team on site, providing background information and on-the-spot suggestions and advice. Most important is the coach or the secondary negotiator. "The coach may hear something that the primary does not hear, and they'll write down on a piece of paper and pass it to you and say, 'Try to go this direction.' They never talk, but they always listen." One negotiator described another role for the coach: "You can't necessarily evaluate yourself in prolonged stressful situations."

The educators I spoke with noted that teacher isolation is a problematic issue that contributes to classroom management issues, and they also stressed the need for teamwork:

> You walk by teachers' rooms and there's paper on the windows and the doors are locked. It's their sanctuary. What goes on in there . . . don't bother me! All the more reason to pull the keys out and go in . . . You have people teaching side by side [but] unfortunately there's not a lot of chat . . . they could learn a lot from each other.

At a conference I attended many years ago, Elliot Eisner, a famous educational theorist, called education the "boudoir profession." "It's all about 'come into my room and close the door!'" he said. Eisner made a strong case for teamwork among educators as a way to help each other learn and grow and as a catalyst for educational reform. Co-teaching, he pointed out, is an obvious solution to teacher isolation. There may be others in the school who can help as well. Sometimes the others we need are not necessarily the people we might expect to get help from. There are times when insight and assistance come from the most unexpected sources. Consider this true story.

At lunch during a full day in-service session with teachers, the special education consultant told us a story about a momentous learning experience. A principal in the district asked him to come and consult on a student that were having difficulty with.

As part of his usual routine, the consultant, Carl, met with the student, a teenager named Donald. Donald was unresponsive and continued to be resistant to Carl's overtures and questions. In these situations, he typically tries to find people in the school who have a positive relationship with the student or some insight into what is taking place. After speaking with a lot of people, he was dismayed to find that the student was universally disliked by his teachers and his fellow students. Finally, in desperation, he asked the principal, "Doesn't anyone like this kid?" After a few moments of stunned silence and reflection, the principal responded. "Well, I don't know if this helps, but I have seen Donald spending time with the school custodian."

Newly energized, Carl ventured down into the bowels of the school maintenance area and found the custodian. "I understand you have some relationship with Donald," he said. "I'm sure you know that he's had some problems in school. Can we talk?"

The custodian looked up from what he was doing and said, "Well, it's about time!" He led Carl to his office behind the furnace room and proceeded to lay out the school problem from Donald's perspective. After a long conversation, Carl returned to the principal's office.

"I have some ideas for an in-service on how to support Donald to succeed," he said.

The principal immediately pulled out his date book. "Let's look at some dates. When are you available?"

"I don't think you understand," Carl said. "I don't need my datebook. I won't be doing the in-service. Your custodian will."

As it turned out, that's exactly what happened.

Ask the Experts

There are times when the best consultants and team members are other students. Vivian Gussin Paley (1993) regularly engaged her very young students in thinking and rethinking many aspects of classroom life, including rules and discipline processes. She mused about the notion of disruption itself here. "Those who never disrupt may be withholding too much. Until they tell us more of what is on their minds, they may not be able to listen to what we have to say."

In her early years as a teacher, Gussin Paley used a "final threat" strategy familiar to many: the time-out chair. "The time-out chair, my punishment of choice, seemed impossible to eliminate, until the inarticulate sadness of the chair's occupants finally began to penetrate my consciousness" (p. 87).

> Being locked up seldom helped a child not do something, though it did notify everyone that the child was bad. I had proof of this the day the chair was missing.
>
> "Where's the blue chair?" Ellen asked.
>
> "Mr. Jackson is fixing it."
>
> "Then nobody will be bad today," she reasoned.
>
> "If there's no time-out chair nobody will be bad?" I repeated, wanting to make sure I understood.
>
> "Of course not. How could there be?" (p. 88)

A student, Angela Gabel, in a book aptly titled *Listening to the Experts: Students with Disabilities Speak Out*, (2006), says, "It's funny how the teachers just assume they know what's best for kids because they're the experts. If teachers would actually sit down with the student and talk for a little while, they would figure out where the problem is and the best way to fix it" (p. 38).

Students often see and hear things teachers don't. They have unexpected insights into the very issues that plague schools most. For example, a friend of ours was involved in an inclusion project in a junior high school. One of the students he'd been working with seemed to have good relationships with the other students in his class but puzzlingly remained consistently isolated and alone in the cafeteria during lunch period. One day, frustrated and at a loss for how to proceed, he asked a couple of the other students why they didn't sit with their friend during lunch. One of the students made a face. "It's that thing he eats with!" (The student was tube-fed, and his lunch was a bag of pureed food suspended on a pole beside him.) "It's gross! Throw a sweater over it or something!" Covering up the pureed food was all it took. From that head-slapping moment on, the student was among his peers in the cafeteria.

"I Didn't Just Come for the Juice and Cookies, You Know!"

Another example is illustrated by a story from a friend. She has a daughter named Sylvia, who had a significant disability. Sylvia used a wheelchair, and when she was in the third grade, she was just beginning to use a rudimentary communication board.

Our friend Lara has always been a staunch advocate for her daughter's educational rights, so Sylvia was in a regular third-grade class. "They call me the mother from hell," she once told us, "and when I come to school, I can clear the hallways in seconds flat without saying a thing!"

For Sylvia's IEP that year, Lara pulled out all the stops. She insisted that not only should Sylvia be present for the meeting but so should her family, friends, and classmates. It became the social event of the season, and invitations were at a premium.

One of the children who insisted on an invitation was a boy in Sylvia's class who had the dubious distinction of being one of the school's worst "behaviour problems." Given the boy's reputation, Lara had qualms about the friendship. But her other children, who also attended Sylvia's school, said, "Mom! He's Sylvia's friend. If it's not broken, don't fix it!" So, despite her reservations, she decided to invite him.

They began the IEP by talking about Sylvia's communication. Maybe it would be more accurate to say they were talking about her lack of communication. Ruefully, everyone admitted she didn't really have much.

Suddenly, from out of the cheap seats, the little boy with the big reputation rose to his feet.

"That's not true, is it, Sylvia?" he said, clearly outraged. Sylvia made a noise that sounded suspiciously like a confirmation.

"Now, when Sylvia wants to go outside, this is how she tells me. When she wants to come in, this is how I know. If she's hungry, I can tell because she does this—" He demonstrated a head movement. "When she's cold, this is what she does." The list went on for a good five minutes. Throughout his speech, Sylvia watched him, occasionally making supportive noises.

The adults in the room, including Sylvia's parents, listened in amazement. "To tell you the truth," Lara told us later, "we had our jaws on our chests. I've got to admit that it was a bit embarrassing to be upstaged so thoroughly by an eight-year-old. You'd swear he knew her better than we did."

Finally, his diatribe concluded, the school's number one behaviour problem pulled himself up to his full height, looked disdainfully at his silent and gobsmacked audience, and said, "Well, I didn't just come for the juice and cookies, you know!"

There is, however, a caveat when it comes to involving other students. At the risk of appearing solipsistic, I am going to quote Norm and me from an earlier publication. (Van Der Klift & Kunc, 1994, 2019).

> A child's classmates may provide useful information about the nature of puzzling behaviours. Sometimes children will see things that remain invisible to adult observers. However, the risk of eliciting input about behaviour may be the development of an increased sense of difference and distance. People with disabilities tell us that it is easier to be ignored than to be patronized or seen as a "class project."
>
> We can still get the information we need without compromising the equity of peer relationships by positing the issue as the school's problem, rather than the child's problem. This way, it is we who do not yet have the insight, experience or information necessary to support the student, not the student who is in need of "fixing." It may emerge that the real issue, one worth discussing, has more to do with how we might make a school more responsive to all its members. (p. 398).

Three Important Components of Problem Solving: Preparation, Practice, and Training

At a certain point, when everyone is calm, we *will* need to solve the problem. One way of doing so is through mediation. Many educators acknowledge the need to develop skills in conflict resolution for use with colleagues and other adults and similarly acknowledge the value of peer mediation programs designed to teach students communication skills to use with each other (Cohen, 2005; Johnson & Johnson, 1996, 2006). However, there are few studies that suggest that conflict management and communication-based strategies might have direct and specific utility between teachers and students during confrontational incidents.

All of the negotiators I spoke with emphasized the importance of learning these skills. One of the most important vehicles they recommended was role-play. In fact, as one negotiator pointed out, candidates who refuse to participate cannot become negotiators:

> We get people that say, "I can't do that type of training." If people tell me that coming in at entry level, I wouldn't select them. I would say, "There's no place for you here because we need to be able to simulate what you might be called upon to do. If we don't do it through role-play, I can't think of any other way we can do it. If you're not into rehearsing, we can't plug you into the real deal." It's huge. Again you have to be careful when you draw up your scenarios that you don't put unrealistic hurdles and traps. They have to be reality based and very carefully and closely monitored. They're very beneficial. Not everything has to be a complete role-play either. You can do communication exercises or a scenario. We can do active listening drills.

He recommended volunteer training on crisis lines as another way to hone and practise the necessary skills.

Mediation and Negotiation in the Classroom and Beyond

The following story illustrates an innovative approach taken by one school. Although initially teachers were mistrustful of the program, over time it became a popular problem-solving approach between students and teachers.

Marisol was a teacher with a particular soft spot for children with learning difficulties and disabilities. In particular, she liked to work with the kids who were labelled as troublemakers, those who were often called challenging or even violent. Her ability to relate well with the students that other teachers struggled with did not go unnoticed by the school principal.

After some time spent observing Marisol's ability to relate well with these students, the principal approached her with an idea. She was asked to consider being the school's behavioural resource teacher. Marisol agreed but with a caveat. "I'll do it," she said, "but I want to make a deal here. I don't want my role to be a 'kid-fixer.' What I see when kids come to talk to me is that many of their issues are not necessarily behavioural problems or even not understandable. A lot of the kids I talk to feel misunderstood and that they're being treated unfairly. So what I'd like to do is create a space to do some mediation between these kids and whoever they have issues with. That includes the teaching staff."

The principal agreed, and with that "Marisol's Space" was born, a place where students could come for guidance, support, and mediation. It was an immediate success with the students. Much to Marisol's surprise and consternation, more and more students came to her with issues that were about relationships with their teachers. "Historically, problems between teachers and students are blamed primarily on the student," she said. "It's the student who has to change. I wanted to take a broader view and work with both the student and the teacher to mediate whatever was going on."

This strategy was not such an immediate success with the teachers. Initially, some were unhappy with Marisol's approach and responded to her requests for mediation with defensiveness and mistrust. She was ostracized, and conversations would stop when she entered the staffroom. It was as if she'd crossed some kind of invisible loyalty line. Marisol believed they were worried that their competence was being called into question. Despite the response, she was undeterred. This was in service of a higher cause. Over time her colleagues began to recognize the value in her approach and realized her intention was not to humiliate them in front of their students but to genuinely broker better relationships.

Marisol had the courage to confront what is often a culture of student blame within schools. Instead of labelling a particular response as a behavioural issue, she reframed it into what was often more manageable: a conflict between two individuals.

Once a difficult situation is viewed as simply a conflict between two people, it becomes less fraught. Conflict can be mediated. As mentioned, the notion that the child is in some way disordered or simply "a behaviour problem" cannot. The additional beauty of this approach is that it allows students, even the youngest among them, to take an active role in problem solving so they can learn to manage conflict productively. It also allows an opportunity for students and teachers to join in an effort to solve the problem together rather than blaming each other. From there, it's much easier to take the approach that this is about "you and me against the problem" rather than "you against me." In the process we build relationships and trust. We all know that if we deal well with each other during conflict, we can trust each other anywhere.

Solution-Focused Problem Solving

Negotiators and authors McMains and Mullins (2006) cautioned that premature "problem solving is a trap that a communicator should avoid" (p. 253). However, we all recognize that in critical incidents, it is a given that some solution, whether temporary or permanent, must be found. In this context, Mike Webster (2008), a hostage negotiator and trainer from British Columbia, made a distinction between "solution *focused* and solution *forced*" (p. 31) problem solving. He noted that the first requires the negotiator to listen and work within the person's frame of reference, whereas the latter is negotiator imposition and should be avoided.

He studied thirty audiotapes of real crisis negotiations in Canada, looking for evidence of active listening techniques. Although he expected a 25 percent usage rate, through detailed content analysis he found that negotiators used active listening only 13 percent of the time. This surprising discovery raised an interesting question: What enabled negotiators to remain successful despite a paucity of active listening? Webster concluded that it was the problem-solving skills of the negotiator that made this possible.

This led him to consider the role of problem solving in more depth. Attempting to determine exactly what kind of problem solving was most effective led him to the field of brief solution-focused therapy. Solution-focused problem solving relies on the use of specific questions to assist individuals in reinterpreting their problems. Individuals are asked to recall times when they were able to handle circumstances more effectively and consider what allowed them to do so. Webster noted, "Problems are not static, they change over time" (p. 31). With this in mind, the negotiator assists the subject in reframing the issue by asking "exception" questions, such as: "What did you do then [when you weren't in this crisis] and how can we bring some of that out now? . . . Was there ever a time in the past when this wasn't so bad? Let's look at what you were doing then. . . . If there was a miracle last night and you got what you wanted, what would it be like?" (p. 7).

It is important to note that this form of problem solving relies on the use of questions rather than suggestions or declaratives. Negotiators confirm the usefulness of this strategy even in high stakes negotiation.

Four Helpful Questions

I asked the administrators I worked with during the course of my study to experiment with similar questions. The four I adapted from Webster (2000; see also Dolan, 2004; Winslade & Monk, 2008) are as follows:

- The exception question: What's going on when X isn't happening?
- The outcome question: Pretend you've solved X. How would your life have changed?
- The coping question: That sounds tough. How do you manage day to day?
- The relationship question: What would so-and-so say is different when you aren't doing X?

These questions allow space for us to wonder with our students about what might be possible. These questions can be useful, but they must be asked sensitively and carefully. They are not "magic bullets" but simply ways to gently offer alternatives to the power struggles that sometimes characterize student–teacher relationships. These moments of open and supportive speculation may be the first time that many students have had to consider with their teachers how they might change the way they are seen by others and themselves.

Asking exception questions, one administrator told me, "worked better for the older kids" and added that "using a short time frame worked best" because these questions can be intense. I feel compelled to counter that I have used these questions with younger children to good effect. She said,

> The coping question was good for face saving because it provided an opportunity to focus on times when the student was able to manage the situation, and it also provided a way for the student to think about the future. One of the things that surprises kids is that they're very personal questions. [So] I ask their permission to ask them tricky questions. It's unfair to pierce that deeply without some warning.

She also found that responses to the use of questions were variable: "Some were grateful, and in a way became more optimistic. Some actually got a bit irritated. They were a little suspicious, or maybe they doubted my sincerity, I'm not sure." She speculated on the reasons for this.

> I think it was contrary to their self-image: "I'm the kid who doesn't have a lot of control over their lives, and I'm someone who shows up late, I'm someone that people get mad at a lot at school, and I let myself and people down all the time." I just wonder [if] some of them were puzzled to have that pointed out to them, "Look, this day, this day, this day you were here on time." One said, "Maybe the teacher just didn't mark me as late." Another was surprised. "Yeah. I guess I did. Isn't that weird?"

This underscores the need to be observant and sensitive to how students may be interpreting our intentions. It also underscores the importance of hearing out any concerns or complaints the students may have non-defensively and with genuine curiosity before we ask about exceptions.

Overall, the administrators found the approach useful: "I want to include this in my ongoing practice on a regular basis." One educator described an incident involving a grade nine student who was having a difficult time with a teacher where the use of problem-solving questions was effective:

> So it was really interesting because it started off that all the teachers are picking on her, all the teachers don't give her a chance, all the teachers look at her as a troublemaker . . . well, [through the use of exception questions] by the end of the session, we were down to one teacher and only one class.

He noted that even when feeling skeptical, it was important to listen, because "that's the way they perceive it, so you have to work with them. Like the [hostage negotiation] research says, if you don't at least lend an ear and say, 'OK, well that could be possible,' you won't make any inroads." Once the source of the problem was more clearly identified, he was able to move forward by asking, "How do things need to be in this particular class to be better?" He used exception questions effectively to de-escalate the student's mother as well. He set out specific times each week to meet and listen to her: "It's been pleasing to see that shift in mind-set as well. You know, we have to work on this together. [It's] getting them off the bench of blame, blame, blame. I'm angry, I'm venting, I'm going to keep yelling. It gets them to completely redirect their thinking onto, 'OK, when the problem's gone, things are going to look like this.' It gets the kids to actually think ahead, and it isolates them from the emotion of the actual incident or incidents. OK when is the problem better? Let's start there."

As mentioned, the use of questions also assists a move to more rational thinking, as confirmed by current brain research (Goleman, 1995; Goulston, 2010; Lynch, 1985).

One Knot at a Time, or Miss Piggy's Third Law

As I mentioned in Chapter 9, Norm is an avid sailor. While I am not a particularly happy sailor, my experience on the sailboat has provided me with a number of useful metaphors. This one has to do with problem solving.

If you've ever done any sailing, you know that as you sail, you have to contend with a large amount of "line" (don't ever call it rope or you'll embarrass yourself, and your sailing buddies will ostracize you forever). From time to time, this line can become tangled on the floor of the cockpit, posing a safety hazard. The first time this happened, Norm asked me to gather up the line and hang it on a cleat at the front of the cockpit. Enthusiastically, I dived in. Within minutes, it was clear that I was making no progress and had made the situation worse.

Patiently Norm said, "You know, there's a better way to do that. What you have to do is find the end of the rope and untie the first knot. Then find the second knot, and the third one. The rope will untangle itself."

I have found this a useful metaphor ever since. When we're confronted with a crisis or a difficult problem, it's easy to see it as a mass of tangles and become overwhelmed. The situation can be made manageable by simply untying the line one knot at a time.

This lesson has been underscored for me many times over the years, but none so humorously as during the early 1990s at a workshop conducted by my late friend Herb Lovett.

Herb was talking to a group of teachers and support staff about supporting people with so-called "difficult behaviour." About twenty minutes into his presentation, a woman from the back of the room stood up and said, "All of this is well and good, but what I want to know is this. What are we going to do about the crack babies?" (In the early 1990s a considerable amount of time and media attention was given to the problem of crack-addicted babies.) "They're coming to school, and we're not ready for them!"

In my visual brain, I had a picture of a long line of small children, lock step with lunch kits in hand, walking zombielike toward the front door of the school. Around the room there was a bit of eye-rolling, but Herb didn't discount the woman's concern. With a perfectly straight face, he said, "In these instances, I like to invoke Miss Piggy's third law." The audience (and the woman with the question) looked puzzled. A ripple of laughter went through the room.

"Yes," he continued. "Miss Piggy says never try to eat anything bigger than you can lift."

The audience promptly dissolved into laughter. But Herb was right. It's only ever one "crack baby" at a time—or one knot at a time, to mix a couple of metaphors. If we can keep from becoming overwhelmed and thinking catastrophically, we will be in a much better position to solve the problems we encounter. Especially during crisis, it is important to keep our heads and think logically. What's one thing we can do? What's the first thing? The next? Proceed from there.

Negotiation Is a Series of Small Agreements

Dominick Misino successfully negotiated the Lufthansa Flight 592 hijacking by an Ethiopian national at Kennedy Airport in New York in 1993. He had only a brief window of opportunity (forty-five minutes before touchdown) to conduct the negotiation, and he had to do it from the aircraft control centre. It's easy to imagine the stress he was under: a short time frame and a highly distraught individual 35,000 feet in the air with a gun aimed at the pilot's head. Through skilful negotiation, Misino was able to defuse the situation, bring the plane to a safe landing in a restricted area, and free the 105 hostages. Amazingly, the hijacker ultimately traded his gun for the pilot's sunglasses.

In describing the incident, Misino noted that "negotiation is always a series of small agreements." I have found this a useful way to think about problem-solving, and it is certainly the way mediators and negotiators in less fraught situations operate. Small agreements are more manageable and are cumulative. Each small agreement can build trust, a sense of safety, and an enhanced relationship, and each subsequent agreement makes it easier to negotiate and arrive at the next one. While this may sound like a daunting enterprise that could take up far too much time, consider the short period Misino had to resolve a highly charged situation.

An amusing postscript to this story: Misino told me that during the negotiation he'd asked for the hijacker's name. The man was reluctant to provide it, so Misino asked him to make something up. "I've got to call you something" he said. "OK," the hijacker replied. "You can call me Jack." Immediately, Misino's coach looked up in panic and said, "For God's sake, Dominick, don't say, 'Hi Jack!'"

Some proactive suggestions about supporting an inclusive, safe school culture are as follows.

Although there are certainly things that individual educators can do to work successfully with individual students who are upset or confrontational, there are also broader, school-wide approaches that can be considered. Katherine Herr (2006) stated, "There is something about merely asking certain questions within the context of a school that sends a ripple through it and begins to interrupt the way every day practices are viewed" (p. 187). Taking time to ask questions about disciplinary practices and their effects is an important beginning. One such question might be: How is a sense of belonging created and maintained in my school, and what are the practices, policies, and attitudes that support it? Conversely: how is a sense of belonging undermined in my school, and what are the policies, practices, and attitudes that contribute to its erosion? What school practices either support or undermine the possibility for student and parent input?

If we truly believe that a positive and inclusive school culture is the best prevention for difficult interchanges, the attention we pay to its development will be time well spent. Below are a few ideas:

- In a large high school in British Columbia, over ninety languages are spoken. Key to creating a sense of belonging is the close attention the principal and his staff pay to acknowledging these many diverse groups. For example, during school dances, they include music that represents the cultural backgrounds of the students. While part of the dance might include rock or indie music, another part includes Bangara and rap. Students are enthusiastic to learn about each other's music, and that is often a catalyst for more interaction and interest between what might otherwise have remained disparate and even hostile groups.

- Many schools are questioning the value of award ceremonies. This practice may seem a positive way to acknowledge student excellence, but the unfortunate side effect is that by calling attention to some students, others may be unintentionally alienated. It also creates a culture of extrinsic motivation. While some might say that receiving an award is an incentive to work harder, for some students such awards remain impossible goals. As some students are celebrated; others will feel increasingly hopeless.

- Many schools are questioning the efficacy and the ethics of time-out and other seclusion practices. Parents and advocacy groups are increasingly critical and vocal about the practice in some schools of isolating students as punishment. In some instances, students have been sent to small locked time-out rooms for indefinite periods. Some schools have reconsidered and removed forcible seclusion as an option. Instead, they have developed sensory-friendly rooms where students can retreat when overwhelmed by the classroom experience, or safe spaces like libraries and empty classrooms. There is a categorical difference between being sent to time-out and choosing the option of finding a safe space to regroup.

- The use of physical restraint is dangerous to both students and educators, and it is increasingly under question for its ethics and efficacy. Schools utilizing restraint are open to expensive legal battles, and the risks cannot be overstated. (See the Garrison interview in Appendix A for an expansion of this discussion.)

- Educators experience significant pressure to "manage" behaviour quickly and efficiently. When difficulties persist, a culture of blame is often the result. Teachers are blamed for poor management skills; students are blamed for causing trouble. Teachers become frustrated and worry that their competence will be called into question and that the other students in the class will suffer as a result of one student's behaviour. The student who is struggling often feels misunderstood and unheard. As students stressed to me, even the bystanders are affected. This destructive cycle most often ends with one of the parties leaving the situation. In most instances, it is the student who is forced to leave. It is clear that when students are systematically excluded, school problems are transformed into social problems.

- Co-teaching and greater collaboration among educators are important ways to improve teaching and provide mutual support and fresh ideas.

- Classroom rules and expectations are often generated by teachers without significant student input. When students are simply told what the rules are, they are not necessarily committed to abiding by them. Teachers have an opportunity to model democracy and gain important insights from students when classroom norms are generated, questioned, and formed collaboratively. Students are often the best resources for finding out what works and what doesn't. Kohn (2018) found that students were often even tougher on themselves than teachers might be, but noted that this also provided a rich opportunity for discussion and negotiation.

It is unfortunate that student perspectives are often underutilized. Asking students to join with teachers and administrators to interrogate rules, policies, and practices of discipline can result in more information and greater insight, and perhaps even more importantly, it can create lasting bonds and foster understanding. This collaboration can be accomplished through individual conversations or through the creation of more formalized committees. Disruptive students in particular are often overlooked as sources of information. Their perspectives can be highly illuminating.

Positing disruption as conflict requires a change of narrative, and the implications of such a shift should not be underestimated. It requires a change in the discourse from blame to curiosity, from telling to listening, from judgment to empathy, and, perhaps most revolutionary, it requires a shift in the power dynamic between educators and students. It is a commitment to partnership. At its heart, this approach asks us to move away from an attitude of "How can we fix you?" or "Where can we relocate you?" to "How can we work together to solve this problem?" Without such a shift, it is unlikely that the superimposition of new and improved strategies onto old paradigms will be effective. It is the underlying philosophy that gives the skills their power.

CHAPTER THIRTEEN

SOME FINAL THOUGHTS FROM NEGOTIATORS AND EDUCATORS

Some Final Words of Advice from Negotiators to Educators

At the conclusion of my interviews, I asked the hostage negotiators to comment on whether they thought the strategies they use in hostage negotiations could be applicable in the educational sector. The response was resounding. "I'm a parent, and I think every teacher should be trained in this!" "What I learned through negotiation training has helped me be a better parent, so I'm sure it would be useful for teachers, too." Consider these thoughts from other negotiators:

> There's a fine line between police officers and teachers. It's all about dealing with people, and kids are people too. My advice would be to be a good listener, to find out what's going on. Because if there's a disruptive kid or there's something going on in class, there is usually something at the root of that. Maybe there is something going on in his life. Being an educator, there's times there's got to be discipline, but it's all about talking to the kid and not being such a disciplinarian as someone who is listening.
>
> If a student's upset, now's the time to get to know them. Like negotiators, you've got a controlled environment, and you have authority figures. But it can't be a dictatorship. If you've got a student who's upset, first you have to make sure

you're not taking away their dignity. Whatever you do, you can't do it in front of the class. You may win temporarily, but you'll lose long term.

If you're an administrator who's saying, "Well, the code of conduct says . . .," you may be inadvertently, while you are trying to do your job, triggering this kid. So learning how to phrase things so it doesn't set the child off is a big, big skill.

You do need to be decisive—but maybe not at that moment. Asking kids if you can help won't make you look weak to other students. You have to have empathy. Unfortunately, some educators are like some law enforcement—they want to just say, "Sit down and shut up." Those aren't good negotiators. There has to be a level of mediation.

Oh, and I think the skills, just the basic skills would help so much! 'Cause, really, what you've got to do . . . just bring them down a bit, get them back, a little more rational. And you've got to appreciate that it might be because his pencil's broken but he's still freaked out because all this other shit's going on. To get the situation under control doesn't always take that much, just that sincerity—hey, this person is interested in me and concerned about me. I think it would be great for educators!

Consider also the following quote from a negotiator who spent significant time as a school liaison officer before becoming a hostage negotiator.

I don't like when I hear we have a zero-tolerance policy . . . I think it's lazy, it's ill advised, and it's ineffective . . . Your front-line educators have to be skilled. They have to have some basic knowledge of nonviolent crisis intervention, active listening, and keep an eye on their students. I don't think punishment generally deters people from acting out, at least in as far as violence goes. I don't like to hear where it's a quick fix in terms of, "OK, from now on, you're out if you do this." I think a team has to convene... knowledgeable people. Take a team approach to most of this stuff... It's fatal to under react. But overreacting I don't think is a happy story either.

Some Last Words from Educators

I asked educators if they felt that learning the skills used by hostage negotiators would be useful, and if so, how would these skills best be taught and learned. The administrators indicated that the skills found in hostage negotiation would be useful in schools. One said, "I've come away with some really solid reminders and a few new facts, and a few new skills. The importance of that calm persona, and lots of questions, and the demonstration that I'm willing to listen." Each of the educators enthusiastically endorsed training in this area for teachers, both in pre-service and ongoing in-service format. Two said,

> There's definitely a use if you're talking training; the mechanics of the conversation. Just to verbalize these concepts increases the level of conscious awareness of what and why, and I think [as] a result of that the effectiveness improves. It would [also] be interesting for people to be forced to look at who they are, how they relate to students.
>
> Providing a different tool and a mechanism for trying to work toward solutions in class instead of sending kids out and yelling at them. Often the beginner teacher will confront kids right in front of the rest of the class, which is problematic.

The educator group agreed that finding opportunities to support teachers in learning and implementing these skills across the district would be useful. As one pointed out, the result could be "a common language, and a common value—like the negotiators have."

These educators confirmed that the most helpful training they received in de-escalation techniques came from counselling, conflict resolution, and other leadership programs accessed outside traditional teacher education. They noted that in order for such training to be useful, participants must have opportunities for practice and in-depth immersion, something not typically offered in either pre-service or ongoing in-service training.

One noted that an optimal situation would involve the larger educational community. She recommended a district-wide approach that would begin with trustee education and move from there to the administrators, teachers, and support staff. Another suggested development of study groups on the topic that paralleled an approach already in existence within the district. She also noted some of the challenges involved:

> Specifically, in terms of a whole orientation, one of the things I'm curious about is how best to communicate that kind of mind set change, that narrative change? I'm also trying to think, how do we work with our staff? Because they're wanting to move toward the positive behaviour support model. That gives me the collywobbles! We talked about when things start fraying at the edges the tendency is to put in more rules. How that doesn't work. I think that's absolutely true.

All the teachers and administrators I spoke with worried about currently increasing budgetary cuts and their impact on school culture and climate. One said, "We're going to be running nonstop with very little reflection time. That compassion, that face-saving, empowering approach is going to be so important. This would be much more satisfying for the people working with students. I think it would feed their souls. Now wouldn't it be wonderful if school was one of the places where you can be heard?"

CHAPTER FOURTEEN

COMPARING PARACHUTISTS TO POTTERS

I began the study that gave rise to this book by asking if the relational, communication-based approaches used by hostage negotiators would have utility for educators in de-escalating disruptive students. Throughout the process I received significant confirmation from people in both fields and even indirectly from students that such a move would prove worthwhile. In fact, I found that some educators were already using some of these skills profitably. However, as I came to the end of this inquiry, I was surprised that the answer to my research question was not entirely clear. Would wholesale adoption of hostage negotiation training in education help educators? At this point, based on what I learned during this project, my best answer is a rousing "it depends."

My hesitation to fully endorse the importation of de-escalation strategies from the field of negotiation to education has little to do with the demonstrated effectiveness of such approaches or the abilities of teachers to incorporate them. It is clear that negotiators are highly successful in connecting with distraught individuals and resolving highly charged situations, and it is also clear that the skills they use are teachable and can be learned. However, during the course of my conversations with negotiators, educators, and students, I began to identify a number of caveats that could not be ignored.

I believe two distinct but related issues must be addressed before any attempt at comprehensive skill training within the educational sector will yield desired results. First, we must acknowledge and actively engage with the larger systemic factors that currently limit and even invalidate the use of these skills in education. For example, outdated authoritarian ideas about how misbehaviour should be addressed and the use of reward and punishment programs are incompatible with these approaches. Second, I believe that the success of this enterprise hinges on a redefinition of disruption from a problem located within the student to a conflict located within the interactive sphere of the student, learning environment, and teacher.

Freiberg and Lapointe (2006) noted that in order for education to fully move into the twenty-first century, "a philosophical change in the way educators think about classroom management" (p. 774) must first take place. According to these authors, such a paradigm shift must be a move away from teacher-directed classrooms and schools to student–teacher partnership and collaboration. In this view, teachers become resources and facilitators of student learning—co-conspirators, if you like. Villa, Thousand, and Nevin (2010) agreed, suggesting that such a change in perspective and practice has the potential to meet twenty-first century goals of democratic education and help increase student capacity in the areas of self-determination and social competence. Villa et al. proposed that such collaboration should move beyond curricular concerns to include how interactions between teachers and students take place. Greene (2008) envisions the role of teachers not as disciplinarians but rather as mentors and collaborative problem-solvers with the challenging students they support. His non-punitive problem solving approach has been validated in many school districts and juvenile detention centres, where rates of detention, suspension, restraint, seclusion, expulsion, and recidivism have been dramatically reduced without the use of rewards or punishment. His ground-breaking work stands as a testimony that working *with* students is far more effective than working *on* them.

A paradigm shift of this kind would provide a philosophically consistent context compatible with the use of negotiation skills. Without such a change, I am concerned that the approaches suggested by hostage negotiators could be used as a quick fix or a way to suppress conflict in service of preserving the status quo. We must go beyond seeing difficult interchanges as problems located within difficult students to a consideration of the larger issue of how education in the twenty-first century takes place.

In advocating for this paradigm shift, Freiberg and Lapointe (2006) brought forward another relevant consideration. These authors noted that classroom management must move from an orientation of intervention to one of prevention and that this would need to be "more than changing strategies" (p. 774) or simply adding more strategies to the teacher's "bag of tricks" (p. 774). Metaphors like the "bag of tricks," "toolbox," or "smorgasbord" are common in the vernacular of educators. These metaphors have a seductive and enduring appeal because they imply that an array of eclectic technologies can be collected, stored, and chosen by teachers for use on an ad hoc basis. Further, and appealing to both idealists and pragmatists, there is an implied promise of situational flexibility and teacher discretion. Is this approach really as effective as the metaphor lulls us into believing? Based on what I have learned during the course of this inquiry, I suggest it is not, primarily because many of the suggested techniques and strategies are in conflict with one another and not part of a unified approach.

As mentioned, many of the currently suggested skills, strategies, and programs for working with disruptive students arise from opposing ideologies. For example, the use of rewards and punishments to gain compliance from students stands in opposition to often stated ideals of intrinsic, pro-social-emotional learning and the development of student responsibility (Kohn, 1993, 2018; Greene, 2008). In addition, exclusionary practices like detention, time-out, suspension, and expulsion undermine the goals of belonging and inclusion espoused by many schools (Kunc, 1992). The dialectical tension created by such contradictory practices cannot be underestimated. Until such contradictions are addressed, I question whether the addition of more strategies into this confusing context would help or hinder.

Freiberg and Lapointe (2006) suggested that what is required is a change in focus from behaviourism to more person-centred approaches (p. 773). If we are to believe these authors, who have stated that education is experiencing an evolution from directiveness to collaboration, we must ask how it is such a change can best be facilitated. I believe that useful perspectives found in the field of conflict analysis and management may be profitably applied to these questions. Within this field, it is generally accepted that conflict is an inevitable part of the interactive human experience. This view represents a shift of narrative away from the more commonly held view that conflict is something to be avoided or suppressed. Conflict practitioners—and the negotiators I interviewed—suggest that conflict need not be considered negative and that it may lead to greater clarity and improved relationships. When managed well, conflict can help disputants to find suitably complex answers to complex problems. Redefining behaviour problems as interactive conflict is a central precursor to any shift from directiveness to collaboration.

Unfortunately, as mentioned in Chapter 1, student behaviour is seldom framed as conflict. Instead, it is more often viewed as an aberration, a deliberate mutiny on the part of the student and something to be swiftly dealt with in order to return to the real work of education— teaching the curriculum. We all know that education is far more than learning content. It is also about developing responsible, caring citizens who are able to deal well with each other. It is not hyperbole to suggest that the world depends on it. Educators have precious opportunities to model and support the development of such skills for students, but in order to do so, the prevailing culture of blame and attribution within education must first be confronted and challenged.

In Summary

It is obvious that effecting sweeping paradigmatic changes are far outside the scope of this book. With the caveats raised above, like the people I interviewed, I remain cautiously optimistic that training and skill development in hostage negotiation strategies might prove useful for educators working to change the paradigms of education.

As we grapple with the larger systemic issues, there is an opportunity that disarmament can simultaneously be brokered between "difficult" students and their teachers in smaller, incremental, and more personal ways.

Twenty-first century education presents educators with many complex problems. Disruptive student behaviour is often a symptom of such larger complexity, and disruptive students may well be the "canaries in the coalmine" of education who show us what is not working in our current educational practices. There are opportunities for educators to utilize the perspectives of students viewed as disruptive to begin to positively reframe the way education takes place. Excluding and marginalizing such students will effectively silence their contributions to the debate. This would be a critical loss since there is much to be learned from their direct experience. In order to determine the direction we must move, all voices and perspectives must be represented and heard.

In this respect, approaches like active listening should never become tools of manipulation or used to suppress uncomfortable truths. The approaches suggested by hostage negotiators in this book are often used as ways to accomplish immediate and pragmatic de-escalation of specific incidents and save lives. Negotiators have only one opportunity to interact with an individual in crisis. On the other hand, teachers have ongoing relationships with their students. This offers more opportunities for them to develop and build positive, respectful, empathetic relationships and to provide powerful role-modelling to their students. In this view, the introduction of communication strategies would not only be useful in de-escalating classroom crises but also a catalyst for educational transformation. It is my belief that when these skills are anchored in a philosophy of partnership, mutual respect, and community, they can go beyond the immediate to become a powerful way of forging the ongoing alliances we need for the future.

During the course of this project, I have sometimes felt that comparing hostage negotiators to educators was a bit like comparing parachutists to potters. Perhaps the divide between the two professional fields is not really so great after all. To quote one of the negotiators I interviewed, ultimately we recognize that "people are people, and behaviour is behaviour." It is my hope that this book will contribute to the dialogue within education as it evolves and changes and, further, might be of assistance to educators in demystifying the process of de-escalation.

Bernard Gassaway observed that "Conflict is like a spark, and there's a number of sparks that eventually turn into a fire. So the job of a teacher is to recognize the sparks. It is about that personal conversation, that personal interaction. I did not function well in classes when I saw the teacher did not like me. Relationships are the key. I will say it three times. Relationship, relationship, relationship."

Ron Garrison is located across the continent from Bernard Gassaway and worked for many years in an equally difficult school district where violence among teens and in the broader community happens frequently. He, too, stressed the need for relationships: "If there is a serious situation going on that is life threatening or has the potential for serious injury, relationships count for everything. It's about relationship, relationship, relationship."

I give these two gifted educators the last words: relationship, relationship, relationship.

EPILOGUE

SCHOOL SHOOTINGS

> You've got to have something to eat and a little love in your life before you can sit still long enough for any damn body's sermon on how to behave.
>
> —Billie Holiday

Initially, I thought this book would be relatively simple to write. However, in light of recent developments, I quickly realized I would need to address a current challenge in education—the incidence of school shootings—before suggesting alternative responses to disruption.

In recent years what appears to be an alarming increase in school shootings, primarily but not exclusively in the United States, has resulted in a public outcry for safety measures that have seldom been proposed in school settings. They include locked perimeter enclosures, more closed caption cameras (CCTV), increased police surveillance and presence both inside and outside schools, regular locker searches, complicated badge protocols, threat assessments, drug testing, sophisticated facial recognition programs, and even profiling to identify students who appear to be doing unusual things. Some people, including the current president of the United States, are even calling for teachers to be trained in the use of guns and allowed to carry weapons to school.

Many of these approaches might have seemed inconceivable a few decades ago, but they are not as new as we might think. For example, as early as 2008, a school board in a small town in Texas authorized teachers to come to school armed, even though there were only one hundred students and no reported crime in the community or the school (McKinley, 2008). Admittedly, this approach was an anomaly. In a Gallup poll conducted in March 2018, 75 percent of educators objected strongly to the idea that they must, in addition to everything else they are asked to do, also become unwilling adjuncts of law enforcement (Brenan, 2018).

In the current climate, such approaches are being seriously considered and implemented, and although many people continue to object, there seems to be a greater public appetite for the application of strong deterrent measures. In many places even zero-tolerance practices are seen as too soft. The danger is that we may now move from policies of detention, suspension, and expulsion to policies that un-hyperbolically include extermination. Rather than looking at gun control, something that many students, parents, and teachers are actively seeking (Jones &Sung, 2018), we are now staring down the barrel of even greater gun presence.

In this context it has become difficult to talk about non-coercive relational responses to crisis. But perhaps now, more than ever, we should be doing so. We must ask ourselves if these hard-line proposals will really help us prevent future events. Will making schools even more like prisons really make them safer? Both history and a proliferation of research suggest it will not(Daniel & Bondy, 2008; Day, Golench, MacDougall,& Beals-Gonzales, 1995; Pollack, Modzeleski,& Rooney, 2008; Mayer & Leone, 1999; Skiba et al., 2006).

The Safe School Initiative

While many of these safety protocols are relatively new to education, the discussion about how to keep schools safe is not. Following the 1999 school shooting that took place in Columbine, Colorado, the United States Secret Service National Threat Assessment Center joined with the Department of Education (2004) to create a document called the *Safe School Initiative*. They looked at the key elements of threat assessment in schools and created a guide for use in the creation of safe school climates.

In 2008 the same group published an ancillary piece called the *Bystander Report*. It included an expanded set of key findings with some interesting and perhaps counterintuitive recommendations. It is surprising that such disparate groups came together to work on this project in the first place—interesting bedfellows indeed—but even more surprising is how few educators are aware of these reports. In the years after each publication, I made a point of asking audiences of educators I spoke to whether they were aware of its existence. In groups of hundreds, and even thousands, over the years, few hands were ever raised. Perhaps this is why the general consensus is that little has been suggested or done to address these issues.

This might be a good time to briefly revisit the findings and recommendations of these reports. They are as follows.

Researchers found that targeted incidents are rarely sudden or impulsive. Despite widespread assumptions that most school shootings occur without previous warning signs and without anyone having previous knowledge, this was not found to be the case. Disturbingly, in many incidents other students not only knew but also were actively involved in some capacity. For example, in a school in Alaska, some students who knew a shooting was going to take place stood on the balcony of the library to watch and even film it. Despite the fact that most shooters didn't threaten their targets beforehand, in almost every case someone was already worried about the attacker's frame of mind.

Unsurprisingly, authors of these studies found that most attackers had access to weapons and were familiar with their use. They noted that many of the shooters had experienced significant losses or personal failures prior to the event and that many had considered or attempted suicide. Bullying, alienation, isolation, and previous suspension and expulsion figured strongly in the rationale and created the backdrop for many of the attacks. The research also showed that most events were stopped by means other than law enforcement and were generally short in duration.

Contrary to public opinion, and critically important in the context of recent events and proposed solutions like facial recognition and heavy-handed student identification threat assessments, the authors were adamant that—with the possible exception of white, middle class boys, (an unworkably large demographic)—no accurate profile of a student likely to engage in school violence exists. This strongly suggests that no diagnostic or predictive approaches will adequately prevent such an episode. This is a significant finding and worth repeating since many of the approaches under consideration and many that have been in place since Columbine are precisely what these authors rejected. Instead, they suggested that the most effective deterrent to episodes of school violence is close attention to school culture. Educators and the community, they suggested, must rely on their instincts and remain sensitive, observant, and aware of what is going on with students. This, it must be stressed, should not be confused with misguided surveillance and profiling efforts. The most effective approaches must be grounded in concern for the welfare of students not further and arbitrary ostracizing of students who appear different.

Technology Will Never Be a Substitute for Relationship

More surprising than the findings in the *Safe School Initiative* were the recommendations. Interestingly, all stressed the importance of relationship, listening, and belonging.

- Assessment of the school's emotional climate
- Emphasis on the importance of listening in schools
- Adoption of a strong but caring stance against the code of silence
- Prevention of and intervention in bullying
- Involvement of all members of the school community in planning, creating, and sustaining a school culture of safety and respect

- Development of trusting relationships between each student and at least one adult at school
- Creation of mechanisms for developing and sustaining safe school climates

What is particularly noteworthy about this list is that there is not a single mention of armed guards, metal detectors, advanced facial recognition, or armed teachers. If we need any more evidence to convince us that technology is not, and never has been, the answer to our prayers, consider the following.

In October 1997, sixteen-year-old Luke Woodham stabbed his mother to death, then went to his high school and shot nine students. Two students died, and seven others were wounded. As part of the *Bystander Report* (2008), interviewers asked Woodham whether metal detectors would have stopped him. His answer is a chilling reminder to us that technology will never be a substitute for relationship: "I wouldn't have cared. What's it going to do? I ran in there holding the gun out. I mean, people saw it. It wasn't like I was hiding it. I guess it could stop some things. But by the time somebody's already gotten into the school with a gun, it's usually gonna be just about too late."

The students I spoke with felt that many of the deterrents being proposed are laughably inadequate. For example, most schools are surrounded by large playing fields with either low fences or no fences at all. Many have banks of windows on the ground floor. Weapons, cigarettes, and drugs are easily tossed over any fence that does exist and could easily be passed through a window, thereby avoiding metal detection. From there, students tell us, despite quick-fixes like transparent backpacks and surprise locker searches, they are easily hidden and moved from place to place. It would be impossible and hugely expensive to have surveillance or human presence in every part of every school property. As we move closer to prisonlike strategies for schools, we should remember that in prisons with even greater security perimeters than schools will likely ever have, it has been impossible to monitor the exchange of weapons and drugs. So what are schools to do?

An Example of a Proactive School-Wide Response

Concerned about what they felt was an increase in disruption and even violence, the staff of one school convened to review a list of all its students. Their goal was simple, and in line with the recommendations of the *Safe School Initiative*: to ensure that each student was connected to at least one adult in the school. To start the process, each staff member identified and assigned themselves to students they already knew and had connections with. They made personal commitments to stay in regular contact with these students. When the first round of student to staff assignments ended, they were startled to note that some students had no one assigned to them. This was a red flag moment. Who were these students who had somehow slipped through the cracks? They went through the remaining list and made sure that every student had an adult liaison, and each staff member personally committed to actively working to create relationships with those students. At the end of the day, no student was left isolated and unaccounted for. This is an example of a simple, low-tech, and inexpensive way in which schools can work proactively to ensure that relationships are built and maintained between teachers and students and that potentially difficult issues are caught before they escalate. Prevention is always better than reactivity.

While an enterprise like this—teachers connecting with students on a regular basis—might seem a daunting task in a large school population, it needn't be. People typically think that relationship building is a time-consuming undertaking. As discussed in Chapter 4, negotiators are adamant that trusting relationships and bonds can be built much more quickly and effectively than people tend to think.

It has been a few years since the *Safe School Initiative* and the *Bystander Report* were published, and it is puzzling that so little has been done to incorporate the findings into mainstream policies and procedures. Many school districts still rely on zero-tolerance policies and the use of triage to deal with disruption. It may seem that these approaches are the most efficacious, but are they? Something we do know is that what most school shooters have in common is a history of detention, suspension, and expulsion. In the years since Columbine, research has unequivocally shown that while zero tolerance may be short term effective, in the long term it is dangerous and counterproductive. When we remove students from one environment, we are simply relocating them to another. As we have seen, these problems can come back to haunt us.

Changing the Conversation

The question after a tragic event like a school shooting is always "How can we make sure it never happens again?" Rightly so. There are actions we can and should take to ensure safety for all members of the school community. The trauma, anger, and fear associated with episodes of school violence can lead us to make reactive decisions. Paraphrasing H.L. Mencken; for every problem there is a simple solution, and it's invariably wrong. Much better to resist simple solutions and, before we take action, stop to consider whether what is being proposed will solve the problem or compound it.

One of the most dangerous and unintended consequences after a school shooting is how anger and fear change the way we think and talk not only about people in crisis but also people who present as noticeably "different." Because we desperately want to understand why these incidents occur and how we can prevent more of them, we are vulnerable to the appeal of faulty assumptions and quick-fix solutions. Let's take as an example the 2018 school shooting at Marjory Stoneman Douglas High School, where seventeen people were killed. Public outrage resulted in an outpouring of vitriol toward the shooter and a plethora of hard-line proposals. Even though the single common denominator in all incidents of school shootings is the presence of guns, and although students from the school have become vocal in protests demanding greater gun control, many of the suggestions that ensued were in favour of greater gun presence in schools (Stolberg, 2013).

Also disturbing was widespread speculation about the mental health of the shooter. The media, politicians, and public suggested that Nikolas Cruz had a mental illness, was autistic or was a sociopath. To date none of these claims have been substantiated. These armchair diagnoses are based on stereotypes and what the general public believes they know about mental illness and autism, both of which are generally misunderstood and overstated. However, these are powerful and dangerous ideas that take hold in the minds of the public and work to dehumanize the perpetrator and others who carry the same labels.

It is tempting, especially after a tragedy like this one, to view people who challenge us as fundamentally other than we are. In the wake of this incident, Cruz was called subhuman, unworthy of consideration or compassion, and not even worthy of living. These may be understandable emotional responses when people are angry and afraid, but they are dangerous. If we allow ourselves to believe there is a clearly drawn line between people like us and people like Cruz, and simply write him off as disordered, we may never learn anything that will be useful in preventing the next incident. Perhaps most alarming is that this line will inevitably shift to include more and more people whom we see as different or unusual. In that moment we risk transforming entire groups of people from "us" into "them." This is when our paranoia makes us most vulnerable to quick judgments and rash actions, and predisposes us to respond to the next student in crisis or the next student who carries a label of autism or mental illness with increasing suspicion and coerciveness. Will our fear then cause us to react fatally the next time a student acts out? History tells us that mob mentality and stereotypical thinking always end badly.

A Graphic Example

> People know what they do; they frequently know why they do what they do. But what they don't know is what what they do does.
>
> —Michel Foucault (1961)

One such misguided response was outlined in an op-ed piece (Barnes, 2018) in the *Oregonian/Oregon Live*. The story recounts an incident that occurred in an Oregon school. A young autistic student was profiled through several anonymous complaints and another student's comment supposedly overheard by the school librarian. The librarian thought she heard the autistic student referred to as "the shooter,". She became alarmed, and reported the conversation to the authorities to the authorities. The student who supposedly made the comment had no memory of saying this and was shocked and appalled at what ensued. He told the reporter that he actually liked and respected the autistic student.

The school, like many in the state of Oregon, was utilizing a threat assessment tool developed by John Van Dreal (2011). Van Dreal's model mandates that a multidisciplinary team meet to discuss any concerns about students. The team consists of school officials, law enforcement, and mental health professionals, and would seem to be a solid plan. However, what happened later was an unfortunate misunderstanding of Van Dreal's work and resulted in the profiling of this student based on several common stereotypes about school shooters. Because Columbine shooters Harris and Klebold wore trench coats and were reputed to have belonged to a "trench coat Mafia," this raised concerns for the team, since the autistic student also wore what appeared to be a trench coat. In fact,it was simply a heavy coat given to him by his father that he wore as a way to help himself regulate. Wearing weighted clothing is often helpful for autistic people. The team was also concerned about the student's keen interest in weapon forging, weaponry, and antique guns. These red-flag issues were compounded by his somewhat unusual social behaviour and unfortunately resulted in the team targeting him as a potential school shooter.

Once so identified, a barrage of interventions ensued, including a police visit to his home, random searches at school, a temporary suspension, and intensified profiling. The student and his family were distraught at the school's response, which they considered unwarranted and unfair. Despite protestations and explanations, the team's perceptions were seen as more legitimate than the family's. Despite numerous requests, the family was never told who the anonymous complainants were.

In the manual used by the school, Van Dreal noted that his model "is not intended to be a complete reference for school climate improvement" (p. 10). This is fair enough, since this is not his area of expertise. But note what happens when a model is indiscriminately applied, and fear and stereotype drive the investigation. Students like this young man are particularly vulnerable to being subjected to profiling. Issues like lack of affect, few friends, literal mindedness, awkward social interactions, and unusual movement and speech patterns (which are sometimes seen as markers of autism) may be easily misunderstood. Likewise, students with mental health issues who behave in atypical ways can be targeted for surveillance. This poses a huge risk for any student who presents as unusual. In the newspaper article, Bethany Barnes wonders, "What if the system was creating the very thing it was trying to prevent?" Angry and disillusioned at the school's approach to their son, the student's parents agreed and believe that what the system effectively did was create a school dropout and a traumatized young adult.

So What *Should* We Do?

> My point is not that everything is bad, but that everything is dangerous.
>
> —Michel Foucault (1982)

Am I suggesting we should do nothing? Of course not. Am I also suggesting what Cruz and other shooters did is OK? Again, of course not. What they did is abhorrent. But are there lessons to be learned from their actions and our responses? I believe there are, and that is the purpose of this book. Hostage negotiators have an interesting perspective that is worth sharing.

However, I'll admit that since the inception of Black Lives Matter and the exposure of how men, women, and children of colour continue to be treated by law enforcement in North America, it has become more difficult for me to talk about non-coercive conflict processes in the context of law enforcement and still be believed. The "shoot now, think later" actions of some police officers, and the response by juries and inquiries to these incidents, have starkly shown the continued and escalating existence of systemic racism. Is it hyperbolic to worry that if we arm teachers, they may kill more black kids than white kids? Many of my friends in communities of colour suggest it is not (Anderson & Accomando, 2018; Harriot, 2018; Jones & Sung, 2018; Scott, 2018).

The Civil Rights Data Collection (CRDC) snapshot of school discipline (2014) shows a shockingly disproportionate number of students of colour and students with disabilities served under IDEA in the United States who are subjected to restraint, seclusion, and other punitive measures like suspension and expulsion. In addition, referrals to law enforcement are far more prevalent within these groups. For example, "students with disabilities (served by IDEA) represent 12% of the student population, but 58% of those placed in seclusion or involuntary confinement, and 75% of those physically restrained at school to immobilize them or reduce their ability to move freely. Black students represent 19% of students with disabilities served by IDEA, but 36% of these students ... are restrained at school through the use of a mechanical device or equipment designed to restrict their freedom of movement" (p. 1). These researchers also note a disturbing trend toward suspension of preschoolers—again, particularly those designated as having disabilities and children of colour.

Who Can We Call on for Help?

These are sobering statistics that actually point to what we *shouldn't* do. The arm of law enforcement—hostage negotiators—that I have brought to this conversation does not support the use of force unless it is the very last resort. They resist profiling attempts and maintain that relational, communication-based responses will always be more effective than hard line interventions. They believe that relational approaches and the others outlined in this book are our best hope for safe resolution. With these negotiators, and many educators, I believe it is critically important that we do not give way to mass hysteria. When faced with unidentified and unpredictable threat, and when we feel most powerless, we risk reverting to stereotypical and simplistic thinking. We must resist that temptation. I am convinced there is a compelling reason that now, more than ever, we need to be thinking about proactive rather than reactive responses to these tragedies. We need to change the dangerous conversation currently circulating in our communities before it inadvertently causes even more carnage. It is to be hoped that cool heads will prevail.

REFERENCES

Abcarian, R. (2018). The tender, terrifying truth about what happened in the Trader Joe's hostage seige. *Los Angeles Times.* http://www.latimes.com/local/la-me-abcarian-hostage-20180803-story.html

Adair, D. C. (2001). Poverty and the (broken) promise of education. *Harvard Educational Review, 71*(2), 217–239.

Alliance for Excellent Education. (2003). *Fact sheet: The impact of education on health and well-being.* Washington, DC: Author.

Alliance for Excellent Education. (2009). *Fact sheet: Students with disabilities in US high schools.* Washington, DC: Author.

Andreas, M. (2011). *Sweet fruit from the bitter tree: 61 stories ofcreative and compassionate ways out of conflict.*Boulder; CO. Real People Press.

Anderson & Accomando. (2018). The cynical red herring of arming teachers. *Psychology Today.* https://www.psychologytoday.com/us/blog/benign - bigotry/201802/the - cynical - red - herring - arming - teachers

Astor, R. A., Guerra, N., & Van Acker, R. (2010). How can we improve school safety research? *Educational Researcher, 39,* 69–78. doi:10.3102/0013189X09357619

Auerbach, C. F., & Silverstein, L. B. (2003). *Qualitative data: An introduction to coding and analysis.* New York, NY: New York University Press.

Barnes, B. (2018). Targeted: A family and a quest to stop the next school shooter. *The Oregonian/Oregon Live.*

Barton, P. E. (2005). *One-third of a nation: Rising drop-out rates and declining opportunities.* Princeton, NJ: Policy Information Center, Educational Testing Service.

Bergin, C., & Bergin, D. A. (1999). Classroom discipline that promotes self-control. *Journal of Applied Developmental Psychology, 20,* 189–206. doi:10.1016/SO193-3973(99)00013-1

Bergin, D. A. (1999). Influences on classroom interest. *Educational Psychologist, 34,* 87–98. doi:10.1207/s15326985ep3402_2

Bohl, N. (1997). Post incident crisis counselling for hostage negotiators. In R. Rogan, M. R. Hammer, & C. R. Van Zandt (Eds.), *Dynamic processes of crisis negotiation: Theory, research and practice* (pp. 45–56). Westport, CT: Praeger.

Bolz, F., & Hershey, E. (1979). *Hostage cop: The story of the NYPD hostage negotiation team and the man who leads it.* New York, NY: Rawson Wade.

Brenan, M. (2018, March 16). Most U.S. teachers oppose carrying guns in schools. *GALLUP.* Retrieved from https://news.gallup.com/poll/229808/teachers - oppose - carrying - guns - schools.aspx

Brendtro, L. K., Brokenleg, M., & Van Bockern, S. (1998). *Reclaiming youth at risk: Our hope for the future.* Bloomington, IN: National Educational Service.

Brophy, J. (2006). History of research on classroom management. In C. Evertson & C. S. Weinstein (Eds.), *Handbook of classroom management: Research, practice and contemporary issues* (pp. 17–46). Mahwah, NJ: Lawrence Erlbaum.

Brouwers, A., &Tomic, W. (2000). A longitudinal study of teacher burnout and perceived self-efficacy in classroom management. *Teaching and Teacher Education, 16,* 239–253. doi:10.1016/S0742-051X(99)00057-8

Burgoon, J., & Hale, J. L. (2009). The fundamental topoi of relational communication. *Communication Monographs, 51,* 193–214. doi:10.1080/03637758409390195

Canter, L. (1988). Let the educator beware: A response to Curwin and Mendler. *Educational Leadership, 46,* 71–73.

Casey, A., Hill, J.,& Goodyear, V. (2014). "PE doesn't stand for physical education, it stands for public embarrassment": Voicing experiences and proffering solutions to girls' disengagement in physical education. In S. B. Flory, A. Tischler, & S. Sanders (Eds.), *Sociocultural issues in physical edutation: Case studies for teachers.* Rowan & Littlefield.

Charles, L. (2007). Disarming people with words: Strategies of interactional communication that crisis (hostage) negotiators share with systemic clinicians. *Journal of Marital and Family Therapy, 33,* 51–68.

Chiu, L. H., &Tulley, M. (1997). Student preferences of teacher discipline styles. *Journal of Instructional Psychology, 24,* 168–176.

Cloke, K. (2001). *Mediating dangerously: The frontiers of conflict resolution.* San Francisco, CA: Jossey-Bass.

Cobb, S. (2013). *Speaking of violence: The politics and poetics of narrative in conflict resolution.* New York, NY: Oxford University Press.

Cohen, R. (2005). *Students resolving conflict: Peer mediation in schools.* Tucson, AZ:Good Year Books.

Cornell, D. G., & Mayer, M. J. (2010). Why do school order and safety matter? *Educational Researcher, 39,* 7–15.

Cothran, D. J., Hodges Kulinna, P., &Garrahy, D. A. (2003). "This is kind of giving a secret away...": Students' perspectives on effective class management. *Teaching and Teacher Education, 19*, 435–444.

Crowley, E. P. (1993). A qualitative analysis of mainstreamed behaviorally disordered aggressive adolescents' perceptions of helpful and unhelpful teacher attitudes and behaviors. *Exceptionality, 4*, 131–151.

Cox, J. (n.d.). K-12 News, lessons and shared resources by teachers for teachers. *Teach Hub.* Retrieved from http://www.teachhub.com/two - ten - classroom - management - method

Curwin, R. L. (1988). Packaged discipline programs: Let the buyer beware. *Educational Leadership, 46*(2), 68–71.

Daniel, Y., & Bondy, K. (2008). Safe schools and zero tolerance: Policy programs and practice. *Canadian Journal of Educational Administration and Policy Issue, 70.* Retrieved from http://umanitoba.ca/publications/cjeap/pdf_files/daniel.pdf

Day, D. M., Golench, C. A., MacDougall, J., & Beals-Gonzales, C. A. (1995). *School-based violence prevention in Canada: Results of a national survey of policies and programs.* Toronto, ON: Earlscourt Child and Family Centre.

De Franco, A. https://www.brainyquote.com/quotes/ani _ difranco _ 377836

De Waal, F. (2009). *The age of empathy: Nature's lessons for a kinder society.* Toronto, ON: McLelland & Stewart.

Dewey, J. (1913). *Interest and effort in education.* Boston, MA: Houghton Mifflin.

Dolan, J. T., & Fusilier, G. D. (1989, April). A guide for first responders to hostage situations. In *Crisis negotiations: A compendium* (pp.

122–126). Quantico, VA: Federal Bureau of Investigation, US Department of Justice.

Dolan, Y. (2004). How to help people go on when nothing is the same: A solution focused approach to the pragmatics of hope. In S. Madigan (Ed.), *Therapeutic conversations 5: Therapy from the outside in: Collected essays, therapeutic questions and workshop handouts* (pp.123–131). Vancouver, BC: Yaletown Family Therapy.

Donohue, W. A., Ranesh, C., & Borchgrevink, C. (1991). Crisis bargaining: Tracking relational paradox in hostage negotiation. *International Journal of Conflict Management, 2,* 258–274.

Donohue, W. A., & Roberto, A. J. (1993). Relational development as negotiated order in hostage negotiations. *Human Communication, 20,* 175–198.

Dreikurs, R. G., & Grey, L. (1993). *Logical consequences: A new approach to discipline.* New York, NY: Plume.

Ellis, J. (1997). What a seriously at-risk student would really like to say to teachers about classroom management. *Education Canada, 37,* 17–21.

Emmer, E. T., &Gerwels, M. C. (2006). Classroom management in middle and high school classrooms. In C. M. Evertson& C. S. Weinstein (Eds.), *Handbook of classroom management: Research, practice and contemporary issues* (pp. 407–437).Mahwah, NJ: Lawrence Erlbaum.

Erickson, E. H. (1963). *Childhood and society* (2nd ed.). New York, NY: W. W. Norton.

Evertson, C. M., & Weinstein, C. S. (2006). Classroom management as a field of inquiry. In C. M. Evertson & C. S. Weinstein (Eds.), *Handbook of classroom management: Research, practice and contemporary issues* (pp. 3–15). Mahwah, NJ: Lawrence Erlbaum.

Fang, Z. (1996). A review of research on teacher beliefs and practices. *Educational Research, 38*(1), 47–65.

Federal Bureau of Investigation. (2003, July). *FBI national crisis negotiation course.* Quantico, VA: Author.

Fisher, R. & Brown, S. (1989). *Getting together: Building relationships as we negotiate.* New York, NY: Penguin Books.

Folger, J. P., Poole, M. S., &Stutman, R. K. (2005). *Working through conflict: Strategies for relationships, groups and organizations.* Boston, MA: Pearson.

Foucault, M. (1980). *Power/knowledge: Selected interviews & other writings 1972–1977.* New York, NY: Pantheon.

Freiberg, H. J., & Lapointe, J. M. (2006). Research-based programs for preventing and solving discipline problems. In C. M. Evertson & C. S. Weinstein (Eds.), *Handbook of classroom management: Research, practice and contemporary issues* (pp. 735–782). Mahwah, NJ: Lawrence Erlbaum.

Froman, L., & Glorioso, J. (1984). Applying communications theory to hostage negotiations. *The Police Chief, 51,* 59–60.

Gassaway, B. (2006). *Reflections of an urban high school principal.* Jamaica: XenoGass ALG.

Gassaway, B. (2007). *Suicide by educator.* www.bernardgassaway.com

Giroux, H. A. (2009, April 20). The tragedy of youth deepens: Ten years after Columbine. *Out of Bounds Magazine.* Retrieved from http://www.counterpunch.org/giroux04212009.html

Glasser, W. (1969). *Schools without failure.* New York, NY: Harper & Row.

Glasser, W. (1986). *Control theory in the classroom.* New York, NY: Harper & Row.

Glasser, W. (1992). *The quality school: Managing students without coercion* (2nd expanded ed.). Harper Perennial, a Division of HarperCollins Publishers.

Glickman, C. D., & Tamashiro, R. T. (1980). Clarifying teachers' beliefs about discipline. *Educational Leadership, 37,* 459–464.

Goergen, M. G. (2006). *Crisis negotiation training.* Minneapolis, MN: Eagle Training.

Goleman, D. (1995). *Emotional intelligence.* New York, NY:Bantam Dell.

Goulston, M. (2010). *Just listen: Discover the secret of getting through to absolutely anyone.* New York, NY: Amacom.

Greene, R. (2008). *Lost at school: Why our kids with behavioral challenges are falling through the cracks, and how we can help them.* New York, NY: Scribner.

Greenstone, J. L. (2005). *The elements of police hostage and crisis negotiations: Critical incidents and how to respond to them.* New York, NY: The Hawthorne Press.

Gresham, F. M., McIntyre, L. L., Olson-Tinker, H., Dolstra, L., McLaughlin, V., & Van, M. (2004). Relevance of functional behavioural assessment research for school-based interventions and positive behavioural support. *Research in Developmental Disabilities, 25,* 19–37.

Gussin Paley, V. (1993). *You can't say you can't play.* Harvard University Press.

Gussin Paley, V. & Coles, R. (1991). *The boy who would be helicopter.* Harvard University Press.

Habel, J., Bloom, L. A., Ray, M. R., & Bacon, E. (1999). Consumer reports: What students with behavioral disorders say about school. *Remedial and Special Education, 20*, 93–105.

Hammer, M. R. (1997). Negotiating across the cultural divide: Intercultural dynamics in crisis incidents. In R. Rogan, M. R. Hammer, & C. R. Van Zandt (Eds.), *Dynamic processes of crisis negotiation: Theory, research and practice* (pp. 105–114). Westport, CT: Praeger.

Hammer, M. R. (2004). *The intercultural conflict style inventory: A conceptual framework and measure of intercultural conflict approaches* (IACM 17th international conference paper). Retrieved from http://papers.ssrn.com/sol3/papers.cfm?abstract_id=601981#

Hammer, M. R. (2007). *Saving lives: The S.A.F.E. model for resolving hostage and crisis incidents.* Westport, CT: Praeger.

Hare, A. (1997). Training crisis negotiators: Updating negotiation techniques and training. In R. Rogan, M. R. Hammer & C. R. Van Zandt (Eds.), *Dynamic processes of crisis negotiation: Theory, research and practice* (pp. 151–160). Westport, CT: Praeger.

Harlow, C. W. (2003). *Education and correctional populations, Bureau of Justice statistics special report.*Washington, DC: US Department of Justice.

Harriot, M. (2018, March 8). Why armed teachers means dead black students, explained. *The Root.* Retrieved from https://www.theroot.com/why-armed-teachers-means-dead-black-students-explained-1823589890

Harris, P. E. (1928). *Changing conceptions of school discipline.* New York, NY: The MacMillan Company.

Herr, K. (2006). Honoring student voice through teacher research. In E. B. Keefe, V. M. Moore, & F. R. Duff (Eds.), *Listening to the experts: Students with disabilities speak out* (pp. 179–198). Baltimore, MD: Paul H. Brookes.

Hickok, G. (2014). *The myth of mirror neurons: The real neuroscience of communication*. W.W. Norton & Company Inc.

Horner, R., & Sugai, G. (2004). *School-wide positive behavioral support: Implementers' blueprint and self-assessment.* Eugene, OR: Office of Special Education Programs and theCenter on Positive Behavioral Support. University of Oregon.

Hyman, I. A., Kay, B., Tabori, A., Weber, M., Mahon, M., & Cohen, I. (2006). Bullying: theory, research and interventions. In C. M. Evertson& C. S. Weinstein (Eds.), *Handbook of classroom management: Research, practice and contemporary issues* (pp. 855–884). Mahwah, NJ: Lawrence Earlbaum.

Hyman, I. A., & Perone, D. C. (1998). The other side of school violence: Educator policies and practices that may contribute to student misbehavior. *Journal of School Psychology, 36,* 7–27.

Ifill, S.(2018, March 5). Children will be the victims of armed teachers. *Time.* Retrieved from http://time.com/5186040/sherrilyn-ifill-black-children-classroom/

International Association of Chiefs of Police & Federal Law Enforcement Training Center. (2010). *Hostage negotiation study guide 2010.* Retrieved from http://www.learning-for-life.org/exploring/lawenforcement/study/hostage.pdf

Ireland, C. A., & Vecchi, G. M. (2009). The behavioral influence stairway model (BISM): A framework for managing terrorist crisis situations? *Behavioral Sciences of Terrorism and Political Aggression, 1,* 203–218. doi:10.1080/19434470903017722

Johnson, B., Whittington, V., & Oswald, M. (1994). Teachers' views on school discipline: A theoretical framework. *Cambridge Journal of Education, 24,* 261–276. doi:10.1080/0305764940240209

Johnson, D., & Johnson, R. (1996). Conflict resolution and peer mediation programs in elementary and secondary schools: A review of the research. *Review of Educational Research, 66,* *459–506.* doi:10.3102/00346543066004459

Johnson, D., & Johnson, R. (2006). Conflict resolution, peer mediation, and peacemaking. In C. M. Evertson & C. S. Weinstein (Eds.), *Handbook of classroom management: Research, practice and contemporary issues* (pp. 803–831). Mahwah, NJ: Lawrence Erlbaum.

Jones, A. & Sung, C. (2018). These parents feel like America already has a target on their kids' backs. Giving teachers guns won't help. *CNN*.Retrieved from https://www.cnn.com/2018/03/08/us/arming-school-staff-race-debate/index.html.

Jull, S. (2000). Youth violence, schools, and the management question: A discussion of zero tolerance and equity in public schooling. *Canadian Journal of Educational Administration and Policy, 17.* Retrieved from http://www.umanitoba.ca / publications / cjeap / articles / jull.html

Kagan, D. M. (1992). Implications of research on teacher belief. *Educational Psychologist, 27,* 65–90.

Keefe, E. B., Moore, V. M., & Duff, F. R. (2006). *Listening to the experts: Students with disabilities speak out.* Baltimore MD: Paul Brookes.

Kennedy, M. M. (1999). The role of preservice teacher education. In L. Darling-Hammond & G. Sykes (Eds.), *Teaching as the learning profession: Handbook of teaching and policy* (pp. 54–86). San Francisco, CA: Jossey-Bass.

Kim, B. (2001). Social constructivism. In M. Orey (Ed.), *Emerging perspectives on learning, teaching, and technology.* Retrieved from http://projects.coe.uga.edu / epltt / index.php?title=Social _ Constructivism

Kohlrieser, G. (2006). *Hostage at the table: How leaders can overcome conflict, influence others, and raise performance.* San Francisco, CA: Jossey-Bass.

Kohn, A. (1990). *The brighter side of human nature: Altruism and empathy in everyday life.* New York, NY: Basic Books.

Kohn, A. (1993, 2018). *Punished by rewards: The trouble with gold stars, incentive plans, A's, praise and other bribes.* Boston, MA: Houghton Mifflin.

Kohn, A. (1996). *Beyond discipline: From compliance to community.* Alexandria, VA: ASCD.

Kunc, N. (1992). The need to belong: Rediscovering Maslow's hierarchy of needs. In R. Villa, J. Thousand, S. Stainback, & W. Stainback (Eds.), *Restructuring for caring and effective education* (pp. 25–39). Baltimore MA: Paul H. Brookes.

Kurtis, B. (1999). Talk to Me: Hostage negotiators of the NYPD. *Investigative Reports.* New York, NY: A&E Television Networks. Retrieved from http://www.latimes.com/local/la - me - abcarian - hostage - 20180803 - story.html

Landrum, T. J., & Kauffman, J. M. (2006). Behavioral approaches to classroom management. In C. M. Evertson & C. S. Weinstein, (Eds.), *Handbook of classroom management: Research, practice and contemporary issues* (pp. 47–71). Mahwah, CT: Lawrence Erlbaum.

Lather, P. (1993). Fertile obsession: Validity after poststructuralism. *The Sociological Quarterly, 34*(4), 673–693.

Le Baron, M. (2002). *Bridging troubled waters: Conflict resolution from the heart.* San Francisco, CA: Jossey-Bass.

Leedy, P. D., & Ormrod, J. E. (2005). *Practical research: Planning and design.* Upper Saddle River, NJ: Pearson Merill Prentice Hall.

Leviton, S. C., & Greenstone, J. L. (2002). The hostage and crisis negotiation's training laboratory: A program to enhance the basic and advanced training of police negotiators. *Journal of Police Crisis Negotiations, 2*(2), 21–33.

Lewis, R. (2006). Classroom discipline in Australia. In C. M. Evertson & C. S. Weinsteind (Eds.), *Handbook of classroom management: Research, practice and contemporary issues* (pp. 1193–1214). Mahwah, CT: Lawrence Erlbaum.

Lewis, T. J., Newcomer, L. L., Trussell, R., & Richter, M. (2006). Schoolwide positive behavior support: Building Systems to Develop and Maintain Appropriate Social Behavior. In C. M. Evertson & C. S. Weinstein (Eds.), *Handbook of classroom management: Research, practice and contemporary issues* (pp. 833–854). Mahwah, CT: Lawrence Erlbaum.

Lindeman Nelson, H. (2001). *Damaged identities: Narrative repair.* Ithaca, NY: Cornell University Press.

Lovett, H. (1996). *Learning to listen: Positive approaches and people with difficult behavior.* Baltimore, MD: Paul H. Brookes.

Lynch, J. J. (1985). *The language of the heart: The body's response to human dialogue.* New York, NY: Basic Books.

Madrigal, D. O., Bowman, D. R., & McClain, B. U. (2009). Introducing the four-phase model of hostage negotiation. *Journal of Police Crisis Negotiations, 9,* 119–133.

Martin, S. D. (2004). Finding balance: Impact of classroom management conceptions on developing teacher practice. *Teaching and Teacher Education, 20,* 405–422.

Marzano, R. J., Gaddy, B. B., Foseid, M. C., Foseid, M. P., & Marzano, J. S. (2005). *A handbook for classroom management that works.* Upper Saddle River, NJ: Pearson.

Matthews, W. J. (2003). Constructivism in the classroom: Epistemology, history, and empirical evidence. *Teacher Education Quarterly, 30*(3),51–64.Retrieved from http://findarticles.com/p/articles/mi _ qa3960/is _ 200307/ai _ n9248485

Mayer, B. S. (2004). *Beyond neutrality: Confronting the crisis in conflict resolution*. San Francisco, CA: Jossey-Bass.

Mayer, G. R. (1995). Preventing antisocial behavior in the schools. *Journal of Applied Behavior Analysis, 28*, 467–478.

Mayer, G. R. (2001). Antisocial behavior: Its causes and prevention within our schools. *Education and Treatment of Children, 24*, 414–429.

Mayer, M. J., & Furlong, M. J. (2010). How safe are our schools? *Educational Researcher, 39*, 16–26.

Mayer, M. J., & Leone, P. E. (1999). A structural analysis of school violence and disruption: Implications for creating safer schools. *Education and Treatment of Children, 22*, 333–356.

McDaniel, T. (1982). How to be an effective authoritarian: A back-to-basics approach to classroom discipline. *The Clearing House, 55*, 245–247.

McKinley, J. C. (2008). In Texas school, teachers carry books and guns. *New York Times*, https://www.nytimes.com / 2008 / 08 / 29 / us / 29texas.html

McMains, M. J. (2002). Active listening: The Aspirin of negotiations. *Journal of Police Crisis Negotiations, 2*(2), 69–74.

McMains, M. J., & Lancely, F. (2003). The use of crisis intervention principles in hostage negotiation: Attitudes, communication and treatment. *Journal of Crisis Negotiation, 3*, 3–30.

McMains, M. J., & Mullins, W. C. (2006). *Crisis negotiations: Managing critical incidents and hostage situations in law enforcement and corrections.* New York, NY: LexisNexis.

Mencken, H.L. https://www.brainyquote.com/quotes/h_1_mencken_141512.

Merseth, K. K. (1996). Cases and case methods in teacher education. In J. Sikula (Ed.), *Handbook of research on teacher education* (pp. 722–744). Boston, MA: Harvard University.

Morgan, A. (2000). *What is narrative therapy? An easy to read introduction.* Adelaide. AUS: Dulwich Centre Publications.

Mulick, J. A., & Butter, E. M. (2005). Positive behavior support: A paternalistic utopian delusion. In J. W. Jacobson, R. A. Fox, & J. A. Mulick (Eds.), *Controversial therapies for developmental disabilities: Fad, fashion and science in professional practice* (pp. 385–404). Mahwah, NJ: Lawrence Erlbaum.

Muller-Pinzler, L., Gazzola, V., Keysers, C., Sommer, J., Jansen, A., Frassle, S., . . . Paulus, F. M. (2015). Neural pathways of embarrassment and their modulation by social anxiety. *NeuroImage119*: 252–261.

Nelson, J. (1987). *Positive discipline.* New York, NY: Ballantine.

Newcomer, L. (2007). Classroom organization and management planning guide. Retrieved from http://www.swpbs.org/schoolwide/Training/files/newcomer_docs/Newcomer08_Classroom_PBS%20Planning_Guide.pdf.

Newcomer, L. (2007). Classroom positive behavaior support. Retrieved from https://www.pbis.org/common/cms/files/pbisresources/B8_Newcomer.pdf

Newman, K.S. (2004). *Rampage at school:The social roots of school shootings.* Basic Books.

Noesner, G. W., & Webster, M. (1997). Crisis intervention: Using active listening skills in negotiations. *FBI Law Enforcement Bulletin, 66*(8), 13–20.

Nucci, L. (2006). Classroom management for moral and social development. In C. M. Evertson& C. S. Weinstein (Eds.), *Handbook of classroom management: Research, practice and contemporary issues* (pp. 711–731). Mahwah, CT: Lawrence Erlbaum.

Nugent, W., & Halvorson, H. (1995). Testing the effects of active listening. *Research on Social Work Practice, 5,* 152–175.

O'Brien, R. (2001). *Um exame da abordagem metodológica da pesquisa ação* [An overview of the methodological approach of action research]. In Roberto Richardson (Ed.), *Teoria e prática da pesquisa ação [Theory and practice of action research].* Retrieved from http://www.web.ca/~robrien/papers/arfinal.html

Oetzel, J. G., & Ting-Toomey, S. (2006). *The SAGE handbook of conflict communication: Integrating theory, research and practice.* Thousand Oaks, CA: Sage.

Olson, K. (2009). *Wounded by school.* New York, NY: Teachers College Press.

Osher, D., Bear, G. G., Sprague, J. R., & Doyle, W. (2010). How can we improve school discipline? *Educational Researcher, 39,* 48–58. doi:10.3102/0013189X09357618

Page, B. (2006). *At-risk students: Feeling their pain, understanding their plight, accepting their defensive ploys.* Nashville, TN: Educational Dynamics Publications.

Pajares, M. F. (1992). Teachers' beliefs and educational research: cleaning up a messy construct. *Review of Educational Research, 62,* 307–332.

Phillips, B. (1999). Reformulating dispute narratives through active listening. *Conflict Resolution Quarterly,17,* 161–180.

Piaget, J. (1973). *To understand is to invent: The future of education.* New York, NY: Grossman.

Pianta, R. C. (2006). Classroom management and relationship between children and teachers: Implications for research and practice. In C. M. Evertson & C. S. Weinstein (Eds.), *Handbook of classroom management: Research, practice and contemporary issues* (pp. 685–709). Mahwah, CT: Lawrence Erlbaum.

Pollack, W. S., Modzeleski, W., & Rooney, G. (2008). *Prior knowledge of potential school-based violence: Information students learn may prevent a targetted attack.* Retrieved from http://www.secretservice.gov/ntac/bystander_study.pdf

Pomeroy, E. (1999). The teacher-student relationship in secondary school: Insights from excluded students. *British Journal of Sociology of Education, 20,* 465–482.

Pulver, C. (2017). *Be a Mr. Jenson.* https://www.youtube.com /watch?v=4p5286T_ kn0

Purdy, M. (1997). What is listening? In M. Purdy & D. Borisoff (Eds.), *Listening in everyday life: A personal and professional approach* (pp. 1–20). Lanham, MD: University Press of America.

Purdy, M., &Borisoff, D. (1997). *Listening in everyday life: A personal and professional approach.* Lanham, MD: University Press of America.

Render, G. F., Padilla, J. M., &Krank, H. M. (1989). Assertive discipline: A critical review and analysis. *Teachers' College Record, 90,* 607–630.

Reynolds, V. (2010).Doing justice as a path to sustainable community work. Dissertation, Tilburg University, Taos Institute.

Rogan, R. G., & Hammer, M. R. (1994). Crisis negotiations: A preliminary investigation of facework in naturalistic conflict discourse. *Journal of Applied Communication Research, 22,* 216–231.

Rogan, R. G., & Hammer, M. R. (1995). Assessing message affect in crisis negotiations: An exploratory study. *Human Communication Research, 21,* 553–574. doi:10.1111/j.1468-2958.1995.tb00358.x

Rogan, R. G., & Hammer, M. R. (2006). The emerging field of crisis/hostage negotiation: A communication-based perspective. In J. G. Oetzel & S. Ting-Toomey (Eds.), *The SAGE handbook of conflict communication: Integrating theory, research and practice* (pp. 451–473). Thousand Oaks, CA: Sage.

Rogan, R. G., Hammer, M. R., & Van Zandt, C. R. (1997). *Dynamic processes of crisis negotiation: Theory, research and practice.* Westport, CT: Praeger.

Rogers, R. R., &Farson, R.E. (1957). *Active listening.* Martino Fine Books.

Schlossberg, H. (1975). *Hostage negotiation.* Calgary, AB: Calgary Law Enforcement.

Schlossberg, H. (1979). Police response to hostage situations. In J. T. O'Brien & M. Marcus (Eds.), *Crime and justice in America* (pp. 209–220). New York, NY: Pergamon Press.

Schlossberg, H. (1980). Values and organization in hostage and crisis negotiation teams. *Annals of the New York Academy of Sciences, 347,* 113–116. Retrieved from http://www.ncjrs.gov / App / Publications / abstract.aspx?ID=70537

Schlossberg, H., & Freeman, L. (1974). *Psychologist with a gun.* New York, NY: Coward, McCann & Geoghegan.

Schwartz, P., & Kluth, P. (2007). *You're welcome: Positive and peaceful behavior supports for the inclusive classroom.* Portsmouth, UK: Heinemann.

Scott, E. (2018, February 18), A big question in the debate about arming teachers: What about racial bias? *The Washington Post.* Retrieved from https://www.washingtonpost.com/news/the-fix/wp/2018/02/23/a-big-question-in-the-debate-about-arming-teachers-what-about-racial-bias/?noredirect=on&utm_term=.ac5d5a034ee5

Skiba, R., & Petersen, R. (1999). The dark side of zero tolerance: Can punishment lead to safe schools? *Phi Delta Kappan, 80,* 372–376.

Skiba, R., Peterson, R., & Williams, T. (1997). Office referrals and suspension: Disciplinary intervention. *Education & Treatment of Children, 20,* 295–315.

Skiba, R., Reynolds, C. R., Graham, S., Sheres, P., Close Conoley, J., & Vasquez, E. (2006, February). *Are zero tolerance policies effective in the schools? An evidentiary review and recommendations.* Retrieved from http://www.pbismaryland.org/documents/Are%20Zero%20Tolerance%20policies%20effective%20APA%20Board%20report%20June%202006.pdf

Skinner, B. (1972). *Beyond freedom and dignity.* New York, NY: Bantam/Vintage.

Skinner, B. (1974). *About behaviorism.* New York, NY: Knopf.

Skinner, B. (1983). *A matter of consequences.* New York, NY: Knopf.

Slatkin, A. A. (2005). *Communication in crisis and hostage negotiations: Practical communication techniques, stratagems, and strategies for law enforcement, corrections and emergency service personnel in managing critical incidents.* Springfield, IL: Charles C. Thomas.

Smith, M.K. (2007). Action research. *The encyclopedia of informal education*. Retrieved from http://www.infed.org / research / b - actres.htm

Smith, R.,& Lamber, M. (2008). Assuming the best. *Educational Leadership 66*, 16–21.Retrieved from http://www.teachhub.com/ two - ten - classroom - management - method

Spaulding, A. (2005). *Looking at school violence through the eyes of secondary, public school teachers in the state of Texas: What role do teacher behaviors play?* Hawaii International Conference on Education, Hawaii.

Sprague, J., & Horner, R. (2000). *Prevention, multi-tiered support and data-based decision making.* Retrieved from http://starfsfolk.khi.is / ingvar / agi / Greinar / Sprague%20%20Horner%20PBS%20 paper.pdf

Stevens, C. (2009). *Listening to the noteworthy practitioner.* Master's thesis. Royal Roads University: Victoria, BC.

Strentz, T. (2006). *Psychological aspects of crisis.* Boca Raton, FL: Taylor and Francis.

Stolberg, S. G. (2013, April 2). Report sees guns as path to safety in schools. *The New York Times*. Retrieved from https://www.nytimes.com/2013/04/03/us/nra-details-plan-for-armed-school-guards.html

Sugai, G., & Horner, R. R. (2006). A promising approach for expanding and sustaining school-wide positive behavior support. *School Psychology Review, 35*, 245–259. Retrieved from http://www.nasponline.org/publications/spr/pdf / spr352sugai.pdf

Supaporn, S. (2000). High school students' perspectives about misbehavior. *Physical Educator, 57*, 124–135.

Taylor, P. J., & Donald, I. (2003). Foundations and evidence for an interaction-based approach to conflict negotiation. *International Journal of Conflict Management, 14,* 213–232.

Tannen, D. (1990). *You just don't understand.* Simon & Schuster.

Tavris, C. (1982). *Anger: The misunderstood emotion.* New York, NY. Simon & Schuster.

Thomlison, T. D. (1991, March). *Approaches for teaching empathic listening.* Paper presented at the Annual Meeting of the International Listening Association. Jacksonville, Florida.

Thompson, G. J., & Jenkins, J. B. (2004). *Verbal judo: The gentle art of persuasion.* New York, NY: Quill.

Thompson, L. (2001). *Hostage rescue manual: Tactics of the counter-terrorist.* London, UK: Greenhill Books.

Thoreau, H. D. (n.d.). Retrieved from https://www.goodreads.com / quotes / 56262 - if - i - repent - of - anything - it - is - very - likely - to

Thorson, S. (1996). The missing link: Students discuss school discipline. *Focus on Exceptional Children, 29*(3), 1–12.

Ting-Toomey, S., & Takai, J. (2006). Explaining intercultural conflict: Promising approaches and future directions. In Oetzel, J. G. & Ting-Toomey, S. (Eds.), *The SAGE handbook of conflict communication: Integrating theory, research, and practice* (pp. 691–723). Thousand Oaks CA: Sage.

Trouble in paradox: Active listening and the use of force in crisis negotiation: Interview with Mike Webster. (2008, January). *Crisis Intervention News,* 5–7. Retrieved from http://www.mediate.com/acrcrisisnegotiation/docs/ACR%20 Newsletter%20Jan2008.pdf

United States Secret Service National Threat Assessment Center & Department of Education. (2004). Retrieved from https://www2.ed.gov/admins/lead/safety/preventingattacksreport.pdf.. (2014). *Civil rights data collection: Data snapshot: school discipline.* Retrieved from https://www2.ed.gov/about/offices/list/ocr/docs/crdc-discipline-snapshot.pdf

US Department of Education Office for Civil Rights. (2014). *Civil rights data collection: Data snapshot: school discipline.* Retrieved from https://www2.ed.gov/about/offices/list/ocr/docs/crdc-discipline-snapshot.pdf

Van Acker, R., Grant, S. H., & Henry, D. (1996). Teacher and student behavior as a function of risk for aggression. *Education and Treatment of Children, 19*, 316–334.

Van Der Klift, E.,&Kunc. N. (1994). Beyond benevolence: Friendship and the politics of help. In J. Thousand, R. Villa, &A. Nevin (Eds.),*Creativity and collaborative learning: Apractical guide to empowering students and teachers.* Baltimore, MD: Paul Brookes Publishing.

Van Dreal, J. (2011). *Assessing student threats: A handbook for implementing the Salem-Keizer system.* OR: Rowman & Littlefield Publishers, Inc.

Van Hasselt, V. B. (2006). Crisis (hostage) negotiation training [abstract]. *Criminal Justice and Behavior, 33*, 56–59.

Van Hasselt, V. B., Romano, S. J., & Vecchi, G. M. (2008). Role playing. *Behavior Modification.* 248–263.

Vigotsky, L. V. (1962). *Thought and language.* Cambridge, MA: MIT Press.

Villa, R.,Thousand, J., & Nevin, A. (2010). *Collaborating with students in instruction and decision-making: The untapped resource.* Thousand Oaks, CA: Corwin Press.

Weaver, G. R. (1997). Psychological and cultural dimensions of hostage negotiation. In R. G. Rogan, M. R. Hammer, & C. R. Van Zandt (Eds.), *Dynamic processes of crisis negotiation: Theory, research and practice* (pp. 115–128). Westport, CT: Praeger.

Webster, M. (2000). *The psychology of managing hostage/barricade incidents: An aide memoire for negotiators and commanders.* Denman Island, BC: Centurion Consulting Services Ltd.

Winslade, J. & Monk, G. (2001). *Narrative mediation: A New Approach to Conflict Resolution.* San Francisco, CA: Jossey Bass.

Winslade, J., & Monk, G. (2007). *Narrative counseling in schools: Powerful and brief* (2nd edition). Thousand Oaks, CA: Corwin Press.

Winslade, J., & Monk, G. (2008). *Narrative mediation: Loosening the grip of conflict.* San Francisco, CA: Jossey-Bass.

Wise, S. (2009, April 21). *pnj.com.* Retrieved from http://www.pnj.com/article/20090421/NEWS01/ 90421012

Wiseman, T. (1996). Listening and empathy: A concept analysis of empathy. *Journal of Advanced Nursing, 23,* 1162–1167.

Wheatley, M. (2002). *The Servant Leader: From hero to host. An interview with Margaret Wheatley.* Retrieved from https://www.margaretwheatley.com/articles/herotohost.html

White, M. (n.d.).http://www.narrativeapproaches.com/resources/quotes/

Womack, D. F., & Walsh, K. (1997). A three-dimensional model of relationship development in hostage negotiations. In R. G. Rogan, M. R. Hammer, & C. R. Van Zandt (Eds.), *Dynamic processes of crisis negotiation: Theory, research and practice* (pp. 57–76). Westport, CT: Praeger.

Wong, H. K., & Wong, R. T. (2009). *The first days of school: How to be an effective teacher.* Mountainview, CA: Harry K. Wong.

Woolfolk Hoy, A., & Weinstein, C. S. (2006). Student and teacher perspectives on classroom management. In C. M. Evertson & C. S. Weinstein (Eds.), *Handbook of classroom management: Research, practice and contemporary issues* (pp. 181–211). Mahwah, CT: Laurence Erlbaum.

APPENDIX A

INTERVIEW WITH RON GARRISON ON RESTRAINT AND SECLUSION

The following is the partial transcript of an interview with Ron Garrison in early 2018. I include it because it gives a comprehensive view of the consequences of coercive responses to crisis events. As mentioned in the introduction and Chapter 4, Mr. Garrison is a retired educator with experience at all levels of the educational sector. He holds a master's degree in school safety and has been an expert witness in more than eighty-five cases involving restraint and seclusion.

Q: Ron, can you give us a brief recap of your legal work and, specifically, your expertise about restraint and seclusion?

RON: Sure. I was a student intern at Napa State Hospital in 1968 and a special education teacher through the 1970s. During the 1980s and 1990s, I worked for an American federal government organization that focused on institutional safety and security. After some time and a lack of continuing grant funding, this profession morphed into private practice, and I became an expert witness in civil litigation. At the end of my career, I had rendered expert legal opinions in eighty-five lawsuits throughout the United States.

Q: Are you a lawyer? How did this work relate to our topic here today on restraint and seclusion?

RON: I am not an attorney but an expert witness lawyers rely on in court to support their cases. Some of those eighty-five lawsuits involved my expert opinions that assisted injured party plaintiffs with their litigation, and some of those cases involved restraint and seclusion.

Q: So before we get into the details, what did you learn from your experiences as an expert witness regarding restraint and seclusion?

RON: Simply put, when many educators, support workers, or family members are in a situation where an individual has become aggressive, self-injurious, or even what is sometimes called noncompliant, they feel like they need to control the situation. They don't know what to do, so they resort to coercive tactics like restraint and seclusion. Although this seems to solve the problem in the short term, in the long term, it actually makes the problem far worse. I believe that using restraint and seclusion is a form of torture.

Q: OK, let's begin by exploring the connection between torture, restraint, and seclusion. To do this, I want to play the devil's advocate and put forth some of the arguments that are often used to justify the use of seclusion and restraint. For example, many people believe certain forms of torture may be necessary at times—for example, in times of war or civil unrest. Are these approaches effective?

RON: One would think so from all of the ideas and images our society is exposed to, both in fictional and nonfictional media representations. But in my opinion, and in the opinion of many others, torture is never useful, nor is it effective. Consider just one modern example, Abu Ghraib. Not only were the techniques used at Abu Ghraib overwhelmingly condemned as unethical, cruel, and inhumane, but also they didn't work!

These strategies are supposedly used to cause pain and humiliation as a way to change behaviour, but it's also vital to recognize that restraint and seclusion are essentially torture as well. So whether restraint and seclusion are used during wartime or in a so-called therapeutic context, restraint is still restraint and seclusion is still seclusion. If it is deemed to be torture in one context, you cannot claim that it is a therapeutic intervention just because you're trying to use it in a different context.

Q: You just talked about nonfictional media representations. Can you give us some examples of the fictional representations you mentioned?

RON: Popular media from *A Clockwork Orange* to *Star Wars* to *Orange Is the New Black* show a variety of torture and coercive techniques as major plot devices in their stories. These torturous practices include shock, deprivation, "force" lighting, and chemical restraints, among others, and are used in various ways to dramatically capture the attention of the viewers. Unfortunately, when people watch movies and TV, they can come to believe that these aversive and coercive techniques are effective in gaining control over a person or situation and should be used in some circumstances—except, of course, on ourselves!

Q: I get that watching restraint and seclusion in movies and on TV can lead a person to believe these techniques are effective. But when you're in court, how do you go about convincing the same juries that may have seen these films and been led to believe this is the best way to respond to crisis situations that restraint and seclusion are ineffective and harmful?

RON: Simply by changing perceptions through the use of evidence. As I said before, restraint and seclusion are often used as torture techniques, and they're still being used even though it has been conclusively shown that they're ineffective and harmful.

They are harmful not only to the person being tortured but also to the person doing the torturing. Darius Rejali writes in his book *Torture and Democracy* that, "organizational torture yields poor information, sweeps up many innocents, degrades organizational capabilities and destroys interrogators." We know that watching abuse also affects bystanders.

Q: How does watching abuse affect bystanders?

RON: There are many studies I can cite: Gregory Janson and Richard Hazler found that repetitive abuse affects bystanders and victims in similarly serious ways at the time the events occur and also later in life. In this context, Darius Rejali describes how a torturer's work apparently never ends. "Memories of applying pain to others tick like a time bomb," Rejali says. In their book *Violence Workers*, Huggins and Zimbardo write, "Torturers suffer from insomnia, hyper-sensitivity, nervousness, emotional problems, alcoholism and potential suicidal behavior." And in another study by Hazler, this time with JoLynn Carney, their conclusions suggest that for bystanders who witness abuse and bullying, stress, trauma, PTSD, damaged relationships, and social mistrust inevitably follow.

When you actually look at the empirical and qualitative evidence about the outcomes of restraint and seclusion, it's clear that these interventions do not achieve any desired behavioural or therapeutic goals. In fact, restraint and seclusion do just the opposite and can lead to deadly consequences.

As an expert witness, I wrote opinions and testified in court in front of juries, arguing that there is a causal link between torture, restraint, and seclusion. Those opinions, of course, were based on fact-based studies like the New York Psychological Association's Task Force. They found, for example, that some of the techniques described as "aversive behavioral interventions" not only constitute corporal punishment but also are included in literature on torture.

Q: I know you have done research looking at the effects of restraint and seclusion on the human brain. Can you talk about this?

RON: Apart from causing significant emotional pain and trauma, experiencing restraint and seclusion damages the person's brain. You see, when we use restraint, seclusion, or other forms of aversive interventions, we flood that person's brain with powerful stress hormones.

Some people assume that using coercion or threatening punishments and pain will create so much stress in the person that they will comply with whatever is being demanded of them. It is also assumed that those stress hormones will go away once the punishment ends and that there will be no lasting neurological damage to the person. This simply isn't true. The stress hormones that flood the brain are extremely powerful and cause long-term brain injury. Dr. Shane O'Mara at Trinity College, Dublin, finds in his research that these stressors substantially compromise memory, mood, and cognitive function.

It's important to note that this is true not only for the one being punished but also for the one doing the punishing, and to the bystanders as well, albeit to a lesser degree.

Q: But couldn't it be argued that this neurological damage is simply the result of the overuse of such methods?

RON: No. Any time we use these strategies, trust and relationships are undermined, and damage occurs. And there's another complicating factor. Unfortunately, it is widely assumed that the people who administer restraint and seclusion will be trained to know when to stop, assess, and calibrate what they are doing, and to come from a supportive therapeutic mind-set.

We presume that the staff will be sensitive, calm, and supportive and work in accord with any agency protocols. However, in the vast majority of cases, this simply isn't true. In the cases that I've testified in, most of the educators and staff that have restrained or secluded individuals have reported being angry, panicked, and in a state of extreme stress.

I've studied the research extensively, and it is accurate to say that restraint and seclusion are very rarely done in a calm and thoughtful way; it is almost always an angry, knee-jerk reaction that comes out of the educator's or staff person's panic and loss of control. To say this another way, restraint and seclusion are rarely simply interventions; they are almost always part of a fight.

Q: Given the brain research you've been quoting here, I'm going to assume that even if restraint and seclusion were used with calmness, that wouldn't really change the physiological outcomes. Would that be fair to say?

RON: Yes, and that's also a fair criticism of programs that teach practitioners and educators how to physically restrain individuals. Quality preventative care is rarely addressed by restraint intervention programs because emergency restraint often becomes physical abuse and a fight for control where calmness and reasoned judgment are nearly impossible to achieve.

Q: So, to summarize what you've said up to now:

- restraint and seclusion can be understood as forms of torture
- many of us have learned from movies and TV that restraint and seclusion are effective ways of gaining control of a difficult situation
- these approaches do permanent neurological damage, and they're often expressions of panic and hostility.

Is there anything else you'd like to add to the list?

RON: Yes. Restraint, seclusion, and other aversive techniques are not only wrong and harmful but also completely ineffective at bringing about any positive outcomes. Restraint and seclusion don't teach; they traumatize. They depersonalize the individual being secluded or restrained as well as the person doing the restraint or seclusion. They typically compromise neural functioning, impair memory, modify mood, and often produce both psychological and physical damage. All of these effects make learning virtually impossible.

But in addition to being wrong, harmful, and ineffective, restraint and seclusion are also incredibly dangerous. I worked as an expert witness on several legal cases involving the deaths of individuals who were restrained by staff.

Q: There is ample evidence that restraint and seclusion programs are harmful and abusive, yet I know sometimes people choose to ignore the research and the experts.

RON: That's correct. In the legal world, if you've been given notice either through precedent or prior knowledge, and choose to ignore that notice, a lawsuit can get very expensive for both the individual and the institution. I learned over the course of my career that being an expert witness for a court action had much more of an impact on individual and institutional change than merely being a consultant.

Q: We know these approaches don't work and are harmful. Are there examples of more effective ways to work with people who may be endangering themselves or others?

RON: Our mutual friend Herb Lovett gave an interview for the Minnesota Disability Law Center where he told the story of a young man who broke glass by going through windows until one day a staff member asked him a question no one else had thought to ask: "Why do you go through windows?"

He said he didn't know why he did it, but breaking glass was important to him. Staff encouraged him to find his own solution to the problem, and he came up with the idea of taking jelly jars, wrapping them up in newspaper, putting them in a paper bag, and stomping on them. He continued to break glass but did so safely.

Instead of staff wrestling with him and trying to physically prevent him from breaking glass, the resolution to the issue was to ask him about the meaning of his actions, then ask him to explore solutions that didn't humiliate him or result in harm.

So the takeaway here for staff and educators is this. You might ask yourself, "What do I really want to accomplish here?" Then ask the client or student to help you figure it out. We don't do that often enough. Most of the decisions about interventions are made without the participation of the individual involved. Herb points out that when we ask people and listen closely to their responses, the solutions often become apparent. It isn't always words we're listening to. Many people who don't speak find other ways to communicate with us, and we simply need to slow down and notice what they're trying to tell us.

Q: Why do you think we don't ask or listen to people?

RON: Unfortunately, in today's world, what we want are "140 character" responses, relationships, and schemes to get the job done quickly so we can move onto some other task.

Q: OK. Are there other alternatives to restraint and seclusion? I'm sure in your legal opinions you had to mention other options and choices.

RON: Sure, over the years there have been many respectful and effective alternatives to restraint and seclusion. But what's important to remember here is that there are often multiple reasons why people become noncompliant, aggressive, or self-injurious. These are the things we need to spend more time exploring.

For example, activist Amythest Schaber, on her YouTube channel "Ask an Autistic," talks about how sensory overload, anxiety, and general life stress led her to engage in self-injurious behavior. Ruth Siegfried talks about how it was vital for staff to give a man they were supporting an exceptionally big boundary when working with him (see Chapter 9).

Many people working in the area of trauma-informed support like Dave Hingsburger from Ontario, Ruth Meyers from Minnesota, and Karyn Harvey from Baltimore talk about how the effects of trauma or PTSD can lead to aggressive or self-injurious behaviour. So it's vital that we try to figure out what is leading to that behaviour before we decide on the best way to support that person. Otherwise, we end up following a one-size-fits-all approach to behavioural support.

Q: What can educators do to be proactive in the way they support people?

RON: Educators and support staff need to take the time to ask the person about their own stories. "Who are the people you really like to see?" "What makes you happy?" "What makes you angry?" Answers to these questions can yield extraordinary insights like, "I miss my brother," "I like to go outside," or "I don't like to be bossed around."

Q: In your experience, what should educators and support staff be thinking about as they are supporting someone?

RON: When we look at alternatives to restraints and seclusion, it's absolutely vital that we look at what we do before the situation erupts. We need to pay attention to three things:

- We need to help a person feel safe.
- We need to develop a trusting relationship with them.
- We need to give them as much control over their own lives as possible.

If we focus on these three things, then it's far less likely that we'll be in a situation where we're tempted to use restraint or seclusion. In order to do this, we need to take the time to talk to and get to know the student. In addition, we need to take the wishes and concerns of the individuals seriously. But above all, we have to remember that restraint and seclusion are not legitimate interventions; they are forms of torture. They specifically destroy what you need to be building up: safety, trusting relationships, and autonomy. Aversive and coercive interventions like torture, restraint, and seclusion destroy one or more of those important needs.

Q: Any concluding thoughts?

RON: Historically, we have done a terrible job listening to those we serve. Restraint and seclusion are not about listening or caring; they're about power and convenience.

I want to sneak in a favorite quote from astrophysicist Ethan Siegel. "Physics has shown us time and time again that our human views of what's logically consistent or preferred are terrible guides to understanding the Universe. Better to ask the Universe itself, and listen to the answers it gives us, no matter how counterintuitive they may be."

I bet you never thought there could be so much overlap between astrophysics and personal support!